Bombay Cinema

Bombay Cinema

An Archive of the City

Ranjani Mazumdar

University of Minnesota Press
Minneapolis · *London*

MI NN NE SO TA

Poetry that is reprinted in this book is reproduced with permission from Rajkamal and Oxford University Press India.

Published by the University of Minnesota Press
111 Third Avenue South, Suite 290
Minneapolis, MN 55401-2520
http://www.upress.umn.edu

Library of Congress Cataloging-in-Publication Data

Mazumdar, Ranjani.
    Bombay cinema : an archive of the city / Ranjani Mazumdar.
        p.   cm.
    Includes bibliographical references and index.
    ISBN 978-0-8166-4941-9 (hc : alk. paper) — ISBN 978-0-8166-4942-6 (pb : alk. paper)
    1. Motion pictures—India.   2. Motion picture industry—India—Bombay.
I. Title.
    PN1993.5.I8M39   2007
    791.430954'792—dc22   2006034883

Printed in the United States of America on acid-free paper

The University of Minnesota is an equal-opportunity educator and employer.

12 11 10 09 08 07   10 9 8 7 6 5 4 3 2 1

For Ma and Baba

Contents

Preface

Several interrelated journeys have taken me in the direction of this book. The first is my love for popular Bombay cinema. Film was for me, like most South Asians, a childhood passion sustained through regular trips to the movie theater and by listening to songs on the radio and on television. This film mania changed when I was introduced to Marxism as an activist in the student movement in Delhi in the early 1980s. Marxism provided answers to complex questions, which allowed many of us in the student movement to deal with the bewildering complexities of a diverse country like India. The ability to categorize, situate, and explore issues based on an underlying theory of social transformation was naturally attractive. The answers were neat, and we were intoxicated by the power of the discourse. Caught between a love for Hindi cinema and a political position against the so-called ideology "the popular" represented, the decade of the 1980s passed by. But at the end of the decade everything changed: the collapse of the Soviet Union and the Eastern Bloc in 1989 and the events in China the same year plunged Indian Marxism into a serious crisis.

Only with the crisis of orthodox Marxism in India did I begin to reflect on the relationship between popular cinema and the city. New questions cropped up, and the city and popular cinema became sites where I began to come to terms with my own relationship to radicalism and critique. In the Indian context, this included an assessment of nationalism and new engagements with issues of identity and sexuality that contemporary globalization brought into sharp focus. I began to look carefully at the range of themes explored by the popular. This search took me in the direction of the "everyday" and of the city, to try to understand the connection between lived experience and the cinema. I began to see the popular as a contradictory site that allowed us access to aspects of experience that needed to be studied with more commitment and enthusiasm, not just through narrow ideological lenses.

Bombay cinema survived the overwhelming tide of Hollywood for various complicated reasons. What is it about this medium that makes it so popular in India? Clearly this was more than just economics. Unlike in Hollywood, premodern forms of expression in India survived right up to the end of the twentieth century, and they show no signs of disappearing. Many in the film industry call cinema a modern technological folk form, for it speaks to specific experience that audiences in a country of uneven modernity can relate to. Popular cinema engages with everyday lives and experiences in ways that are unique. A culturally and historically specific mode of address has not only made both the content and the form successful but has given it a special power to restrict Hollywood's expansion in India.

A third aspect of Bombay cinema has influenced the writing of this book—my own experience as a documentary filmmaker in Delhi. Filmmaking allowed me to travel throughout India and opened my eyes to a range of complexities and new experiences. Moving between the countryside and the city in my film work brought into focus the specific context of the urban experience in largely agrarian societies like India and China. I began looking for clues and traces that would help me mount popular cinema's archival potential. The urban experience could be read via the cinematic, would allow me to ask different kinds of questions about the experience of modernity in India.

During the writing of this book I have seen the making of a neoliberal consensus in so many of our media institutions. I have also seen the indifference of the political and cultural elites vis-à-vis the growing inequalities that are surely part of global capitalism today. All this makes a new radical critique of our time more urgent than ever before. The film experience refracts through new dream worlds, conflicts, and miseries of our present in ways that account for its power and its pleasures. Recognizing this, I have attempted to search for a critical vocabulary to understand cinema in a way that is neither an uncritical populism of the present nor an ideological dismissal. In the pages that follow, I have tried to deal with both my love for the practice of cinema and my desire to understand its cultural force. The result is *Bombay Cinema: An Archive of the City*, the book in your hand.

Delhi, March 2007

Acknowledgments

There are a number of friends and colleagues to whom I am indebted for what this book has finally become. In New York, Robert Stam's intellectual presence, sense of fun, and democratic spirit have been invaluable to the writing of this book. I am very grateful to Toby Miller for his immense generosity with time, his detailed comments, his ideas, and, above all, his solidarity with the project. Robert Sklar inspired me to think through difficult questions of history. Zhang Zhen and Una Chowdhary provided thoughtful and encouraging comments that have found their way into the book. Nitin Govil not only provided me with stimulating intellectual insights but also handled so many of my mundane affairs in New York. Our passionate agreements and disagreements have been useful in shaping the arguments of the book. Radhika Subramanium and I share a deep bond on issues relating to the city. Our endless conversations over cups of tea and on the telephone were invaluable to the writing process, and I cannot thank her enough for both her intellectual insight and emotional support. Ira Bhaskar, my friend and now colleague at Jawaharlal Nehru University, has been a supportive, encouraging, and happy presence whose critical insights and careful reading of the manuscript have been very helpful. I am thankful to Parag Amladi for our endless conversations about cinema. Rachel Moore's intellectual presence and warmth will always be remembered. Tejaswini Ganti gave me access to a rich body of material on the Bombay film industry. Denise Mckena provided insights on popular culture and technology. Isabelle Freda has always been an inspiring presence with her deep commitment to the study of politics in the cinema.

I am fortunate to have lived and worked with friends with whom I have experienced a diverse world of cinema. I thank my compatriots in the Mediastorm film collective in Delhi for their support and interest in the project. Shohini Ghosh shared her rich collection of newspaper articles and ideas on popular culture. Our early morning telephone conversations will always be remembered as the right combination of *adda* and intellectual debate. I thank Shikha Jhingan for her comments and for codirecting with me a television series on Bombay cinema that proved very useful to the writing of this book. Sabeena Gadihoke provided valuable comments on many sections of the book, particularly chapter 3, along with a healthy dose of entertainment and encouragement. Sabina Kidwai was always around as a friend and willingly helped me edit a sequence of film clips to go with the book. Charu Gargi's house in Bombay was always open to me as a second home during research.

In Delhi and Bombay, a number of friends helped out with the book. Ravi Vasudevan generously shared his rich collection of tapes, books, and ideas. His comments on many of the chapters have been invaluable. Subodh Verma and Shaswati Mazumdar translated some of the songs that appear here. Ravi Kant Sharma first introduced me to Hindi poetry about the city, then typed the text for the manuscript. Awadhendra Sharan (Dipu) gave me valuable references and encouragement. Jeebesh Bagchi, Shuddhabrata Sengupta, and Monica Narula of the Raqs Media Collective have been a constant support, egging me on in my intellectual life. My young friends Bhrigupati Singh, Ankur Khanna, Debashree Mukherjee, and Prerna Singh have always been a great source of inspiration, helping me out whenever I was in a bind. In different ways that were crucial for the development of my ideas, Ashis Nandy and Anurag Kashyap inspired me to engage provocatively with the cinematic city. Anurag also helped me procure many stills for this book.

At Princeton University, where I was a fellow at the Davis Center in 2003–2004, I acquired many friends who played an important role in my intellectual and social life. Two chapters were written during my fellowship year. I thank my housemate and colleague, Christina Jimenez, for her warmth, support, and intellectual generosity. Aruna Prakash, Helen Tilley, Michael Gordon, Frank Romagosa, Ann Maria, Judith Hanson,

Pamela Long, William Jordon, Elizabeth Lunbeck, Jennifer Houle, Belinda Davis, Angela Craeger, and many others made my stay in Princeton very enjoyable. I am especially grateful to Gyan Prakash for his thoughtful and incisive comments after a careful reading of the entire manuscript; I cannot thank him enough for his intellectual support, generosity, friendship, and a great sense of fun, all of which made the Princeton experience memorable.

Many friends have been a source of support over the past decade. I would like to thank Aditya Nigam, Abhilasha Kumari, Vibhu Mahapatra, Nivedita Menon, Rajni Palriwala, Indu Agnihotri, Javed Akhtar, Shabana Azmi, Frances Guerin, Alisa Lebow, Suresh Chabria, Saumya Gupta, Sheyphaly Sharan, Lita, Rahul Roy, Suzanne Goldenberg, Chitra Padmanabhan, M. K. Venu, Sidharth Varadarajan, Nandini Sunder, Zainab Bawa, Shonali Bose, Richard Allen, Lawrence Liang, Nasreen Reheman, Vidyun Singh, Pankaj Mehra, Sumit Ray, Vinod Kaul, John Mcmurria, Bela Amladi, Shawn Shimpach, Manorama Chandra, and Subhash Chandra.

I thank all the Mazumdars—my parents Shankar and Vina Mazumdar, my sisters Shaswati and Indrani, and my brother Surajit—for their presence, encouragement, solidarity, and, above all, for the passionate arguments and fights that helped sharpen the arguments of this book. Support also came from the extended family of T. K. Rajalxmi, Vaasanthi, R. K. Sundaram, Hari Sundaram, Akhila Yechury, Ashish Yechury, Rustam Mazumdar, and Subodh Verma. Joan, Frank, Leela, and Babu were like a second family in New York, providing me with shelter when I desperately needed it.

The following institutions and fellowships funded various stages of this project: the American Institute of Indian Studies; the Jay Leyda Memorial Dissertation-Writing Award of the Department of Cinema Studies, New York University; the American Association of University Women; the Dean's Dissertation Writing Award of the Graduate School of Arts and Sciences at New York University; and the Shelby Cullom Davis Center for Historical Studies at Princeton University.

I am grateful to Thomas Blom Hansen for his comments on the manuscript; to Jason Weidemann at the University of Minnesota Press for his support, patience, and commitment to the book; and to Adam Brunner, Jeni Henrickson, Dan Leary, and Nancy Sauro for their careful work on the manuscript. Bhagwati Prasad worked with me to organize the stills for the book. Yogender Dutt and Guntupalli Karunakar helped typeset the Hindi text. Sudhir Mishra, Anupama Chopra, and Anjum Rajabali helped with the hunt for stills. Without the help of Surya Prakash, it would have been hard to maintain any of the press's deadlines.

Ravi Sundaram, as always, has been the greatest help and support. With him, I began this journey into the city. Our common interests and long discussions have found their way into the book. He has been around through all the ups and downs in my intellectual and emotional life. Without him, this book would not have happened.

INTRODUCTION

Urban Allegories

Film in India has always testified to the powerful public presence of modernity. The sheer vastness of the film public points to the overwhelming presence of a vibrant film culture. The Bombay-based film industry resonates throughout the world, in places where the Indian diaspora has settled and in places where nonnative speakers appreciate its unique choreography of music, melodrama, fantasy, and spectacle. Much of popular cinema's success can be attributed to what many in the industry refer to as a "techno folk" form, which combines folk traditions with new cinematic technology. What appears to the uninitiated as exotic, bizarre, and wild is in fact a dynamic form that draws its sustenance from everyday life and experience. Throughout its history, Indian cinema has responded to local traditions, displaying a strong desire to maintain a distinctive form.[1] Drawing on various visual, literary, and artistic traditions, each with its own distinct history, popular Indian cinema is an evolving, unabashedly hybrid cultural form that narrates the complicated intersection between tradition and modernity in contemporary India.

Film production started in India almost simultaneously with other filmmaking countries, beginning in 1896. In the years after independence, Indian cinema circulated outside the country to audiences in Russia, the Middle East, Africa, and Latin America. In the more recent past, Indian diasporas in different parts of the world have ensured a continuing audience for Indian cinema. Today, a vast and growing urban filmgoing public in India supports film culture and circulation. India has for many years been the world's largest film-producing country, with an output in several different languages. In the year 2002 alone, almost 1,200 films were produced. Bombay is home to the most powerful section of the industry, producing films in the Hindi language. Popular cinema in India has survived the overwhelming tide of Hollywood's world domination by addressing people's experiences in surprisingly inventive ways.

Bombay Cinema attempts to enter the complex world of popular cinema by bringing together a range of cinematic practices and the urban experience. My purpose is to engage with the dynamism of popular cinema in the country's sprawling metropolitan life. The city as a concept remained a crucial absence in much of Indian nationalism's history. The nationalists instead invested in the imagination of the village as one of the secure sites of citizenship, reflecting the social base of anti-colonial mobilization. The interesting feature of Bombay cinema is that it has never been at one with the nationalist prioritization of the village. While cinema also looked at rural life, it is the urban experience that has dominated its landscape. The coming together of cinematic practices and the urban experience offers a useful way of transcending the imaginative limits imposed by nationalist narratives on culture.

The imagined city of cinema is born at the intersection of mental, physical, and social space. It is in this imagined city that we get access to what Baudelaire called "the fleeting, the ephemeral, and the transient" (1986) that shapes the rhythm and movement of contemporary city life. The traffic between the "real" city and the represented cinematic city is a complicated movement driven by a subjective and psychic projection. Journeying through the traffic of codes and signs that move between the physical spaces of the city and the topography of its cinematic production, I argue that popular Bombay cinema is a legitimate and powerful archive that provides us access to a range of urban subjectivities. This book sets itself within the political and historical transformations of the past three-and-a-half decades, which witnessed a deepening crisis of India's developmentalist/nationalist state in the 1970s and the onset of globalization in the 1990s. Negotiation with the urban—which in itself is conflictual and implicated in new codes of violence, utopian yearnings, and social movements—has opened up entirely new debates on film practices in India.

Cinema's relationship to the city is both complex and historical. Cinema emerged in the background of the transformation of Western capitalist society into an urban industrial one. This transformation produced an entirely new experience of the metropolis. The new landscape of urban spaces resulting from the expansion of industrial capitalism not only shaped the transition to a *modern* way of being in the world but was also impacted by the culture of the *moderns*. Like many other visual forms, cinema became implicated in the process of change even as it played a role in documenting and commenting on the pace of change. "Thus, the spectacle of the cinema both drew upon and contributed to the increased pace of modern city life, whilst also helping to normalize the frantic, disadjusted rhythms of the city" (Clarke, 3). Early cinema's success lay in its capacity to combine technological innovation with an ability to respond to the new social forms of metropolitan life. The new experience of (urban) modernity was disenchanted and fleeting, generating rapid stimuli that were reproduced in early cinema. "In a film perception in the form of shocks was established as a formal principle," wrote Walter Benjamin in his work on Baudelaire (1969, 132).

The shock-like experience of modernity is the decisive element that has shaped the work of almost all the writings on cinema and the city. While this has been an extremely useful intervention, a deeper understanding of the uneven and complex articulation of modernity across different cities of the world, in both the early and the contemporary periods, has not been adequately addressed. More than one hundred years since the birth of cinema, we need a greater elaboration of both the cultural contexts within the contemporary and the politics of the cinematic city. While the body of work dealing with film noir explores the psychology of the postwar experience in American cities, non-Western cities remain inadequately debated in relation to film. *Bombay Cinema* is in many ways both a departure from and an addition to the previous work on cinema and the city, while at the same time bringing a perspective from India.

The immediate difference when looking at the city in South Asia, as opposed to the city in the West, is the continuing presence of a large countryside where the majority of the population lives. The countryside supplies the city with a constant flow of migrants and labor.[2] In the periphery, the "givenness" of the modern West's urban experience does not have any reference point. By the twentieth century, the urban had become the typical form of experience in the West, something that is not true in India even in the early twenty-first century. In India, the city constantly acknowledges its rural other, a point that is explicit in the history of cinematic representation. Thus the Western "street," a space of detached observation (home to the *flâneur*), of terror (film noir), of "alien" anxiety (science fiction), becomes in Bombay cinema a site of community and crime, dance and violence, madness and freedom, death and renewal. The "street," which could be the "footpath" in Bombay cinema, is part village community, part cosmopolitan city street—a symbolic organizer of a set of contradictory impulses that generates intense performances.[3] Various themes common to modern urban life the world over are also integral to the book: the tension between the idea of the city as the typical embodiment of reason versus the production of sites of marginality; the urban experiences of hope and loss, yearning and nostalgia, terror and fear; the mapping of identity and difference; and the spectacles of contemporary consumption.

It was the crisis of Indian nationalism in the 1970s that led to Bombay cinema's reflection on urban life in terms that had not been possible earlier. By the 1970s, the dreams of the "development decades" held by the new leadership of post-independence India had run aground. Unemployment rose rapidly and social movements with strong urban referents emerged throughout the country. For the first time, the confidence of post-independence nationalism was shaken. The space of the village, which was central to the imaginary constitution of anticolonial nationalism (the Gandhian imaginary), had started fading in cinematic representation. There was now a greater acknowledgment, even centrality, of urban space. While political, consumption, and lifestyle movements today take the city almost as a given, the cutting edge of this new concern has come from the world of cinema. This has not only generated critical contradictions within the cinematic narrative but has also allowed for a certain *distinction* from the nationalist narratives of the past. The point is not that Bombay cinema's themes on the urban experience were discrete narratives, *separate* from the national, but that in the historical crisis of postcolonial nationalism, the cinema emerged as an allegory of the urban experience.

Taking the crisis of the 1970s as the starting point of this book, I move forward into the contemporary period of globalization, which made its presence felt in India in the 1990s.[4] Over the past three decades, urban India has seen rapid expansion and transformation. The growth of many towns outside the big cities has brought the urban experience to a vast, newly urbanized population. This includes the experience of mass crowds, urban violence and chaos, consumption and spectacle, and the spread of television. Shock, anxiety, and the tactile pleasures of urban life are now experienced by millions, something that has accelerated rapidly and radically after globalization. With the explosion of urban crises, city spaces have become focal points of critical reflection. Films like Yash Chopra's *Deewar* (1975), Raj Kumar Santoshi's *Ghayal* (1988), Vinod Chopra's *Parinda* (1989), and Vikram Bhatt's *Ghulaam* (1998) address this new sensibility.

Globalization has spurred a rapid profusion of urban consumption, scores of satellite television channels, and a new, expanded music culture centered on the film industry. At the time of writing, India has close to seventy television channels, compared with two state channels a decade ago. One of the world's largest music markets, India is the region's advertising headquarters, and its print and television industries give wide coverage to the fashion industry. India now also has a large software industry geared toward export, with millions employed in a supportive service industry. Scores of cities and small towns are nodes of consumption paralleled by urban crisis, violence, and expansion. India's cities have been overtaken by a frenzy of chaotic construction: flyovers, shopping malls, multiplexes, hotels, and highways. A massive automobile boom has further added to what can be called an urban delirium. Streets and markets are awash with new electronic gadgets, mobile phones, computers, and DVDs, each promoting diverse advertising strategies on walls, on billboards, and on lampposts. New forms of lighting have transformed the experience of the night in commercial areas. The shift from the previous modes of urban experience cannot be emphasized more.[5]

It is no exaggeration to say that after globalization, city life witnessed an accelerated flow of images at every level. Everyday life became infused with a new visual display of signs, which were shock-like intimations of the commodity space. This global regime of signs has affected all forms of representation in India—music, television, radio, print, and film. The temporal acceleration of this process has revealed the vulnerability of various forms, as deeply contradictory forces emerge in the world of representation, particularly in Bombay cinema. Spectacular new productions like Suraj Barjatya's *Hum Apke Hain Kaun* (Who am I to you, 1994) and Aditya Chopra's *Dilwale Dulhania Le Jayenge* (We will take the bride away, 1995) focus on consumer-oriented joint families, speaking to "tradition" yet geared to global mobility. The urban references are not just Bombay and Delhi, but London and New York.

The experience of a new delirium of urban life has come to India in the context of increasing migration, growing urban inequality, and an increased visibility of the destitute in the streets of the Indian city.[6] Violence, fear, and terror are as much a part of the delirium as the cheerful spectacle of the "good life" circulating in the major metropolises. The term "urban delirium" provides us with a powerful metaphor to stage the mise-en-scène of city life after globalization. This delirium is a complex configuration or a "buzz" that exists like a "shapeless substance into which politics and gossip, art and pornography, virtue and money, the fame of heroes and the celebrity of murderers, all bleed" (Foster, 7). *Bombay Cinema* situates the cinema within the discourse of the delirium. The nature of the delirium takes different forms in the range of films produced by the industry. Therefore, like an archaeologist, I attempt to make sense of this delirium as it expresses, shapes, and draws sustenance from the cinematic city.

Imaginative Urban Journeys

The imagined city comes to us through a variety of journeys. These journeys mediate visual, literary, and sociological forms that embody a range of perspectives, images, and narratives (Donald). In India, the journey into the texture of modern life has come up against the overwhelming centrality of the nation-state in cultural and political discourse. This framework of the nation and its attendant discourses has created a situation in which the tissue and texture of everyday life remains subsumed under an overarching analytical category. This proves to be a limiting exercise whenever scholars are forced to confront experiences that exceed or exist irrespective of the nation. The context of the Indian city as a metaphor, as a space, as a conundrum of diverse human experiences, and as an imaginary landscape of deep psychic dislocations is one of the casualties of what Gyan Prakash has called "the historicist discourse of the nation" (2002, 6). In the field of cultural production, however, this paradox is complicated, because literary creativity, artistic expression, and popular perceptions have created an entirely different kind of articulation.

Even during the heyday of nationalist euphoria immediately after independence, urban space was critically negotiated. In the films of the 1950s, the self-image of the nation was forced to confront several instances of dislocation, which complicated the issue of national identity. For example, in films like *Sri 420, Awara, Bazi,* and *Kismet,* a modern sense of space and movement is negotiated even as the narratives yearn for the security of a world lost through uprootedness (Vasudevan 1994, 93). The opposition between the city and the countryside is the most common form of dislocation addressed in these films. Further, there is a sense of trauma that prevents the characters from engaging with the present. The relationship to the new order is that of ambivalence, rendered visible through new spatial and temporal adjustments of the city (93).

The importance of the urban can be traced in the work of many Hindi writers. While pre-independence literature was overwhelmed by the anticolonial struggle, rapid industrialization in the post-independence period led to a complex engagement with urbanization in literature. Hindi writers in northern India confronted a range of urban themes: the dialectic of the country and the city; the emergence of the lonely hero; alienation and the loss of traditional values; the crisis of the joint family (Goswami). The Hindi language itself is forced to change in order to powerfully communicate the complexities of the urban experience in India (Goswami). In the field of poetry, the city's disciplining and controlling power is a popular theme. Dhumil, a well-known Hindi poet of postcolonial India, writes:

धूमिल

नगरपालिका ने मुझे बाएँ रहना सिखाया है
(सफल जीवन के लिए
कारनेगी की किताब की नहीं,
सड़क के यातायात चिह्नों को समझने
की ज़रूरत है)

चौराहे पर क़वायद करते हुए
ट्रैफ़िक पुलिस के चेहरे पर
मुझे हमेशा, जनतंत्र का नक़्शा
नज़र आया है। (राजकमल, १९७२)

The municipality has taught me to keep left
For a successful life, we do not need Carnegie's book,
But knowledge of traffic signs.
In the face of the traffic policeman
Who strains himself at the crossroads
I have always seen, the map of democracy. (1972)

Hostility to the city as a space that evokes order, discipline, and the power to control is a recurring theme in literature and poetry. In Dhumil's poetry, a casual encounter in the street, a fragment of daily life, is used for a philosophical and political mediation on the concept of modern "democracy." While Dhumil interrogates the disciplining mechanism of the state (through the image of the traffic policeman), poet Jan Nissar Akhtar yearns for the village while walking through the city. Akhtar writes:

जाँ निसार अख़्तर

शहर के तपते हुए फुटपाथों पर गांव के मौसम साथ चलें
बूढ़े बरगद हाथ जो रख दें मेरे जलते शानों पर

On the burning footpaths of the city,
May the seasons of the village accompany me,
May the old banyan tree lay a hand
on my burning shoulders.

While Akhtar is simply evoking nostalgia in this couplet, the use of the "footpath" as the space that triggers an imagination of the village is significant. The space of the footpath is the "mimic village." In an instant, Akhtar brings the village into the city to express loss, yearning, and uprootedness. As I show in many of the chapters in this book, the space of the footpath acquires a powerful mythical dimension in Hindi cinema. The footpath emerges as a reference point for childhood memories and homelessness, as a mark of marginality, and as a different imaginary of the cinematic city.

Given the city's presence in diverse literary and cinematic representations, its absence in political and historical discourse may seem baffling. The crucial question when discussing the cinematic city is the lack of any systematic reflection on urban life within Indian nationalism.[7] This is all the more intriguing given the widespread nationalist mobilizations in large cities and small towns during the colonial period, and because of the fact that a large section of the nationalist leadership was of impeccable urban origin. For an answer to this paradox, we have to turn briefly to Indian nationalism's engagement with modernity.

Debating the Historical Context of the City in India

Beginning with its origins in the nineteenth century, Indian nationalism mounted a wide-ranging critique of Western modernity that sought to locate a sovereign sphere from which an argument for self-determination could be launched. The issue of defining this sovereign space was crucial to realizing the nationalist goal of independence. From Bankim Chandra Chatopadhyay in the nineteenth century to Gandhi and Nehru in the twentieth century, the colonial encounter provided the basis for an increasingly complicated discourse on subjectivity, selfhood, exploitation, and power (Chatterjee 1993, 24). The drive to define a *different* imaginative sphere from that of the West dominated the nationalist enterprise. The insistent demand for a nation-state was an urge to establish a "modernity of one's own," one that differed from Western modernity:

> This was a defining feature of Indian nationalism because, being an anti-colonial project, it had to articulate its aspirations as a critique of Western modernity and as a desire to institutionalize a culturally specific community. (Prakash 1999, 201)

As Partha Chatterjee has shown, nationalism resolved the issue of a different modernity by constituting a sovereign inner sphere of the "spiritual," to which the colonial subject had privileged access and which was outside the colonial domain of power. This is Chatterjee's well-known formulation:

> The material is the domain of the "outside", of the economy and of state-craft, of science and technology, a domain where the West had proved its superiority and the East had succumbed. In this domain, then, Western superiority had to be acknowledged and its accomplishments carefully studied and replicated. The spiritual, on the other hand, is an "inner" domain bearing the "essential" marks of cultural identity. (1993, 6)

The terms of asserting this sovereign sphere of culture varied from the more elite nineteenth-century narratives[8] to the Gandhian intervention in the twentieth century. Gandhi's own work mounted a general critique of industrial capitalism, which he saw as based on unequal exchange between the city and the countryside, a model that could not be adopted for an agrarian society like India. Gandhi was skeptical of socialist solutions favored by Nehru, who was influenced by European social democrats and by Soviet state planning. In the public realm, no two leaders could have seemed more different than Gandhi and Nehru. For Gandhi, no amount of socialization could remove the evils of industrialism. His own symbolic reference point was the village community, which now entered the domain of the inner spiritual world. Only through a network of self-reliant village communities could India escape the evils of industrialism and urbanization. However, the divisions between Gandhi and Nehru or Gandhi's alleged anti-urbanism seem exaggerated. In producing the village as a site of authenticity, Gandhi was in fact drawing from one of modernity's oldest discourses (Prakash 1999). Ashis Nandy has spoken of how Gandhi, a person of impeccable urban origins, came to see the village as the source of anticolonial struggle and as a spiritual reference point for the independence struggle (Nandy 1980).

Nehru emphasized state-centered planning and industrialization, which, he believed, would be attentive to Indian traditions and "our unique history" (Prakash 1999). In his *Discovery of India*, Nehru draws attention to the horrors of Western-style industrialization, whose capitalist character had destroyed the fabric of urban life and led to sharp inequalities. Nehru argued for planned growth, which would attend to India's "civilizational heritage." The invocation of the inner sphere continued in Nehru's model. The external sphere of the state and the economy had to be reworked in the postcolonial period to accommodate the "spiritual" heritage of India.[9] The Nehruvian model strongly influenced the post-independence regime. What is interesting in the nationalist reading of modernity in the post-independence period is the commitment to republican democracy, in contrast to most Third World elites of that time. However, Nehru remained ambivalent about the village; there was a certain apprehension in the post-independence period about the powers of a newly enfranchised peasantry (Kaviraj 1996, 121). This apprehension was resolved by the construction of the technocratic institutions of the state, which were autonomous from the day-to-day functioning of political power. Institutions like the Planning Commission took on the task of organizing development programs. Independent of daily politics, these structures functioned as autonomous state bodies seeking to map larger national goals.

The nationalist legacy posed a version of sovereign political space that became increasingly abstract in the postcolonial period, a space that was accessible only to political and cultural elites who operated as modernizers of the nation. Power operated through republican democratic politics and a panoptical vision of control. As has been argued, "a *sui generis* constitutionalism, rather than the city (as in the West) was the preferred basis for regulating citizenship" (Sundaram, 100–101). State-centered and technocratic, this political space became the imaginary reference point for much academic and elite discourse after independence, dominated by work on political economy and the state. This constellation enabled little reflection on the meaning of daily life in India's cities and towns.

Critical responses to the nationalist legacy often came from Marxist traditions. A large body of Marxist thought in India before the 1970s also tended to be state-centered, weaving-in issues of class and ideology. Nationalism, as such, was rarely questioned; it was castigated only for its failure to live up to the promises of genuine sovereignty and equality.[10] Indian Marxism was critical of Gandhi, whose aestheticized politics articulated issues of daily life and experience. The Left's fascination was more with Nehru's spectacular modernism and "nation building." Radical social historians, who dissented from the Marxist mainstream, raised issues of reflexivity, subject position, and the need to engage with alternative possibilities outside the nationalist problematic (Guha and Spivak). Much of this work undertaken by the Subaltern Studies Collective focuses on the pre-independence period. However, work on the contemporary urban everyday remains to this day largely absent from the intellectual history of the Indian Left.[11]

It was the crisis of nationalism that led to a concerted engagement with the city in cinema. From 1973 onward, India witnessed a series of urban movements of students and the unemployed in Gujarat, Bihar, and other parts of northern India (Kothari). Inflation and unemployment created a growing disillusionment with the rhetoric of developmentalism. By the 1970s, it was clear that developmentalism had made little difference to the experience of everyday life. By 1975, various movements posed a significant challenge to the Congress regime[12] and a state of emergency was thus declared and all civil rights were suspended.[13]

The Emergency saw the institutionalization of a repressive regime aimed at curbing political dissidence by fostering a climate of fear and paranoia in India's cities and towns. The urbanization programs of the Emergency period perceived urban crisis as a disease. Bureaucrats, who tended to see the city as a monster to be controlled, often cleaned up the city through authoritarian planning and displacement of the poor. Urban areas witnessed demolition drives against the poor, and compulsory sterilization drives aimed at urban youth. The Congress regime was defeated in the elections held after the Emergency.[14] Throughout the 1980s, successive regimes continued to speak in an increasingly diminished Nehruvian nationalist language. The old social coalition, which had ruled the country after independence, came under increasing stress from backward caste movements, regionalism, and the new impulses of globalization. The most dramatic political development in the 1980s was the rise of an aggressive Hindu nationalist movement, which challenged the Nehruvian heritage of secularism inscribed in the Indian constitution. Hindu nationalism used urban centers as points of early mobilization, with violent campaigns resulting in many attacks on the Muslim minority.

Political developments since the 1970s form the backdrop to the journey into the cinematic city made in this book. The political events exist in the background as reference points, not as dominant codes affecting the contour of the imagined city. Political and social events and the everyday coexist in *Bombay Cinema,* not as discrete categories but as a labyrinth of experiences shaping the cartography of the cinematic city. Against the tide of an engagement that looks at the represented city as a purely modernist construction (Bruno 2002; Clarke; Donald), *Bombay Cinema* engages with the culture of modernity as it manifests itself in the historical and social space of South Asia, relying on a detailed delineation of urban life and practice as they unfold through the tissue and texture of cinema. Moving against the desire to trace an overwhelming national history through the cinematic form, each chapter in this book negotiates experiences that offer us a discontinuous sense of history. The city slides into the terrain of the urban experience where the historical, the political, the anecdotal, and the textual coexist and unfold in the magical world of popular cinema. "The city" was the typical space of modernism, usually seen through the visual map of iconic figures: the flâneur, the prostitute, and the avant-garde artist (Baudelaire). The "urban experience" is of more recent vintage, which, while recognizing earlier references, privileges the contemporary. Debates on the urban experience have the merit of drawing in various forms of the popular, not just through the iconic references of the past, but through the re-invention of hybrid, polymorphous, and performative figures (Hebdige 1979).

Interpretive Strategies

While the city of Bombay plays a crucial role in my understanding of screen narratives, the attempt here is to raise broader issues of the urban experience in India. Jonathan Raban, in his now-classic book *Soft City*, presents us with a magical journey into the experience of city life. In Raban's sensuous engagement, cities, by virtue of their plasticity, can be molded into images that in turn influence the urban form. The relationship between humans and material forms that unfolds in the creative play of urban living is an art that can be best captured through the vocabulary of art and style. For Raban, "the city as we imagine it, the soft city of illusion, myth, aspiration, nightmare, is as real, maybe more real, than the hard city one can locate in maps and statistics, in monographs on urban sociology and demography and architecture" (4). It is this combination of movement, performance, and transition within the urban experience that I find useful for my work. While much has been written on urban sociology, *Bombay Cinema* looks at the cultural imagination of the city and its intersection with the cinema.

Walter Benjamin said, "In thousands of eyes, in thousands of objects, the city is reflected" (cited in Gilloch, 6). It is the task of the urban physiognomist to read the experiences of the metropolis through the many fragments offered by the city (Benjamin 1999). The act of reading fragments has to rely on an allegorical gaze. Allegory is the recurring desire to compensate for an awareness of loss through saturated and fragmentary experiences. At the same time, the allegorical mode seeks to unravel the phantasmagoria of the city as "progress," through images of ruin and catastrophe (Gilloch; Buck-Morss 1990). The allegorical gaze reorders its objects to offer a new reading embedded within the surface reality of what is available at "first sight."[15] There are two levels of engagement here. The first is the cinematic medium, which I argue is the archive of the modern that houses allegorical images of the city. The second level of engagement constitutes the role of interpretation in reading the cinema, in which the allegorical mode is deployed to unravel cinema's negotiation of the urban experience in India. These twin engagements are central to the writing of *Bombay Cinema*.

Georg Simmel developed a slightly different approach to the study of modernity, outside of a well-defined "method" in the strict social-science sense. He was criticized by many of his contemporaries for lacking the conceptual ability to systematize his material. Simmel's approach to contemporary life relied on a reflexive mode that recognized the sociologist's particular mode of experiencing social reality. In his *Philosophy of Money*, Simmel interrogates the impulse for empirical phenomena by suggesting that

> the theory according to which everything held to be true is a certain *feeling* which accompanies a mental image; what we call proof is nothing other than the establishment of a psychological constellation which gives rise to such a feeling. No sense perception or logical derivations can directly assure us of a reality. (1990, 452)

This intuitionism enabled the creation of a "sociological impressionism" that was rooted in an aesthetic mode of approaching social reality (Frisby, 53). For Simmel, the fragmentary, fleeting, and contradictory reality in metropolitan life found its best expression in the aestheticization of social reality. The clue to the modern experience of the city lay in the superficial ensemble of "styles" and fashion, in the movement of the crowd and the "topography of space." Through impressionistic journeys, Simmel embarked on an interpretation of the momentary, in the process creating an aestheticized and novel approach to understand the "soul of the city."

In a very different context, Ashis Nandy attempts to engage with issues of the modern experience in India, in ways that go outside the ideological. Nandy's use of the anecdotal, his allegorical invocation of the slum as a metaphor for cinema, his recent work on the decline of the imagination of the village from public life, and his attempt to read the mythical persona of Karna in the *Mahabharata* as a tortured urban figure all point to interesting possibilities (1997, 1998). In many ways, Nandy's approach is reminiscent of Benjamin's fascination with the "archaic in the modern," wherein the dialectic of antiquity and modernity is deployed to reveal the world of myth as it permeates the world of contemporary "newness." Nandy, however, does not fit within the ideological tradition of established social sciences in India. Almost iconoclastic in form, he offers controversial yet perceptive insights into the contemporary.[16]

Drawing on such perceptions on the city, *Bombay Cinema* has been written with the desire to generate a debate that can deal both with the similarities and the distinctiveness of the urban experience in India. Cutting across disciplinary boundaries, the debates on the city mediate other debates within film historiography and theory. I look at the public discourse generated around the reception of cinematic images in the mass/popular media. Detailed interviews with scriptwriters, actors, and other professionals from the industry are also woven into the fabric of this book.[17] I adopt a narrative that combines the anecdotal with the theoretical, the philosophical with the political, and the textual with the historical. These different forms of knowledge are integrated to present cinema as *the* most innovative archive of the city in India. Defending the act of interpretation as an inevitable process when encountering works of art, Tom Gunning emphasizes that this process must not only involve the progressive discovery and uncovering of a film's surface texture, but also present us with a narrative of *surprises* (2000, x). This intention informs the writing process of the book.

The Cinematic City: An Intervention

In his introduction to *The Cinematic City*, an anthology on cinema's negotiation of the urban sphere, David Clarke writes about the lack of theoretical or historical work on the relationship "between urban and cinematic space" (1). Clarke forcefully argues for a conscious effort to understand the cinematic city without imposing a single a priori interpretation (10). While Clarke's initial disappointment at the lack of work on the cinematic city may now change as theoretical engagement with the cinematic city grows, a deeper exploration of the uneven articulation of urban modernity across different cities of the world still remains to be done. Drawing on and acknowledging the importance of existing work on the cinematic city, *Bombay Cinema* takes a slightly different journey that attempts to move beyond the initial shock of modernity and its technological exegesis as witnessed in the cinema and cityscapes of the West. This is a book about the power and value of popular cinema in India. In mediating the complexities that have shaped the trajectory of Indian film studies, I make a conscious attempt to create a space for a different kind of inquiry and engagement with the world of popular cinema. Existing accounts of Indian cinema have tended toward three major trajectories: nationalist, ideological, and biographical/historical. The nationalist account attempts to restore the study of Indian cinema to an academic mainstream that vilifies it; the ideological approach charts the politics of the cinematic form and the subjectivities and pleasures it engenders; and the biographical approach eulogizes the complex history of Indian cinema through the hagiographies of well-established stars and auteur/directors. *Bombay Cinema* recognizes the contributions of such studies, while at the same time it looks specifically at the relationship between popular cinema and urban life.

Sumita Chakravarty's *National Identity in Indian Popular Cinema* (1996) is perhaps the first comprehensive book-length study on Bombay cinema, followed by Madhava Prasad's *Ideology of the Hindi Film* (1998) and Lalitha Gopalan's *Cinema of Interruptions* (2002).[18] Prasad sees Bombay cinema as the articulated expression of the Indian state. Through an analysis of the historical and material practices that shaped the cinema, Prasad draws ideological conclusions about the role, politics, and culture of the cinema. Chakravarty, on the other hand, sees the image saturated with the gaze of the "national." Cinema performs the "national" and becomes the impersonation of Indian national identity. Through readings of several films, Chakravarty explores the "structure of feeling" of Indian society. In *The Cinematic ImagiNation* (2003), Jyotika Virdi looks at the narratives of thirty films and argues that the configuration of the nation is central to popular Indian cinema. Gopalan, however, argues against generalized readings of popular cinema in which the exploration and uncovering of hegemonic ideology is offered as the only possibility. Using the categories of "pleasure" and "cinephilia" to trace specifically cinematic techniques of narration, Gopalan suggests that popular Indian cinema is a "cinema of interruptions." Identifying these interruptions as song and dance sequences, the interval, and censorship codes, Gopalan attempts to explore the different ways in which these cinematic interruptions are playfully and creatively negotiated by directors to weave in their own storytelling style. Prasad, Gopalan, Virdi, and Chakravarty provide us with interesting insights into the different kinds of representational strategies adopted by popular Indian cinema. Though very different in their approaches, all four authors display a desire to categorize Indian cinema within a framework of either "dominant ideology" or the "nation" and "state," thus situating cinema within networks that constitute nationalist and ideological discourse.

Ravi Vasudevan takes the formal dimension of the image and dissects the network of gazes that create meaning within the cinematic narrative. Nationalism, modernity, spectatorship, and narrativity coincide in his work, which focuses primarily on the cinema of the 1950s. Vasudevan's detailed formal analysis is premised on three central narrative concerns: the use and deployment of the iconic mode,[19] the organization of characters within the tableau frame,[20] and the use of continuity editing as developed by Hollywood cinema. Vasudevan suggests that through these techniques, the narrative of Hindi cinema provides the spectator with an entry into a "national space." The genre of the "social"—through which the cinema attempted to deal with issues of modern life—is premised on a strategy of excess and containment, a melodramatic mode that deploys binary oppositions to push a moral universe through the narrative (Vasudevan 1995, 2000).

Similarly, in a well-known essay (1993), Ashis Rajadhyaksha deploys the term "epic melodrama" to understand the rise of the melodramatic mode in the post-independence period as a form that suppressed other generic formations within the Bombay film industry. Through a parallel genealogy of state and nationalist discourses, Rajadhyaksha suggests that the aesthetic category of realism was used in a melodramatic mode, to create national fictions. Renarrativizing a variety of earlier genres, the epic melodrama (like the mythologicals and the costume dramas) turned "into a major cultural hegemony within a broader ideological container of the nationalist allegory and its several more abstracted metaphors" (Rajadhyaksha 1993, 60). Rajadhyaksha then makes a distinction between an avant-garde realism and the melodramatic use of realism, positing the radical initiative of the former against the hegemonic function of the latter. Rajadhyaksha maintains this distinction, as a political point, even in his *Encyclopedia of Indian Cinema* (1999), for it is through this distinction that a political critique of the popular cinema is launched.

Nationalism's overwhelming ubiquity in the debates on Indian modernity is obvious in the work of almost all the authors writing on Indian cinema. Even this book does not claim to be innocent of this influence. The issue is further complicated when the film industry gets defined as a "national cinema." India has four powerful film industries located in different parts of the country, each addressing cultural specificities and contexts. While there are many similarities and overlaps in the narratives, the differences are equally striking in both content and form. Any attempt to locate or club all these industries within the category of a "national cinema" would only suppress the textures that go into the making of these diverse films. Therefore, assumptions about "the national" speaking through "the cinema" need to be attentive to this diverse reality.[21]

When categories of nationalism, the state, the mode of production, ideology, and secularism get retailed as typical formations of "Indian modernity," the texture, fluidity, and fragmentary character of urban life seem to get lost. As I show in the following chapters, the landscape of urban life has powerfully enriched the archive of cinema. Consider the space of the footpath, the flyover, housing, spatial claustrophobia, the discursive space of language, the spectacles of fashion, and the practices of violence, suspicion, and the *stranger* in the urban crowd, to name just a few. The cinema thus constitutes a hidden archive of the Indian modern. I use the words "cinematic modern" with deliberation, as it is through the fleeting yet memorable forms of urban life in popular Bombay cinema that the texture of modernity in India can be understood.

With the urban experience as the prism that enables the privilege of a refracted gaze, I read a set of films to draw on their embodied nature as texts that are saturated with themes that the contemporary city in India tries to grapple with. At no point do I suggest that my reading of a limited number of films can speak for the entire volume of production emerging from the film industry. Nor do I suggest that the urban experience, as I understand it, is the dominant mode of experiencing the social or the cinematic. Instead, I see my project as an intervention that seeks to interrogate received orthodoxies in which the cinema is categorized within what is seen as hegemonic or ideological in Indian history and politics. I resist the desire to read the popular as an instrumental sphere steeped in ideological structures or "national" allegories (Jameson 1986). With such an approach, there is little to learn from the dynamic of form or in-depth historical investigation into the textures that constitute the world of cinema. Subsuming the popular within a "hegemonic mode" or "ideological structure" rules out any critical engagement with issues of experience and cinematic practice, which the popular cinema has enabled in so many contradictory ways.

In this book, I attempt to show how the city and Bombay cinema form force fields through which categories of the national, cultural authenticity, and globalization can be complicated and addressed in new ways. Through unorthodox journeys into the world of cinema, I present the cinematic city as an archive that is deeply saturated with urban dreams, desires, and fears. Popular cinema is not just an arena of competing discourses, but a powerful lens that provides a complex vision of the cinematic city. By engaging with various cinematic aspects, such as characterization, acting/performance, plot, mise-en-scène, language, editing, and music, *Bombay Cinema* explores the complex decentering of landscapes to accommodate action and spectacle. The effort here is to enable a critical reflection on the "significant tension between the place in film and the space in film" (Aitkin and Zonn, 17). It becomes important here to understand the tension produced by the interaction between film's visual performance, on the one hand, and its narrative drive, on the other. The power of cinema rests in the medium's spectacular visual excess and performance, which spill out of the narrative to speak a unique language. In the introduction to a recent anthology on film and the city, the authors argue that the cinematic form is a peculiarly spatial system that allows one to explore the relationship between urban social space and cinematic space. Arguing that cinema is more a spatial system than a textual system, the authors suggest that spatiality is what gives the medium "a special potential to illuminate the lived spaces of the city and urban societies, allowing for a full synthetic understanding of cinematic theme, form, and industry in the context of global capitalism" (Shiel and Fitzmaurice, 6). I find this approach suggestive and useful. It is for this reason that *Bombay Cinema* privileges mise-en-scène and sequential fragments over narrative analysis.

An argument for the "cinema of attractions" is also relevant to this book. Tom Gunning's pioneering intervention into the history of early cinema to suggest a pre-classical narrative desire for visual intensity is extremely relevant to my discussion and approach to Indian cinema. In Gunning's argument, the spatial mise-en-scène of early framing privileged the act of display rather than storytelling. This "cinema of attractions" was the preferred mode of cinema whose fundamental grip on spectators depended on an ability to arouse their curiosity for visual spectacle. Through a framing device that mobilized display techniques, early cinema drew on the visual spectacle of the fairgrounds, amusement parks, vaudeville performances, and so on, in which shock, surprise, and sensational pleasure evoked the new landscape of urban modernity. The "cinema of attractions" became subsidiary to what later emerged as the predominant form of classical narration, but survived in the structures of early avant-garde films and in the musical genre in which an explicit frontal address and display techniques were privileged in the musical numbers (2004). In the context of the form of popular Bombay cinema, Gunning's argument has been evocative since song sequences and their function as a landscape of "attractions" sitting within the narrative make popular cinema available for different kinds of display techniques. These issues are discussed at length in chapters 3 and 4, in which fashion and panoramic architectural design are mobilized by the song sequences to privilege display over storytelling. Given the unique form of popular Bombay cinema and my own desire to understand its relationship to urban space, this book, while taking the story form seriously, privileges mise-en-scène and sequential fragments as against narrative analysis.

Each chapter in this book arrives at a problem of representation within the contemporary by tracing a historical genealogy of the issue at hand. The first chapter is on the cinematic articulation of anger. The cinematic city in this chapter dialogues between the political turmoil of the 1970s and the culture of suspicion and strangeness that emerged in the city of the 1990s. The city, in this opening chapter, is the site of tragedy and myth, as we engage with the figure of the "angry man" and the "psychotic."

Chapter 2 situates the body language and speech of the cinematic *tapori* (vagabond) within a historical debate on language both within and outside the film industry. This chapter also shows the intertextual embeddedness of the tapori within the wider circulation of masculinity and rebel-male images of Hollywood cinema.

Chapter 3 traces the historical formation of a moral discourse on women that sought to divide their existence within the modernist categories of public and private space. This discourse offers us interesting insights into women's relationship to the city, which was in cinema to a large extent mediated through the figure of the westernized *vamp*. In the 1990s, the new landscape of song and dance sequences brought about the death of the vamp, whose performative stance, combined with techniques of fashion photography and window displays, is today used to present the heroine on-screen.

Chapter 4 looks at the rise of panoramic interiors as a new fetish form through which cultural identity is negotiated. This landscape of the interior combines design techniques with architectural spaces to produce a "virtual city" in which the new global family can displace the physical spaces of the city and also reinvent tradition and modernity. Chapter 5 looks at the cinematic articulation of terror in the new gangster films, as a mode of expression that is trying to grapple with spatial anxiety, claustrophobia, and the experience of the uncanny within the city of Bombay.

Bombay Cinema therefore attempts to situate the city within a set of related practices and discourses that in turn have influenced the way the cinema has represented and archived the urban experience in India. In this century of cinema, the city can hardly be understood without taking cognizance of the visual world. Entering the world of the cinematic and the urban experience through a form of engagement that is markedly interdisciplinary, this book attempts to indicate how other readings can be drawn upon to push the possibilities of popular Bombay cinema. It is my hope that by illustrating cinema's ability to surprise us with its mediation on everyday life and experience, *Bombay Cinema* can con-tribute to our collective and ongoing effort to understand the complex texture of modernity as it unfolds in the space of metropolitan India.

CHAPTER ONE

Rage on Screen

Anger, says scriptwriter Salim Khan, is a powerful human emotion that lends itself to creative possibilities.[1] The articulation of a tragic and divided urban subjectivity has played an enormous role in cinema, working primarily through the performative power of anger. When combined with revenge, anger allows one to create a temporality of past, present, and future through which the revenge plot reaches its climactic resolution. In the revenge narrative, the past is the site of traumatic memory to be settled in the future. Constructed as journeys driven by a sense of rage, revenge narratives can play out an unusual cartography of the mind and its relationship to the past and to memory. When revenge unfolds within the landscape of the city, it can be deployed to provide access to an urban topography. Anger, revenge, and urban subjectivity in popular Bombay cinema was perhaps most influential during the "angry man" phenomenon of the 1970s and 1980s, personified in the figure of actor Amitabh Bachchan. Bachchan's brooding, inward-looking anger was symptomatic of the time. It was an anger that mobilized the experience of alienation and suffering to navigate an urban geography and also to lash out at a system of social injustice. The "angry man" phenomenon faded away during the 1980s. While revenge continued to play an important role in cinema, it was not until the psychotic films of the 1990s that revenge was mobilized again for a novel exploration of selfhood.

In this chapter, I place the "angry man" phenomenon in dialogue with the psychotic figure[2] in order to trace the relationship between anger and the cinematic city. Engaging with this dialogue through the visual dynamics of two cult films, *Deewar* (The wall, Yash Chopra, 1975) and *Baazigar* (The player, Abbas Mastan, 1993), I journey through the many experiences of urban life and the city that these films embody. The urban landscape of *Baazigar* is clearly very different from that of *Deewar*. *Baazigar* speaks to an experience of the 1990s, while *Deewar* addresses the social crisis of the 1970s. And yet these films need to be placed in dialogue with each other so that the changing urban landscape of the last three decades can be delineated. Also, Javed Siddiqui, the scriptwriter of *Baazigar,* saw the protagonist's characterization as an extension of the "angry man" phenomenon. Thematically, what binds together *Deewar* and *Baazigar* is the deployment of anger and revenge to negotiate an urban cartography.

Deewar looks at childhood memory, the trauma of separation from an "originary" space outside the metropolis, the yearning to project the past onto the future, and a relentless drive toward death as the only utopian possibility. *Deewar* is in many senses the film that marks the acknowledgment of the crisis of postcolonial nationalism. Disenchantment with the settled categories of nationhood is mediated through the crisis of the family, fratricidal conflict, and tragedy.[3] It is this disenchantment that spoke (albeit complexly) to a society convulsed by social struggles that culminated in the imposition of the Emergency.[4] *Deewar* is a deeply contextualized text: there is an "elective affinity" (Weber) between the "moment" of the film and historical transformation.

Baazigar is the first of the psychotic films and is very different from *Deewar*. The psychotic does not speak the broad social language of the earlier "angry man," but remains within a world of seemingly unrelated individual obsessions. The psychotic is desiring of both a family and the family's ultimate destroyer, who kills even as he loves, evoking passionate emotions of love and hate through, for example, his obsession with a young woman in the films *Darr* (Fear, Yash Chopra, 1994) and *Anjam* (The result, Rahul Rawail, 1995), and through the mother in *Baazigar*. What makes *Baazigar* interesting is its narrative rendering of a contemporary experience of evil to present the *stranger* in the city. This new stranger is not an easily identifiable type—that is, he is not a villain or someone belonging to an ethnic group. What marks this character is his ordinariness and his ability to lead a deceptive life.

A feature common to both *Baazigar* and *Deewar* is the use of the idea of homelessness as a master trope that lends credibility to the urban hero's imaginative performance. The Indian city, says Ashis Nandy, has "re-emerged as the location of a homelessness forever trying to reconcile non-communitarian individualism and associated forms of freedom with communitarian responsibilities, freely borne. Apparently, the city of the mind does not fear homelessness; it even celebrates homelessness" (1997, 19). Homelessness evokes a certain morality and power. It has the ability to capture contemporary imagination by situating the city as a site of *ruin*, from within which a range of discourses can emerge. Homelessness has always had a powerful appeal in India's literary and cinematic traditions, for it magnifies the experience of loss, deprivation, and anger. As a powerful metaphor signifying community, loss, solidarity, and conflict, homelessness has been extensively deployed by popular cinema to navigate the urban experience. The "footpath" in the city is usually the imagined space of homelessness, where millions without a home sleep. It is the imaginary reference point for many narratives in which the experience of childhood on the streets provides the moral justification for the protagonist's actions (as, for example, in *Awara*, 1951; *Deewar; Muqqaddar Ka Sikander*, 1978; *Baazigar*). Homelessness also infuses the nonlegal cultures of the street with a moral integrity that gives legitimacy to the journey of the antihero.

Homelessness has been a recurring theme in popular cinema since the 1950s. Over the last three decades, the pathos that influenced earlier narratives of homelessness has all but disappeared.[5] In contemporary cinema, homelessness introduces scars that cannot be easily erased. The metropolis is now the place where memory and homelessness converge to create a range of complex representations. One of the central features of the moral universe of homelessness since the 1970s is the cathartic and powerful use of violence and revenge. Revenge and violence can link loss to action, creating a new breed of antiheros, whose journey through life becomes deeply connected to the experiences of the "unintended city."

The "Unintended City," the Crisis of Democracy, and the Melodramatic Mode

Debates on modernity and the metropolis have overwhelmingly emerged in the context of technological changes as they were experienced in major Western cities. This is evident in the work of several writers engaging with the cinematic city. A few examples help substantiate this. In his book *The Films of Fritz Lang,* Tom Gunning approaches the theme of modernity by presenting Lang as an auteur filmmaker (2000). Gunning suggests that Lang's technique goes beyond the shock element of modernity (captured so vividly in early silent cinema) to deal primarily with its systematic nature, wherein the human will is forced to encounter the sinister power of modern technological machines. Lang's best-known and most controversial film, *Metropolis* (1927), is "the allegory of the future as the triumph of the machine" (Gunning 2000, 55). *Metropolis* is in many ways the pretext for Ridley Scott's science-fiction film *Blade Runner* (1982), in which a future Los Angeles is presented as bleak, decaying, and fragmented. Providing us with a thorough and extensive reading of the film, Scott Bukatman presents *Blade Runner* as a text that contains rich insights into the experience of space as simultaneously imprisoning and liberating. The city in *Blade Runner* appears both crowded and empty. Bukatman draws attention to Simmel's theses that in the city the human as an object of economic relations is in conflict with the human as a unique individual being. Bukatman suggests that Simmel remains valid even today: films like *Blade Runner* "make a place" to "test the tensions, and play out the contradictions, of concentrated cities, spectacular societies and the continuing struggle to exist in the bright dark spaces of the metropolis" (Bukatman 1997, 86).

Both Gunning and Bukatman locate their core argument in the context of the Western metropolis and its overwhelming experience of technological dominance. While important, this fact does not provide us with the lens to view or comprehend the complexities of different sites of the modern metropolis. One of the key distinctions between the urban experience in India and that in the West is that in South Asia the urban form has neither been overwhelming nor hegemonic. The city itself is marked, even scarred, by the fuzziness of lines between the "urban" and the "rural." In imaginative terms, the "village" is never absent from everyday life in the city. The narrative of migration and departure from home is a key part of urban life. The street in the city is a site for the flow of both rural and urban imaginations. Part consumption space during the day, the street also becomes home to the homeless at night. Thus the term "footpath" seems more relevant and has been used extensively by Bombay cinema to conjure a powerful and mythic space in the city. The "footpath" evokes a whole range of experiences related to loss, nostalgia, pain, community, and anger. There are innumerable examples of heroes referring to the "footpath," either to legitimize their actions or to draw attention to their roots or their past. The imagined space of the "footpath" in cinema is contradictory and complex, generating intense performances. These performances articulate the experiences of the "unintended city."

Following Max Weber, the Indian architect and social activist Jai Sen defines the "unintended city" as "the often unintended result of planning and social work programs and policies, as opposed to direct exploitation" (1976). This "unintended city" is the underside of the original master plan, whose focus has always been the "official city."[6] The "unintended city" is needed by the official city for its survival, "but it cannot own up to its 'unintended' self" (Nandy 1998, 2). Weber first put forth the brilliantly ambiguous formulation on the unintended consequences of modernity. In doing so, he problematized the disjunction between intention and consequence, between the neat architecture of modernist projects and the contradictory results that were actually obtained. The idea of a perfect city has held the imagination of a variety of thinkers since the time of Augustine. In India, urban life was subjected to a process of careful control and regulation beginning in the colonial period (Chakrabarty 1991; Kaviraj 1997; Bannerjee 1989). The regulating projects of both colonialism and nationalism, which were sometimes ambiguous and sometimes brutal, quickly generated their own "unintended" results. Practices, flows, and contradictory movements emerged, often outside the grasp of planners of the urban and the political classes. "Unintendedness" seems to capture the very soul of postcolonial Indian cities.

The bulk of the people in the "unintended city" are poor migrants who flock to cities in search of work and a better life. While planners build the city for cars and the urban elite, causing many hardships for those belonging to the unintended city, the juxtaposition of a "master plan" and its unintended consequences gives rise to a space where both the rural and the urban coexist, sometimes in conflict with each other and sometimes in harmony. Jai Sen vividly describes the buzz of a Calcutta street to drive home his point:

> A cart overloaded with hay swaying along Bondel Road, pursued by the horn blasts of an impatient bus. Laundry in a rickshaw being brought across Chittaranjan Avenue at midday, the rickshaw-wallah all but gets run over by a state bus. (33–34)

This tension between the "official" and the "unintended" city is at the heart of the urban imagination in India and is perhaps true for many other parts of the Third World. Uprootedness combined with rejection by the "greater" city produces deep resentment and anger, born out of the inability to change the logic of "unintendedness." The result of this simmering anger is deep despair and desperation. For this reason, "the toilers come to constitute a mass of people infused with a deep discontent and a searing sense of loss, an army in search of an enemy, of a target to hit out at" (Pendse 1996, 23). Unintendedness faced its biggest crisis during the 1970s, with the rise of powerful urban movements.

The early 1970s saw social protest concentrated in India's cities and towns. A whole new generation of unemployed youth, who saw little in the inflated claims of developmentalism, took to the streets (Kothari, 216–19). There was a slow erosion of the exaggerated, almost overwhelming presence of the state in urban daily life. A significant nonlegal urban subculture (filled with illegal supply chains, distribution, and petty crime) emerged. This subculture spread to those spheres of urban life that were vacated by the state, from which the rhetorical claims of nationalist growth had long evaporated. In fact, the regime had waged massive campaigns against smugglers and black marketers, often without great success. There is little doubt that the movements and the public cynicism in cities and towns in the 1970s marked an important break in the relatively settled period of the first two decades after independence. Urban life now entered an ongoing period of crisis and conflict.

In 1973, railway workers all over India went on strike, bringing the economy to a standstill. The scale of the strike was unprecedented in the history of postcolonial India and was all the more remarkable because it happened just two years after the regime had claimed victory in its war against Pakistan in 1971. The strike was brutally repressed and its leaders sent to jail. In that same year, there was a large student movement in the western state of Gujarat that paralyzed the state. It was quickly followed by an equally large student movement in Bihar. By early 1975, a vocal opposition coalition led by Jai Prakash Narain, a Gandhian, besieged the regime. In mid 1975, the Congress government declared a state of national emergency, citing threats to national security.[7] With civil rights suspended and the media censored, thousands of opposition activists were thrown in jail (Frankel). The postcolonial republican model now lay in shambles.[8]

In this period, the critiques of development and the increasing author-
itarianism of the post-independence regime carried urban referents—
even the bulk of protests against the Emergency were held in cities. During the Emergency, the regime carried out its visions of social engineering:
mass sterilization of the urban poor, forcible resettlement of millions of
migrant workers from the inner cities to suburbs, and the constant use
of the language of disease as a substitute for democratic politics (Tarlo
2003). It is not surprising that this period, which is referred to as the
"crisis of democracy" (Kaviraj 1996, 114–38), witnessed the emergence of
nonlegality as a popular trope in Bombay cinema. Reworking a certain
vision of modernity in which the state is the sole repository of legitimate
action, the hero took on the role of smuggler *(Deewar)*. As sections of
the state became criminalized and corrupt, a nonlegal sphere gained
social legitimacy. The moral divisions between the legal and the nonlegal, the legitimate and the criminal, grew increasingly fuzzy, opening
up a reflection on dystopian forms in urban life. The older relationship
between ethical action and the genealogy of the Bombay film hero
could not always be easily maintained.

The antihero can be seen as a performative figure that emerged from
a cynical political culture in which the division between "good" and "evil"
was becoming increasingly blurred. This is not to suggest that a film like
Deewar is functional to a cynical culture, but rather to suggest, as Elin
Diamond does, that performance "could produce consciousness, make
meanings, provoke contestation" (6). To produce new trends and sites
of contestation, it is important not only to read these performative sites
in a manner that recognizes the context within which the production
and reception of the films are embedded, but also to show how sense is
being made of the social and cultural context. For an understanding of
the anithero's performative power, it is imperative that we understand
why the melodramatic form became the ideal mode to narrate the urban
conflicts of the 1970s.

The urban landscape is akin to a melodramatic form in which conflicting practices play themselves out in spatial, aural, and bodily configurations (Raban, 11–32). Stories of the rich and poor in conflict inhabit
empowering narratives of social justice articulated best through a melodramatic form. Melodrama draws the social world into the realm of the
family to present heartrending conflicts through extremes of emotion,
nightmarish conditions, and tragedy. Placing the individual as a figure

in a harsh modern world, melodrama attempts to resolve the injustices of the world by creating oppositions between different sets of moralities; these conflicts are then redeemed through the power of poetic justice. It is a form that expresses the insecurities of modernity and then seeks to resolve the chaos and crisis of the world through some kind of utopian myth. Combining heroism with sensational excitement, violence, and cosmic ambition, melodrama is a kind of expressionism that is driven by a hyperbolic rhetorical mode, playing out our deepest desires and subjective emotion within the realm of popular culture (Brooks 1976; Gledhill 1987; Singer 2001). The melodramatic structure in film plays with color, music, light, and a particular style of performance, using cinematic techniques to present its central thematic. That which is not always possible in real life is played out as an emotionally saturated performance of excess.

If melodrama is seen primarily as an emotionally charged form, then Ben Singer's more recent intervention has drawn attention to the tactile sensationalism of modernity most vividly present in cityscapes as an important component of the melodramatic spectacle (2001). In many ways, Jai Sen's descriptions of the cart and the horn blasts, the rickshaw with laundry, and the bus in the streets of Calcutta appear like snapshots that conjure the same experience of hyperstimulus that Singer evokes in his engagement with melodrama. The powerful collision between premodern and modern forms of experience produced "an anxiety about the perilousness of life in the modern city and also symbolized the kinds of nervous shocks and jolts to which the individual was subjected in a new environment" (Singer 2001, 69). The experience of the "unintended city" produces the social codes for the melodramatic rendering of the urban landscape. With powerful urban movements questioning the logic of "unintendedness" in the 1970s, it is not surprising that Bombay's melodrama became the ideal vehicle for the narration of this urban conflict. Thus emerged the figure of the "angry man," who addressed the crisis of the period as a figure representing the margins of society.

The Urban Warrior: Amitabh Bachchan and the "Angry Man"

It is difficult to discuss the "angry man" phenomenon without the screen persona of actor Amitabh Bachchan, who was often known as Vijay on-screen. So linked and intertwined are the two that any analysis of one has to deal with the other. Amitabh Bachchan has been described as the "first urban-industrial man in Indian popular cinema, one who made the earlier chocolate-pie heroes obsolete" (Nandy 1997, 26). The height of his stardom is yet to be matched by any other actor. Writing in the newspaper *Pioneer* more than two decades after the birth of the "angry man" image, journalist Avijit Ghosh noted, "Never before had an actor and his screen persona typified and embodied his times and its con- sciousness so closely and so graphically. Hindi cinema was to be affected in every form" (1).

Bombay scriptwriter Javed Akhtar (who coauthored, with Salim Khan,[9] most of the "angry man" films) attributed the genre's success to a break- down of the legal system and of traditional lifestyle in India (Gehlot 1995, 234). The hero, as a criminally minded vigilante, "mirrored the rage and disillusionment of the youth in the seventies. They saw them- selves in his roughhewn screen persona, and fantasized about the power they never had" (234). Psychoanalyst Sudhir Kakkar saw the "angry man" phenomenon as a direct product of development and moderniza- tion (1992, 38).

In director Shyam Benegal's perception, a sense of idealism in the post-independence period is articulated in the cinema right up to the end of the 1960s. This idealism is evident in the films of Raj Kapoor and in films like *Naya Daur* (New era, B. R. Chopra, 1957). "And then comes the despair, of things not quite moving, aspirations not being met or the law not working quite well. This is when revenge and vengeance emerge through the figure of the "angry man."[10] Clearly, filmmakers, academics, and critics do not hesitate to link the "angry man" phenome- non to a rising social, economic, and political crisis. However, what seems missing in these sociological perceptions are the complex ways in which the urban experience is navigated both by individual film narra- tives and by Bachchan's own performances.

Bachchan's rise to stardom was epitomized by his complex and varied portrayals of the "angry man," a screen space occupied by the star for well over a decade. Bachchan's dialogue delivery, sense of timing, and superbly crafted restraint in acting ushered in a new kind of anger on the screen, an anger generated primarily by his physical gestures and movements. The brooding, inward-looking yet outwardly searching, vulnerable anger of Bachchan was symptomatic of its time. Bachchan's ability to absorb and transmit both the "modern" and the "traditional," the Eastern and the Western, through a novel body language is perhaps the single most important reason for his unmatched star status in the history of Bombay cinema. Bachchan was neither completely "Indian" nor totally "Western." The son of a well-known Hindustani poet who grew up in the Indian city of Allahabad,[11] Bachchan was exposed to Western culture as part of the cultural intelligentsia. This background seems to have privileged Bachchan with a body language that was always projected in his screen persona. Javed Akhtar says:

> Amitabh Bachchan cannot be compared to any other actor. Bachchan is an exceptional actor. He has been fortunate enough to be living in a kind of no man's land for a very long time, between the eastern oriental Indian and western culture. So that is how and that is where he has been able to imbibe from both sides. Today in modern India (whether the writer or the actor or the director), only those people will be effective who have the best of both worlds. If you are too westernized then you get alienated by the audience, you get too far—if you are too Indian then you cannot fulfill their aspirations because their aspirations are different. So you have to be the synthesis of Indian and western influences and I think fortunately Amitabh had the background and circumstances for that. (Mazumdar and Jhingan, "The Legacy of the Angry Man")

Clearly, the synthesis that Akhtar refers to here speaks to the peculiarity of the urban experience in India. An uneven modernity needs complex performances that can address a range of experiences. It was Bachchan's ability to combine multiple narratives and yet retain their distinctness that made him such a popular star for so long (Mazumdar 2000, 238–64).

Bachchan's on-screen persona, Vijay, was an angry hero, torn between a desired future and an unhappy and turbulent past. As the "good bad hero," Vijay's "badness is not shown as intrinsic or immutable but as a reaction to a developmental deprivation of early childhood, often a mother's loss, absence or ambivalence towards the hero" (Kakkar 1992, 37). Operating within private worlds and the turbulent public arena of political citizenship, the crisis of legality, and received notions of order and individual freedom, Vijay emerged as the quintessential urban hero whose sense of loss became the driving force of all the "angry man" narratives. It was the combination of a performative mode that could deal with a deep sense of loss performed through restraint,[12] a cosmopolitan demeanor (as elaborated by Akhtar), and a blend of Eastern, Western, traditional, modern, small-town, and big-city styles that helped Bachchan

Amitabh Bachchan *(right)* as the "angry man" in *Deewar* (1975). Courtesy Trimurti Films.

in his march to stardom. Bachchan's ability to deal with "interiority" made him the most suitable actor for the character of Vijay, whose "inner exile" had to be performed with tremendous complexity on-screen. Vijay was a character whose past was traumatic and haunted him throughout his life. Vijay was driven by his past, constantly yearning for peace but self-destructive in his journey. The combination of loss, anger, and revenge, which coalesced in the "angry man," drew heavily on the epic structure of the *Mahabharata* and one of its most fascinating figures, Karna.

Karna is a major figure in the *Mahabharata*, a well-known Sanskrit epic that narrates the story of a war between cousins. Rich in philosophical and ethical negotiations, the *Mahabharata* continues even today to occupy a significant place in the public and private imagination of Indians, particularly urban Indians. One of the central themes of the *Mahabharata* is the rendering of unfulfillment as the normal condition of humanity. As Iravati Karve says, "to some extent each major figure in the *Mahabharata* is defeated by life, but none so completely as Karna" (138). Karna was the illegitimate son of a princess, Kunti. Abandoned by his mother for fear of a scandal, Karna was put in an ornate casket, which floated down a river. A charioteer named Adhiratha found the casket and brought up the child as his own. Kunti later married Pandu, the king of Hastinapur, and, along with his second wife, became the mother of five sons. After the death of the second wife, Kunti became the sole mother of the five brothers who were known as the *Pandavas*. Karna grew up as a *Suta*[13] but always hoped for the status of a *Kshatriya*,[14] since he knew that when he was found in the casket, he was dressed like a *Kshatriya*. Karna became a great warrior whose bravery, generosity, and self-destruction became legendary.

In the course of the epic, Karna joins the Kauravas (the rival cousins of the Pandavas, who are Karna's blood brothers) to fight the great battle between the cousins at Kurukshetra. On the eve of the battle, Karna discovers from Kunti that the Pandavas are his real brothers, but he decides to remain loyal to the Kauravas. Karna dies when Arjuna, Kunti's third son and Karna's archrival, attacks him.

Throughout his life, Karna was haunted by feelings of rejection and he desperately tried to transcend his lowly status. Insecure and defiant because of his uncertain parentage, Karna was unwilling to accept his status as the son of a charioteer. Karna's persona seems to "symbolize the predicament of the self made person in a society not fully receptive to individualism" (Nandy 1997, 25). As a powerful force whose individuality and aggressive posturing could give voice to the wretched, discarded, and marginalized outsiders of the city, Karna's image could very well provide the "unintended city" with a sense of pride and performance, without losing the experience of a deep anguish. Karna was forever haunted by his past and the memory of his lost childhood. The struggle to master the narrative of fate, and still become caught in the cycle of that fate, marks Karna's personality development. In a provocative treatise, Nandy evokes Karna's persona in order to trace "the course of India's ambivalent relationship with the urban industrial vision" (1997, 21). Karna's particular place in an urban space deeply implicated in uprootedness, loss, and fear can be related to the experiences of the "unintended city."

Nandy succinctly develops the connection between Karna's mythic image and the rise of contemporary cinema's "urban warrior," who negotiates life through "the technology of violence" (1997, 26). Nandy sees in Karna the elements that mark the rise of a modern hero, whose journey through life ends in tragedy, unfulfilled and full of despair. Nandy provides us with the connections between Karna, an ambivalent industrial vision, and cinema, without going into the actual contours and cartography of the cinematic city. While Karna's presence in the "angry man" persona is undeniable,[15] the most unself-conscious and direct acknowledgment of Karna's presence as an "urban warrior" can be seen in *Deewar*, the film that catapulted Bachchan to absolute stardom.[16] A detailed analysis of *Deewar* thus becomes necessary to understand not just the cinematic city of the 1970s, but also the troubled and tragic journey of the antihero.

The Urban Cartography of *Deewar*

Deewar, directed by Yash Chopra,[17] is the story of two brothers who follow different paths. One brother, Vijay (played by Bachchan), becomes a dockworker/smuggler; the other brother, Ravi (played by Shashi Kapoor), becomes a police officer. *Deewar* develops various strategies to confront social crisis, by acknowledging the existence of widespread poverty and inequality and the ineffectiveness of the regime. But *Deewar* also develops a striking acknowledgment of urban space. In *Deewar*, the city loses its fundamentally diabolical character, as found in earlier cinema, becoming instead a space where the hopes and yearnings unleashed by the promise of nationalism are either fulfilled or dashed.

The entire story of *Deewar* is presented in flashback as Ravi is honored by the state for performing his duty in an "exemplary" manner.[18] The flashback relates the story of a militant worker, Anand Babu (played by Satyen Kappu), forced to betray his comrades in order to protect his family. The posing of the family versus the community of workers sets the tone of the film and resonates throughout the narrative. As Anand runs away in shame and humiliation, the older son (the young Vijay), is caught by the workers and taken to a man who tattoos the boy's arm with the phrase *Mera Baap Chor Hai* (My father is a thief). This tattoo marks the different paths taken by the two brothers and influences Vijay's personality and character development. Vijay is scarred, physically, symbolically, and metaphorically. The scar becomes a signifier for marginality and social displacement, soon taking Vijay outside the pale of the family.

Caught in the conflict between the two brothers is the overarching figure of the mother, who clearly evokes the mythical conflict of Karna/ Arjuna as the underlying grid of the narrative. The mythical language of the *Mahabharata* becomes in *Deewar* "a type of speech chosen by history" (Barthes 1993, 110). It is not the eternal play of the epic, but a historical reworking of its ethical and philosophical dimension.[19] The reemergence of Karna and his particular significance in the 1970s "angry man" genre shows how the image of the "angry man" helped in negotiating the political and social turmoil of urban India. *Deewar* carries two distinctly opposed voices; one represents the state and goes on to cherish the dream of the Emergency, while the other offers us a critique of the "system." Nikhat Kazmi, a leading film critic with the *Times of India,* attributes the success of *Deewar* to its new kind of hero:

> The success of *Deewar* largely lay in the fact that it brought to the fore a new hero. One who was drawn from a different milieu altogether. When it came to retelling tales of poverty in films, it was mostly the rural poor that had hitherto found representation in popular cinema. For the rest, the characters were usually drawn from the frightfully rich or the comfortable middle class. Here for the first time was a hero who not only emerged from the working class, but whose silence and suppressed rage lent a voice to the angst of the urban poor. The unprecedented migration of destitute villagers into cities and towns had manifested itself in a mushrooming of slums all over. There in the underbelly of every big city were the hundreds of haphazard bustees (slum dwellings), spilling over with the down and outs, the unemployed, the underpaid strugglers and drifters. Chopra's protagonist found his alter ego in the umpteen angry young men living in the shadows of the high-rise concrete jungle. Hence the unstinted applause for him and his ilk (124–25).

The angry persona of Amitabh Bachchan became the archetypal imagination deployed to render a state of urban despair. *Deewar*'s success and power lies in its skillful deployment of melodrama to heighten the conflict between the two brothers. To a large extent, this is achieved through a strategy of contextualizing the two characters sociologically to represent a form of urban conflict and drama. This sociology, which is intricately woven into the plot, is aimed at presenting a causal explanation for the sequence of events and for Vijay's estrangement from his family, the law, and the city. What is significant in the film is Vijay's development as an alienated loner, a man who suffers from an "inner exile." *Deewar* follows Vijay's pain through a narrative that explains every action and decision he is taking. All these explanations are grounded in the memory and experience of urban poverty, homelessness, and deprivation, seen closely through his family's journey.

Vijay's transition from childhood to adulthood takes place in the early part of the film with the screenplay dwelling on different spaces in the city—construction sites, under bridges, hutments, high-rise buildings, schools, and places where children work. Vijay sees his mother struggle at a construction site where a contractor is harassing her. His anger erupts one day when the contractor dismisses his mother after humiliating her. Vijay reacts to his mother's pain by throwing a stone at the contractor. Later that night, we see the family in their home, which is literally the street under the bridge. As the narrative of poverty is emphasized, the mother reprimands Vijay for reacting the way he did. Several characters in the film repeat her statement that the poor need to watch their steps. The under-bridge space, which is also referred to as the "footpath," here acquires a mythic dimension as the site that becomes the meeting point for the two estranged brothers as adults.[20]

The film's childhood sequence also presents us with the state of children in the city. Vijay and another boy are shown polishing shoes for rich men. One day a man throws money at the boys after getting his shoes polished. Vijay reacts and says the money should be given to them in their hands and not thrown at them. He emphasizes that they have polished shoes, not begged for the money. This is another moment to which the narrative later returns.[21] Childhood sequences such as this one are central to Vijay's character development and offer us a sociological explanation for the life of crime that he finally adopts.

Deewar's sociology of urban poverty is emphasized even in the adult life of the two heroes. There are two separate incidents that shape the decisions made by both brothers. In Vijay's case, the narrative focuses on the lives of dockworkers. The dockworkers have to deal with organized extortions conducted by local crime bosses. A major extortion sequence in the film begins with the workers standing in line, each placing two rupees in a small container as they pass the extortionist. A new worker, Satyadev Dubey, asks Rahim Chacha (a Muslim worker) why they should give their hard-earned money to the extortionists. Rahim tries to reason with Satyadev, saying that this is the fine they must pay for their poverty. The worker is still unconvinced and talks about his family back home who relies on the money he sends. He also talks about his sister, who cannot get married unless he saves money for her dowry.

The conversation testifies to the relationship many workers in the city have to their families living either in villages or in small towns.

The mother (Nirupa Roy) with her two sons in *Deewar*. Courtesy Trimurti Films.

Here the village appears like a hidden backdrop with the worker clearly established as a migrant, whose real home is outside the metropolis. Satyadev's statement initially seems to suggest that the village needs to be taken care of. However, the imagined space of the village, mired in "patriarchal traditions" and a struggle for survival, is juxtaposed with the plight of the dockworkers. This juxtaposition presents a certain continuity of crisis rather than a counterspace to the city. The village of imagination here is no utopian space. Instead the sequence tells us that all narratives of the village are now imagined through the prism of the urban experience. The village is inconceivable as a space without the gaze of the city (Nandy 1997, 10; Prakash 1999).

When it's his turn to place money in the container, Satyadev refuses. He is subsequently roughed up by the extortionist and pushed in front of a speeding truck. As Satyadev's money flies out of his clutched hands, the truck hits him. In the next shot, we see the workers running to look at their critically injured coworker. The camera zooms in on Vijay's face, almost imprinting him with the chain of events he has just witnessed. The staging of Satyadev's death in the dockyard is an important event. Vijay sees in the action before him the suffering and misfortune of a coworker. Vijay now becomes the bearer of the "tragic cause," internalizing Satyadev's tragic death. The event seems external to the hero, and yet marks him in a way such that Vijay's journey does not just seem rooted in individual experience, but emerges out of a shared and collective experience.

In the film's next sequence, the workers are drinking tea in the canteen. The conversation centers on the coworker who died on the way to the hospital. Rahim Chacha says the poor must always think before doing anything, and that in all the twenty-five years of his working life, he had never seen anything like this. Another worker says Satyadev lost his life for just 2 rupees. In the midst of this conversation about Satyadev's death, the fate of the poor, and the power of criminal gangs, the camera zooms to Vijay's thoughtful face. He finally responds, saying, "What has not happened in twenty-five years will happen now. From tomorrow, one more worker will refuse to pay money to the extortionists." The shot ends with Vijay slowly standing up as the camera tilts to a close-up to capture his expression. The way the camera dialogues between the context and the hero here is of great significance. There is a spatial positioning of the actor, through which the exploration of the hero's internal

Dubey's death in *Deewar*. Courtesy Trimurti Films.

thoughts and conflicts are enhanced by camera movements that im-
print the hero with the knowledge of his context, symbolizing an order
of dialogue in which the "outside" and the "inside" are interlocked. "It is
generally accepted," says Barry King, "that film poses limits on the representation of interiority, inclining towards behaviourism, showing the
surface of things. . . . Films tend to re-site the signification of interiority
away from the actor and on to the mechanism" (177).

Vijay's subjectivity is explored from the point of view of the world at
large, attempting a dual objective of identification and distance, creating a diegetic strategy of positioning the protagonist. The narrative strategy here emphasizes an internalization of external events that finally
makes Vijay resist the extortionists the next day. Through this buildup
we get a glimpse into the world of dockworkers—their struggles, their
hardships, and their acceptance of a life of humiliation. Vijay's resistance to this life is an effort to transcend the cycle of poverty and powerlessness that is sociologically narrativized in *Deewar*. The dockworker
sequence is staged to open a series of events that leads up to Vijay's transformation into a rebel. All these sequences operate as vignettes of independent events strung together through the hero's personality.

Just as Vijay's anger is contextualized through his childhood experiences and his life as a dockworker, Ravi's development is presented
through a sociology that is distant from him, but that leads him to confront family bonds. In a powerful sequence, Ravi is chasing a boy, Chander, for stealing. Unable to stop Chander, Ravi finally shoots him in the
leg. As Chander falls, Ravi runs up to see what he has stolen. The sight
of *rotis* (bread) covered with a crumpled paper shocks him, as the full
realization of what he has done hits him. This chase across the railway
tracks is also significant because it takes us to the space of the "unintended city," right next to a railway station.

In the next sequence, we see Ravi knocking on a door, a packet in his
hand. The door opens to show an old man, his wife, and a child (a young
girl) standing in a corner. The father assumes Ravi is a friend of their
arrested son Chander, who is now in the hospital. Ravi offers the packet
to the father. Placing it on the table, Ravi unwraps the packet to show
the *rotis*. The closeup of the bread is intercut with the girl's hungry face.
The bread here acquires monumental significance as the narrative of
hunger and poverty is condensed in its image. Ravi finally introduces
himself as the officer responsible for shooting their son. At this point,

the mother picks up the bread and throws it at Ravi. The mother insists that Ravi leave the house and says that they do not want his pity or charity. The mother taunts lawmakers for their bias against the poor, for their hypocrisy, and for their inability to fight the wealthy and the powerful. The mother's diatribe instills a deep sense of guilt in Ravi, evident from the silence he maintains throughout her tortured screaming. The father (a retired schoolteacher) apologizes for his wife's behavior, saying the existence of millions who are poor should hardly justify stealing. This statement further needles Ravi's conscience. The narrative use of the poor family, with three distinct responses to his charitable gesture, forces Ravi to confront the nature of inequality in the city. It also convinces him that he must confront his own brother, now a powerful smuggler in the city. A narrative of social guilt pushes Ravi to challenge family bonds as, in the next sequence, he agrees to investigate his brother. Ravi clearly stands on the side of "virtue," the law, and the state.

Deewar's contextualizing strategy for the development of the two heroes of the film appears at times like a journalistic gaze, searching desperately for "documentary evidence" to lend authenticity to the narrative. The particular use of cameo characters in different situations— the family on the other side of the rail tracks, an unemployed youth desperately searching for a job,[22] the dockworker who dies at the hands of the local mafia—all point to this conscious strategy adopted by the screenplay. These "reality driven representations" embedded within the drama of the rising conflict between the brothers points to the close relationship many films display between fiction and documentary, in which the fictive slides into the documentary form and vice versa. This narrative strategy of inhabiting two domains of the cinema (Renov, 3) enables the overwhelming sociological stance of the screenplay to emerge as a major historical document on the city of the 1970s. *Deewar* does not just resurrect the mythical dimension of the Karna-Arjuna conflict, but "makes the myth into something that reproduces history, and at the same time into something that integrates history into itself as its own episode" (Blumenberg, 633).

Mythic and Monumental Space

Henri Lefebvre points out that "a monument transmutes the fear of the passage of time and anxiety about death into splendor" (1997, 139–40). The monument exudes tranquil power, erasing the presence of violence, death, aggression, and negativity. The monument thus freezes movement, conflict, and memory (140). The monumental space can be any structure that provides a certain splendor, prestige, and power to the city. The city of *Deewar* offers us images of the street, the flyover, the railway tracks, and high-rise buildings, all of which are shown as fragile.

In perhaps the best-known and most popular sequence in the film, Vijay evokes the metaphor of the bridge, which morally separates the identity of both brothers within the city. Vijay requests that Ravi meet him under the bridge, and he recalls their shared childhood experience in the squat under the bridge. Vijay is worried that Ravi's life is in danger, because members of Vijay's gang want Ravi dead. At the meeting, Vijay suggests that, despite the loss and breakdown of all the bridges that connected the two brothers, the physical bridge imprinted with shared childhood memories is the only bridge that cannot be broken. The opening of this sequence is significant. We see Ravi waiting under the bridge at night, the same bridge beneath which the two brothers grew up. A popular nationalist song is playing on the soundtrack. The song is used both to recall a moment in Ravi's childhood[23] and to make an ironical statement through its lyrics, which talk about the beauty of the greatest country in the world (India). This juxtaposition, of the ugly underside of the bridge with the song about how beautiful India is, goes beyond a simple narrative moment, imbuing the sequence with mythic power.

As the sequence continues, Vijay gets out of a car and walks up to Ravi. The tableau-like framing of the two brothers, with the soundtrack playing in the background, makes this sequence appear like a fragment of the "totality" of the history of the characters framed within it. A deeper experience of the city lays buried beneath the cinematic framing and the mythic elements contained in the conversation between the brothers. To historically unpack this moment, the mere surface coherence of the image needs to be destabilized (Kracauer, 52). A photographic image is like a spatial entity within which a whole history is embedded. But a photograph cannot actually grasp history; it merely collects elements. It is the look of the spectator that can reveal what is not available at first sight (Kracauer, 52). Likewise, the under-bridge sequence in *Deewar* needs to be unraveled to understand the politics of monumental and mythic space in the exploration of the cinematic city.

In his analysis of *Deewar*, Madhava Prasad focuses on the conversation under the bridge as an important sequence negotiating the politics of memory. Prasad then focuses on the overarching figure of the mother, whose presence and absence in the lives of the two brothers creates the wedge that separates their identities:

> For Vijay this bridge of memory is the only remaining link between him and Ravi and he wants to reactivate it. Ravi does not yield to the unifying power of memory. Frustrated, Vijay boasts of his achievements, his worldly possessions, beside which Ravi's sub-inspector salary is a pittance. "I have all this, but what do you have?", he asks, to which Ravi replies "I have mother". This scene pre-figures Vijay's tragic destiny. It is here that we learn the differences between the new figure that is representative of the law and the old one. One is possessed by the past and seeks to be possessed and dominated by the mother, who is a figure from the past. The other, emancipated from the past, is able to "have the mother", to possess her as a part of his familial affective realm. (151)

While this is certainly a useful reading of the sequence, it misses the irony of the song, the song's significance in the conflict between the brothers, and the deeper excavation of memory that Vijay insists on. We need to reread this sequence through an alternatively juxtaposed pattern that can produce a different kind of illumination.

The bridge acquires a monumental presence whose physical structure may provide an illusory mask, hiding the overwhelming presence of the underside, which in this case is the footpath. Yet the conversation between the brothers is meant to shatter that illusion. While Ravi appears not to see the mask, Vijay tries to draw Ravi's attention to life behind the illusion, thus providing an emotionally charged critique of the modern metropolis. The wall that separates the two brothers shows two visions of the metropolitan experience. One brother wants to move on, leaving the past behind; the other wants to recall the experience of homelessness in the past, to emphasize the burden of a lived experience. This subtextual layering of the conversation is significant in the way it articulates the specific tensions of the time, namely the rise of urban conflict during the Emergency. At a broader level, the Emergency saw a concerted attempt by the state to put into motion a new authoritarian order deploying the architecture of social engineering. Cities were reconstructed by large-scale drives against the poor, who were brutally displaced from inner-city squats. This displacement was paralleled by large-scale construction projects. The discourse here was between (authoritarian) legality and order, as opposed to criminality and illegal squatting by the poor. *Deewar* seems to prefigure the crisis and politics of the Emergency, something that has been acknowledged even by scriptwriter Akhtar (Mazumdar and Jhingan, "The Legacy of the Angry Man"; Kabir, 75). By placing the official and the unofficial city in direct conflict with each other, *Deewar* speaks to some of the most immediate experiences of the Emergency—the transformation and politics of city space. One writer describes Delhi during the Emergency as an

> Amoral city, its roads get wider and sleeker . . . unreal city, the posh new architecture could be on the outskirts of Rome or Milan, Nice or Marseilles: but the *jhuggis* (slums) next to the elegant structures are as filthy and desolate as those in darkest Calcutta; every few weeks, at dead of night or in the early hours of the morning, the police will mount well organized surprise swoops; the *jhuggis*, which were put up without authorization by the wretched tramps, will be demolished, and the land will be restored to the Development Authority which will see to it that more posh constructions come up uninterrupted. (Mitra, 111–12)

The terror of losing even the little space they had became a living nightmare for many urban poor during the Emergency. Using the language of cleansing, beautification, and disciplined organization, the state conducted demolitions in many cities in India. This cleanup program was an operation that reflected the direct spatial conflict between the elite and the underclass in the cities.

It is this tension, which had been building up for years prior to the imposition of the Emergency, that gets projected in the mythic and melodramatic conflict between the two brothers in *Deewar*. While Vijay constantly focuses on the experience of the "unintended city," for Ravi that experience has little to do with his concept of "principle." The bridge and its invocation of a past life, hidden from the glitz and surface reality of the city, becomes the point of separation/tension for the brothers. Vijay wants to scratch the surface of the mere functionality of the bridge to show its deeper embeddedness in the semantics of the city. Vijay's scar marks him for life with a memory of loss and deprivation, while Ravi adopts a posture of forgetting the past. Metaphorically the brothers reproduce a familiar dialectic of the city—the juxtaposition of marked and unmarked elements, for "there exists in every city, from the moment that the city is truly inhabited by man and made by him, this fundamental rhythm of signification which is the opposition, the alternation

Amitabh Bachchan *(far left)* as the smuggler in *Deewar*. Courtesy Trimurti Films.

and the juxtaposition of marked and unmarked elements" (Barthes 1997, 168).[24]

The spatial conflict presented through the focus on the bridge also addresses the tension between "lived" and "conceived" spaces of the city. The bridge may be an abstract, conceived space for the "objective" gaze of architects and planners of the "official city." The underside of the bridge (the footpath), however, is the space of real users—homeless people whose lived experience introduces an everyday subjectivity to the space. The conflict between this "space of subjects" and the "objective" master narrative of planners is significant, because what emerges as a result is the production of a space where the "private" realm asserts itself to vigorously challenge the public one (Lefebvre 1997, 145). While Vijay evokes the bonds of the family, a shared childhood, and the concreteness of everyday reality, Ravi represents the public language of abstract citizenship; he is objective in his principles and vision and does not relent to his brother's desperate attempts to recharge the present with the concreteness of lived experience. Ravi as the symbol of the official city thus has to press the conflict to its logical end by killing his brother in the course of duty. Vijay is the weakness that could destroy Ravi's attempts at becoming an exemplary citizen. Ravi dons the symbols of the state and uses the language of principles *(adarsh)* to push the already widening schism between him and Vijay. Vijay, on the other hand, is marked, scarred for life, with a tattoo that clearly separates him from Ravi.

Recalling Memory: The Tattoo and the Badge

The separation of the brothers' identities is repeatedly experienced in the narrative. In one of the childhood sequences, we are introduced to Vijay's rebellious personality when he throws a stone at the contractor who humiliates his mother at a construction site. The mother tries to reason with Vijay that night under the bridge, asking him why he is so different from his brother, who has a calm personality. Vijay extends his tattooed arm and says, "This is the biggest difference between us." Here the scar becomes the signifier of a traumatic past whose burden is carried by Vijay until his death. Vijay's tattoo is the mark of experience, an index of memory, a regulator of his practice, a constant intrusion into his life, and a reminder of his marginality. As a narrative device, the scar/tattoo is a brilliant innovation, whose periodic introduction in the course of the film regulates the hero's journey.

The scar's presence seems to stress a return to origins, the shame of childhood. For example, following the conflict with the mafia at the dockyard, Vijay, when confronted by his mother, replies, "tum Chahte ho ki main bhi mu chupake bhag jaun?" (Do you want me to also hide my face and run away?). The reference here is to the failed/absent father, whose exit brought the family to the brink of disaster, whereupon the family left for the big city. Vijay justifies his actions as part of a redemptive strategy dealing with historical pain—pain that has been inscribed on the body of this hero. At the close of the sequence, while Vijay sleeps, the camera dwells on his tattooed arm. This is the first time in the film's depiction of Vijay's adult life that the tattoo is shown; its appearance here, through the gaze of the mother, paves the way for a narrative transition in the hero's life. When confronted by his inspector brother, Vijay uses his tattoo to justify his transition to criminality. As Ravi demands his brother sign a confession, Vijay evokes memories of their childhood, their mother's humiliation, and, finally, the tattoo. In an emotionally charged reply, Vijay says he is prepared to sign the document if his brother gets signatures from all those who destroyed their childhood.

Another important moment that focuses on Vijay's scar is when Vijay's girlfriend Anita (played by Parveen Babi), unable to accept his anguish, asks him to remove the tattoo through plastic surgery. Vijay replies that the tattoo has left deep marks on his body, soul, and arm and that no plastic surgery in the world can remove it. In a shot with both stars in the frame, we see Anita bending her head to kiss the tattoo, an erotically charged moment during which she proclaims her solidarity with Vijay's past/pain. At the funeral of Anand, the long-lost father, the camera moves from the fire of the funeral pyre to Vijay's arm as he lights the pyre. The tattoo is highlighted, embodying Vijay's burden of shame/revenge. In family-reunion dramas, meaningful objects are often highlighted to recall and resolve the broken home. In *Deewar,* however, the tattoo is constant and publicly exhibited, to be carried by Vijay until his final redemption by death. The past and its shame are important regulators of Vijay's trajectory in *Deewar.* The damaged past is the site of constant referral and the justification for criminality; a tragic death is the narrative's resolution of Vijay's defiance of the system.

The number 786 (in Islam, 786 is sacred; it is the numerical total of the chant "Bismillah E Rahmane Rahim")[25]—the number on Vijay's dockworker identification badge—operates as a symbolic object that involuntarily negotiates memory through chance encounters. The badge assumes the status of a fetish object, whose phantasmic powers are summoned periodically through the film. The badge becomes the object of memory, evoking a multilayered realm of meaning. The status of the badge changes when Vijay changes his proletarian clothing to become a smuggler—no longer worn on his arm, the badge rests uneasily in his pocket. Its magical powers are exaggerated by its very ability to transcend its initial functionality in Vijay's *coolie* (dockworker) stage.

In the *Mahabharata,* Karna dies at the hands of Arjuna when Karna's chariot wheel gets stuck in the mud. Karna gets off the chariot to unhinge the wheel. Flouting all the accepted norms of battle, Arjun kills Karna in this helpless state. It is this story of Karna's death that is evoked in *Deewar* through the use of Vijay's badge, an object closely related to Vijay's fate.

At one level, the badge inscribes Vijay's identity as an adult, his class status, by merging with his body. The badge also regulates Vijay's transition to upward mobility (when he joins a mafia gang), by acting as a magical guarantor of life. Having escaped death twice, Vijay is finally caught by death when his body is separated from the badge—he is shot by his brother just after the badge falls out of his pocket. The badge is thus deployed to negotiate the space between the mythic and the everyday. It recalls the tragic moment of Karna's death, imbuing Vijay's journey with a certain inevitability, and it organizes Vijay's identity as a dockworker. Through this play between the mythic and the everyday, the badge operates as a device that, along with the tattoo, visually helps negotiate the politics of urban memory.

At another level, the badge may be contrasted with the tattoo in organizing the narrative of the "angry man's" journey. While both the badge and the tattoo serve as sites of memory and, to some extent, regulate identity, they operate at different levels of temporality and inscription. The scar is posed as a historical given for Vijay from childhood; the badge, on the other hand, maintains an uneasy relationship to the body, allowing Vijay to move between different social spaces—notably his transition to a higher lifestyle. This displacement of the badge from the arm to the pocket evokes a desire for class ascendancy, while at the same time it draws attention to his "origins." The use of the badge and the tattoo heighten Vijay's identity, marking him as different from his brother. While Vijay is not able to transcend his fate, Ravi manages to do so.

At the end of the film, Vijay dies as a martyr, whose journey through life presents us with a complex narrative on the city. Vijay's death in his mother's arms after a chase through the city is the climactic moment of tragedy. Tragedy occurs here because each brother sees it as necessary to act in his own way. Death represents the moment of redemption, but also introduces a critique of the city through tragic suffering. Tragedy occurs in *Deewar* because, in the words of Friedrich Schopenhauer,

> characters of ordinary morality, under circumstances such as often occur... [are] so situated with regard to each other that their position compels them, knowingly and with their eyes open, to do each other the greatest injury, without any one of them being actually wrong. (cited in Williams 1966, 38)

Deewar, however, plays another very important role, clearly juxtaposing antiquity with modernity. As with Benjamin's idea of the dialectical image, *Deewar,* like a "flash of lightning," brings the past and the present into a new constellation, a dialectical relationship in which "the past and the present recognize each other across the void which separates them" (Gilloch, 113). While the present relates to the past in a purely temporal continuous way, the past enters the present in a dialectical and imagistic way. Dialectical images are therefore historical and different from archaic images (Frisby, 220). While the mythic, Mahabharatic conflict between Karna and Arjuna is played out through a competition between the brothers to keep the mother's love, the concrete everyday experiences of the contemporary city penetrate the mythic with the actuality of the present. Like Benjamin's dialectical image, the continuum of historical time here is destroyed, if only to make the image genuinely historical. The recognition of Karna, the discarded hero of the *Mahabharata,* through a negotiation of the urban experience in *Deewar,* turns the present into a battleground for the past. In the dialectical image, the forgotten is captured to redeem the past through remembrance (Gilloch, 114). The city is negotiated in *Deewar* as the repository and site of myth. The Mahabharatic theme is redrawn for a deeper understanding of a contemporary moment. There is no eternal repetition of the epic, but a historical remembrance of the forgotten. Through the melodramatic conflict between the brothers, *Deewar* presents the metropolis as the site of both forgetfulness and remembrance, which together constitute the urban experience. Unlike Nandy's dark vision of history, myth here is redeemed by history.

The Bachchan phenomenon, and films like *Deewar,* slowly faded away, leaving traces in certain kinds of films during the 1980s. In the 1990s, Shahrukh Khan[26] made his film debut with *Baazigar,* the first of the psychotic films. Directed by Abbas Mastan,[27] *Baazigar* dramatically reinvented the antihero as a self-destructive force withdrawn from the world. The spectacle of psychological violence unleashed by some of the psychotic films alluded to changed social circumstances that required a different kind of narrative. The desire here was to move away from the social context into a world where despair had turned into a personal nightmare. Sociological explanations can rarely explain the layered, hidden, and secret life of the city. The rapid onrush of transformation in the city increases its incomprehensible quality.

Today, the city remains almost unreadable—a complex cartography whose imagination wanders everywhere. Religious riots, violence, expanding crowds, spatial conflict, distrust, and hypervisuality inform the landscapes of cities in postglobalized India. In the midst of this maze, the psychotic figure in cinema speaks to the paranoia and anxiety of the urban nightmare. The urban crowd, fragmented and scarred by inequality, violence, and terror, is now suspicious of one another. The crowd is steeped in fragmentary perceptions that can cohere in situations of conflict and tension. The fleeting and the everyday is the space where the idea of "strangeness" is created. The stranger takes on the garb of the uncanny, not as an extraordinary force, but as the fear of the person who lives next door.

Violence and Suspicion in the City

In an interesting essay on the changing narrative strategies of Hindi cinema, Rashmi Doraiswamy compares the "angry man" persona of the Bachchan films with the psychotic persona of the 1990s. Doraiswamy suggests that in the films of the 1990s, considerable "film time is first devoted to the extenuating circumstances that cause the hero to embark on his path of revenge, and only evil is dispensed with evil, thus retaining a sense of justice in the moral universe created" (173). In the cinema of the 1990s, says Doraiswamy, "the segment providing the logic for the behaviour of the protagonist rarely occurs in the beginning: it is provided much later in the film. As such the actions of the protagonist have to be taken at their face value, the spectator having no clue to the origins of this pathological behavior" (173). To say that this is a strategy of the 1990s cinema is perhaps a generalization, but there is no doubt that such a technique is deployed in many of the psychotic films. The unpredictability of the psychotic's actions is heightened in the narrative through the repression of causality that Doraiswamy refers to. Thus, within the accepted codes of the film narrative, the psychotic emerges as a stranger, whose performance and action have no relationship to the images of past antiheroes.

Trying to make sense of the emergence of screen characters that exist on the margins of "normalcy," scriptwriter Shantanu Gupta says, "We are going to see more unhinged characters on screen. Today madness has become entertaining" (cited in Chandra, 88). Director N. Chandra locates the fascination for cinematic violence in a culture of economic liberalization and competitiveness that produces losers living on the fringe. "The emphasis on materialism, money and success in a jungle-like society where only the fittest survive will create the unhinged man. Soon our society will have its share of psychopaths that we used to see only in American films" (cited in Chandra, 88). The conflict and instability of everyday life, which has reached an unprecedented scale in the last decade, is the other reason offered by many. Earlier images of villains, says film critic Anupama Chandra, "will no longer disturb an audience numbed by bombs, riot and daylight murders" (89). Kamlesh Pandey, the scriptwriter of *Khalnayak* (The villain, Subhash Ghai, 1993), says, "Just as Amitabh Bachchan became the vehicle for an entire generation's anger so has Shahrukh Khan become the expression of this generation's cynicism" (cited in Chandra, 89). Clearly, the popular discourse on the fascination with violence is being attributed to a general breakdown of morality, political culture, and the experience of extreme violence in the decade of globalization. This perception is amplified in Anupama Chandra's references to bomb blasts and riots, which show how she is trying to make these connections. It seems that such perceptions on the culture of violence belong to a huge archive of popular discourses on the transformations taking place in contemporary city life. Media critics and the film industry share a certain notion of the contemporary as an incomprehensible space, a wild zone where violence is routine and everyday. There is also the perception that something new is required to capture the experience of the present.

In an insightful essay, Veena Das and Ashis Nandy problematize the language of silence that usually exists around issues of violence. Das and Nandy believe violence tends to be viewed with a certain degree of ambivalence in all cultures. Because this ambivalence is rooted in philosophical doubt, "it invites not only elaborate structures of representation but may also be surrounded by silence and the breakdown of signification" (177). Though these authors are writing on the experience of violence during the partition of India into India and Pakistan, the argument seems relevant here as well. Das and Nandy look at Sadat Hassan Manto's short story "Toba Tek Singh," in which Toba Tek Singh is a "madman" who is unable to make sense of the madness that has gripped the collective community of people involved in the riots. The very people who had kept Toba Tek Singh at a distance from their "normal" world are now involved in the violence of the riots. Das and Nandy ask the question, "Could Manto be suggesting that the voice of the madman is the only sane voice that could be heard in the midst of these events?" (190). This question pushes us to think through the difficulties of representing violence. In some ways, there is a similarity between Nandy and

Das's question and Chandra's perception. The story of "Toba Tek Singh" deploys the language of madness, which allows Manto a certain ability to communicate terror. During a moment of historical crisis, the "sane" and the "insane" exchange places. The formerly insane are now endowed with the power of perception that seems to have escaped rational "normal" communities.

Along a slightly different track, Radhika Subramaniam maps a culture of suspicion in the everyday routines of the city. Trying to make sense of the Bombay riots of 1992–93,[28] Subramaniam navigates the city deploying the gaze of an ethnographic surrealist who picks up sounds, expressions, conversation, images, and direct speech to build a vast archive of terror and suspicion. The culture of suspicion is buried in the everyday. In trying to make sense of the violence, Subramaniam suggests that our attention be "directed to a cultural elaboration of dread and unease that does not throb with overt hostility but is fleeting and everyday" (151). The urban crowd is central to Subramaniam's narrative; she presents the violence through the spatial dimensions of the city. Violence is latent in an urban situation. The experience of the urban crowd in situations of conflict can be debilitating and painful. It is within this culture of suspicion, which is at once ordinary and capable of erupting into extreme forms of violence, that the idea of *strangeness* is born. The Bombay riots saw the slaughter of thousands of Muslims by crowds that included neighbors and former friends. The events of 1992–93 were a watershed in the imaginative rendering of a city, so crucial to Bombay cinema. After 1993, the deep emancipatory moment of the urban modern, which spoke to new visions of community, independence, and freedom, was shattered. The city of citizens was transformed into a city of strangers marked by the ubiquity of "evil."

While media critics and filmmakers observe that a new culture in the city has numbed film audiences, creating a burning desire within them for something different that is also extremely brutal, Nandy and Das try to draw attention to the difficulties of representing violence. Subramaniam, on the other hand, develops a vast archive of the fleeting and the everyday impressions of the city in order to understand the latent existence of violence in the urban crowd. While these three critics differ in perspective and approach, they exhibit a general dissatisfaction with existing narratives that explain the eruption of terror in an urban context.

The themes of dread, unease, fear, madness, anxiety, and suspicion inflect the perception of everyone trying to make sense of the contemporary. It is here again that the idea of *strangeness* offers us another entry into the heart of the urban nightmare.

Adventures of the Mind: The Stranger in the City

The *stranger* is an important type whose presence within the urban crowd has been central to discussions of urban violence, crime, and the culture of suspicion. The stranger plays an unusual role in shaping identity and notions of otherness within the space of the city. It was Georg Simmel who first wrote about the stranger as a social type within the urban milieu. Simmel's stranger is not someone with a fleeting presence, but a person who "is fixed within a certain spatial circle—or within a group whose boundaries are analogous to spatial boundaries—but his position within it is fundamentally affected by the fact that he does not belong to it initially and that he brings qualities into it that are not, and cannot be, indigenous to it" (1971, 143). The stranger is thus attributed with qualities that make him both remote and close within a spatial entity.

Cities and the discourse of urban planning have always had an ambiguous relationship to strangers. The stranger could belong to the vast multitude that belongs to the "unintended city." Constantly intruding on the idea of urban order and civic control, the stranger disrupts the aesthetic appeal of the "rational" city. When the vision of a rational urban utopia guides planning for the city, *strangeness* and *strangers* are often the first targets (Bauman, 129). The stranger occupies a fuzzy space between insider and outsider. There is no guarantee that yesterday's outsider may not become tomorrow's insider, a problem that has haunted every authoritarian vision of urban order.

The stranger combined with "the notion of adventure expresses the experience of the 'extraordinary,'" says David Frisby (65). For Simmel, adventure is a form of experience through which one is able to wander through space and time in a manner that enables the adventurer to drop out of "the continuity of life" (1971, 187). Adventure allows one to transcend boundaries, norms, and entanglements. It is central to our experience and existence, "it is a foreign body in our existence which is yet somehow connected with the center; the outside, if only by a long and unfamiliar detour, is formally an aspect of the inside" (188). In the figure of the psychotic, we see both the surface constellation of the stranger and the "experiential tension" of the adventurer. Governed by nothing except a drive toward death, the psychotic's adventure marks a decisive shift in the rhythms of the urban experience.

Baazigar: Adventure and Interiority

Baazigar is the story of a boy named Ajay (played by actor Shahrukh Khan), who grows up with vivid memories of his father and sister dying under tragic circumstances instigated by a man called Madan Chopra (played by Dalip Tahil). Chopra, a junior officer in Ajay's father's firm, swindles the father and takes over as the new director of the firm. Ajay's family is rendered homeless. The father and sister die under tragic circumstances, resulting in the mother's loss of sanity. Ajay's childhood memories of these events are not revealed to the audience until late in the film, through two important flashback sequences. It is his family's destruction, however, that turns Ajay, the protagonist, into a ruthless killer with a single-minded obsession for revenge.

The mother (played by actress Rakhee) provides legitimacy and motivation for Ajay to emerge as a psychotic. There are also two younger women in the film, Seema (played by Shilpa Shetty) and Priya (played by Kajol); both women are daughters of Chopra. Ajay becomes romantically involved with both sisters. He kills Seema, along with witnesses to her murder. He is then set for marriage with Priya, through whom he intends to take over the firm that originally should have been his. Ajay does manage to take over the firm, in exactly the same way as Chopra had done earlier. The chain of unfolding events that leads to Ajay's exposure as a murderer disrupts this cyclical maneuvering, and Baazigar ends with Ajay's death.

Ajay's movements and his ability to disrupt the repetition so central to the Hindi film narrative (particularly the predictable conflict between the hero and the villain) allow him the mobility and freedom to create a narrative that introduces newness, shock, and confusion, in much the same way adventure does for Simmel. What is also striking about the psychotic figure in Baazigar is that the narrative is structured in a manner that takes the spectator through a journey of confusion, provoking him or her to abandon the codes of perception the spectator is used to in Hindi films.[29] The spectator thus becomes part of the adventure. As Simmel writes:

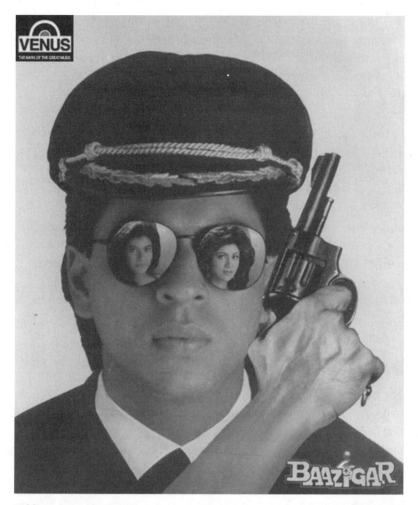

Publicity image for *Baazigar*.

Adventure has the gesture of the conqueror, the quick seizure of opportunity, regardless of whether the portion we carve out is harmonious or dis-
harmonious with us, with the world, or with the relation between us and
the world. On the other hand however, in the adventure we abandon our-
selves to the world with fewer defenses and reserves than in any other relation, for other relations are connected with the general fun of our worldly
life by more bridges, and thus defend us better against shocks and dangers
through previously prepared avoidances and adjustments. (1971, 193)

The shock of the urban, of sound and space, of terror and violence,
require articulation and representation. What is the language available
to develop and communicate the inner world of pain? How can such a

language evolve from within the structure of the Bombay film narrative? The most significant aspect of the shock introduced by the psychotic lies in a combination of violence and the expression of "interiority." There is a desperate attempt to speak from *within*, from inside the core of the protagonist. This expression of "interiority" takes place within a changed urban context of distrust in the neighbor and of the recognition of the stranger within the city, as an internal rather than an external factor. The psychotic's adventurous stance takes us on a new journey of excess, destroying the representational limits of the popular film "formula,"[30] to articulate the depths of the urban nightmare.

Baazigar does not provide us with a sociology of the city. Rather, the protagonist internalizes an experience that is expressed through innovative cinematic techniques. Ajay's persona, style, and odd behavior situate him differently in relation to other popular heroes and antiheroes of Bombay cinema. The film's ability to express a kind of contemporary subjectivity makes *Baazigar* unusual. In breaking many of the boundaries usually set forth for the hero, Ajay creates a new space for the articulation of pain and interiority.

Interiority and Death in the City

The narration of "interiority" is presented in *Baazigar* through the use of flashbacks. Ajay makes his entry from childhood to adulthood in a cut that seems like an exact copy of *Zanjeer*[31] (Chain, Prakash Mehra, 1973); the transition takes place via negative images of childhood memories of his family's destruction and subsequent homelessness. In *Zanjeer,* the transition is a haunting dream—a fragment of Vijay's (played by Amitabh Bachchan) childhood memory and thus an unclear image. As a child, Vijay witnesses the murder of his parents through a gap between cupboard doors, behind which he is hidden. His frame of vision is limited. The spectator, however, is allowed the privilege of knowing what Vijay's dream actually refers to.

Interestingly, in *Baazigar* Ajay controls the unfolding narrative in its totality. The negative film images are meant to mask the audience's entry into the child's memories. The audience is allowed entry into that past only when Ajay wants them to, through two very important flashback sequences. Since the flashbacks appear post-festum (after the psychotic's brutality), the viewer is confronted largely by a narrative that is strange, unmotivated, and frightening. Ajay's action "constructs" the past through selective, episodic filters, in contrast to Vijay in *Deewar*, in which the flashback from Ravi's point of view appears more as a functional strategy of storytelling.

The first flashback in *Baazigar* takes place after Ajay, following a cleverly worked-out plan, wrests his dead father's business empire back from Madan Chopra, the usurper. As the director's chair on which Ajay is about to sit starts revolving, we are taken into the character's past. Since Ajay is sitting in this room alone, the flashback is directly addressed to the spectator in narrative terms. Ajay conducts an internal dialogue with the past and his psyche, while simultaneously addressing the spectator. Since the reenactment of the past via the flashback shows the child witnessing the gradual disintegration of his family, the child, as the spectator of all the events, imbues the flashback with the notion of a perceived past. The recounting of the flashback sequences at crucial moments within the narrative again constructs the imagined spectator, by narrating a series of traumatic events emerging from childhood fixation, making possible the pleasure of loss and suffering, all of which takes place within the diegesis of *Baazigar*. Childhood memory in *Baazigar* is preserved and controlled by the protagonist. The flashback is important because of its ability to foreground a well-developed notion of the past. The past is the site of such deep scars that it not only tears apart and creates the psychotic figure, but also provides the justification for a cyclical repetition of the past through revenge. Childhood scars can neither be healed nor forgotten.

The second major flashback takes place toward the end of the film, as Ajay completes the story of his past for Priya, the second daughter of the villain. With the jigsaw puzzle finally revealed, *Baazigar* resolves the dilemma for both Priya and the spectators. Through this second recounting of a *perceived past* (a "subjectively focalized narrative," to use Maureen Turim's words) *Baazigar* finally moves on to the gruesome climax whose causal inevitability is now available for us. This strategy of allowing the protagonist to control the narrative betrays a fascination for the character, through whom a certain melancholic adventure is experienced. *Baazigar*, like many other psychotic films, deals with "interiority," identifying quite clearly with the psychotic's gaze. Scriptwriter Javed Akhtar provides one explanation for this fascination:

I suppose we respect perfection. We respect freedom, there is an evil in all of us, there is a sadist hidden in each one of us, but our morality has imprisoned it and when we see somebody whose evil has broken all the moral norms and now he's a complete person in himself, even in his ill doing, we admire that person because he is a law unto himself, he's a morality in himself. We respect that power. We don't want to imitate him, but that power fascinates us. (cited in Mazumdar and Jhingan, "The Legacy of the Angry Man")

What is fascinating about Akhtar's statement is the acknowledgment of an attraction to a form of power that breaks all norms. This was clearly central to the scripting of *Baazigar.* Javed Siddiqui, who wrote *Baazigar,* sees the psychotic as an extension of the "angry man," the only differences being in motivation and impact. The "angry man's" compulsion contained a dialogue with society on issues of justice. The psychotic fights only for himself. This drive toward death, imbued with a radical evil, is surely Bombay cinema's Nietzschean moment. In an interesting interview, Siddiqui says:

I think Shahrukh's image is an outcome of the earlier angry hero because what Amitabh and Salim Javed managed to do in the 70's was now being transcended. The difference is that the earlier hero selflessly fought for others, while today's hero fights first for himself. Its the same old story of revenge. The question was how to narrate it differently. We wondered how a character who could cross the limit lines, demarcation lines and the boundaries of society appear on screen. (Mazumdar and Jhingan, "The Legacy of the Angry Man")

Both Akhtar and Siddiqui see the breakdown of all morality within the narrative as enabling a new form of communication. Here the breakdown of signification in the repetitive narrative form of Hindi cinema is pushed to create a new space for communication.[32] One could suggest that the breakdown of signification is an expression that articulates the crisis of the everyday, precisely because new imaginaries are required to negotiate this contemporary subjectivity.

By breaking the long-standing hold of the repetition central to popular-film formula and the star system, the psychotic's image seems to question the more "rational," restrained, and controlled anger of the 1970s "angry man" era. Bachchan's portrayal of the wronged urban man, unstable but always "morally" bound, an outlaw but committed to the family and the "honor" of the women in his life, seems a different image from that of the psychotic whose apparent retreat on screen from the values of social justice seems to embody the melancholic subjectivity *within* contemporary urban existence. This melancholia is perhaps a result of both a fascination with and a fear of the stranger.

Ajay's character in *Baazigar* is complex. He carries the burden of a bitter life. The street and homelessness are central to his experience. During the credits at the beginning of the film, images of the little boy cleaning cars, polishing shoes, washing dishes, and serving tea, form the backdrop for the titles. Such a beginning is crucial, for it presents the summary of a childhood that can later be connected to the climactic moment of the film—when Ajay's identity is truly revealed to Priya. Until the end of the film, he remains a stranger for all the characters. Ajay only reveals his identity to himself, through prolonged monologues with his mirror reflection or just talking in an empty room, looking at the spectator. But he is able to slide in and out of any situation and place.

Ajay occupies several spaces of the city in *Baazigar*. He is a student at a college, a racing sportsman who enters student hostels, college parties, five-star hotels, airports, nightclubs, and, obviously, the streets. The murders take place in a college hostel room, in a five-star hotel room, and on the top floor of a skyscraper. The film shows Ajay approaching his victims like a stalker slowly walking up to his prey. It seems that no one is really safe from the killer.

In Seema's case, murder acquires a different aura. Seema has no idea that the man she loves and wants to marry is going to kill her. Her closest friend is her biggest enemy. Many critics have commented on the chilling quality of the sequence when Ajay pushes Seema off the top floor of a skyscraper. The murder will perhaps be remembered as a significant moment of shock in Bombay film history. In many ways, the shock effect of the sequence evokes the world of danger and hyperstimuli so central to the debates on urban modernity (Singer 2001, 69). Seema's fall from the terrace of the skyscraper and her instant death capture the experience of impending peril inscribed in the city experience, providing *Baazigar* with a different kind of melodramatic coding. This is the first murder in the film and it completely destroys well-established and accepted codes of the popular-film "formula." The psychotic's action presents the spectator with a shocking puzzle, the answer to which is revealed much later in the film. It is this technique of revealing the action before exposing the cause that presents the psychotic as the stranger in the city. He is close and distant, known and unknown, charming and horrific.

His actions acquire an adventurous quality, since he breaks all the stable forms of narrative perception to create a new space for the expression of a hidden "interiority." Ajay's ability to walk with ease through these diverse spaces makes him present everywhere but unknown to the others around him. The quality of strangeness is partially known to the spectator, but not to other characters in the film. Using the detective mode, the parts are slowly put into a whole just before the climactic moment.

In occupying the traditional space of the villain within the "formula," the psychotic seeks to explode the regulated desires of the iconic hero, on whom the codes of morality imposed by the "formula" are at play. This complex interplay of a social morality and a rewritten geography of desire takes place within a new configuration of the "formula." The psychotic figure's experience of pain and pleasure can be read as both the externalization of an agonized subjectivity and as a schizoid movement toward "irrational" fulfillment. Ironically, this "retreat" from the old imaginary of the 1970s opens up new possibilities, the least of which is the changed architecture of *desire,* in which the psychotic's action holds out the utopian possibility of breaking all boundaries.

In giving a peculiarly distorted expression to an agonized subjectivity that is born out of a particular negotiation of memory, the psychotic aspires to freedom that is elusive within the codified nature of the "formula." As the expression of "interiority" fights for a public space, filmic constructions exaggerate the movement through a narrative of *excess.* However, this excess is justified through a confessional mode deployed by the film. As Ajay's conversations with his mirror image, the flashback sequences, and other forms of personal dialogue suggest, Ajay is given ample opportunity within the narrative to provide the causal links required to justify his actions. Structured as they are at crucial moments within the film, Ajay's dialogue and the style and mood of the mise-en-scène acquire the aura of a confession that is directed at the audience for sympathy. As Ajay stretches the limits of narrative possibilities, there emerges a character—frightening yet attractive, illusory yet "real"—who defies and yet encourages identification.

In his *Origins of German Tragic Drama,* Benjamin shows how the Trauerspiel (the mourning play) was an allegorical intervention vis-à-vis the continuum of the historical catastrophe of the Thirty Years War. The conventional form of tragedy—with its focus on the tragic, heroic resistance of the hero and what George Steiner calls an "aesthetic of reticence" (cited in Benjamin 1997, 18)—could not articulate the magnified pain and terror of the times. An engaged response, says Benjamin, could only be in the form of allegory—the Trauerspiel. Breaking with the conventions of tragedy, the Trauerspiel magnifies negativity, evil, lamentation, and gesture—the central themes are decay, ruin, and the personification of evil in the corpse. The Trauerspiel does not "address" history, but is the expression of historical crisis:

> The *Trauerspiel* does not offer some manifest commentary on these
> historical events. Rather, the experience of historical catastrophe itself
> is incorporated into the structure and content of the work, becoming the
> controlling premise of dramatic action, the fixed metaphorical referent
> for the generation of dramatic language. (Pensky, 75)

Like the Trauerspiel, the psychotic films seek to generate a new discourse of pain, dispersed morality, and a violent drive toward death. Like Benjamin's allegory, the psychotic image is a fragment in the current constellation of images present in Bombay cinema.[33] And like in the Trauerspiel, the image in the psychotic films allows us entry into forbidden realms of desire, pain, and subjectivity inaccessible through given narrative structures.

Ajay experiences a freedom in death. The torture that leads to death, the pain inflicted on the body, is both pleasurable and painful. In a sense, the psychotic embodies the pain of a scarred and torn city expressing an agony that needs to be shared. "It is through this movement out into the world," says Elaine Scarry, "that the extreme privacy of the occurrence (both pain and imaginary are invisible to anyone outside the boundaries of the person's body) begins to be shareable, that sentience becomes social and thus acquires its distinctly human form" (170).

The power of evil and blind fate is central to the narrative of tragic action (Williams 1966, 37). This is, however, one version of tragedy in which the concept of heroism is actively destroyed to develop a closer connection with death and evil. *Baazigar* displays a similar drive, wherein a sense of despair emerges out of a fundamental absurdity that ultimately takes the hero toward suicide.[34] The climactic end of *Baazigar* is a violent battle between Ajay and Madan Chopra. The battle is excessive, brutal, bizarre, and tactile. Everyone is killed as Ajay drives himself toward death, in order to ensure Chopra's death. The film ends with Ajay's body sprawled on the ground, his mother crying beside him and Priya looking on. Ajay's dead figure is the site of tragedy. This fatalistic end of the film builds on the theme of personal sacrifice as the solution for revenge. Revenge of this kind ultimately has no meaning, for it proposes a cyclical form of survival. Revenge here breaks all norms to repeat what has already happened.

What is striking about *Baazigar* is that the imagery of loss and homelessness is compressed into the pre-title and title sequence. The rest of the narrative becomes a nightmare within which the history of the protagonist is embedded. It is the detective's gaze, operating through Priya, and the police inspector's investigation that bring the whole story together by revealing the stranger who is nestled within us. Cities get more complicated and masklike when diverse urban crowds become a mass presence. When impenetrability of the crowd informs the cityscape, the notion of the uncanny, the hidden secrets of the city, says Richard Lehan, begin to appear in literary and artistic imagination. Rooted in the familiar, the uncanny emerges in many different situations when the familiar appears strange (Lehan, 74). It is this sudden force of the uncanny that makes *Baazigar* unusual, since the psychotic operates in the film as "one of us" who later becomes a stranger.

Fredric Jameson writes in *Marxism and Form* that the utopian impulse, while unable to abolish death, may "rob it of its sting." Death cannot abolish life "fully realized" in a "perpetual present" (142). In the case of the "angry man," the city is the canvas that provides a utopian counter to the tragic death of the hero. The city retains its character as a site of the unrealized utopian impulse of the hero despite the redemptive death of the protagonist in *Deewar*. For the psychotic, the urge for freedom is never separate from that of evil. The nihilistic surge from all restraint in *Baazigar* produced a force field that was both radical and evil. Death was stripped of its mythic qualities, lacking the beauty of tragic martyrdom. For the psychotic, death is unrelated to the utopian impulse of the city: the act of dying seems emptied of meaning and fulfillment. Yet, even in the image of the psychotic, a weak utopian urge shines through, perhaps in an allegorical allusion to the possibility of freedom in schizoid action. While in *Deewar* the hero leads us through a well-defined journey of redemption, in *Baazigar* the psychotic fleetingly poses the unimaginable during a moment of historical ruin, destruction, and death in the city.

CHAPTER TWO

The Rebellious Tapori

If a simmering rage drove the "angry man" and the "psychotic" in their explorations of the city, then the *tapori* (vagabond) speaks to a structure of feeling strongly rooted in the hybrid cultures of Bombay's multilingual and regional diversity. Performance and performative gestures are crucial to the tapori's agency. This performance deploys sharp street humor and an everyday street language, in addition to a deep skepticism toward power and wealth. Using the popular *Bambayya* language as his weapon against an unequal world, the tapori creates a space through insubordination that endows him with a certain dignity in the cinematic city. Drawing attention to the self through linguistic and stylistic performances, the tapori creates a space where control is possible. Deploying an irreverent masculinity that contrasts with the dominating male presence of the "angry man" era,[1] the tapori stands at the intersection of morality and evil, between the legal and the illegal, between the world of those with work and those without work. Lacking a home but longing for a family, the tapori occupies the middle space between the crisis of urban life and the simultaneous yearning for stability. Part small-time street hood and part social conscience of the neighborhood, the tapori embodies a fragile masculinity that is narrated through a series of encounters with the upper class and the figure of the woman. In performing and depicting marginal figures whose narrative predicaments seem to mirror their psychological states of marginality, we see a verbal and social alienation expressed in the tapori's performance. This alienation is countered through style and gesture to both shock and play with the signs of the everyday.

The tapori's hybrid speech creates the possibility of transcending various other identities. It is important to stress this point because the Hindi film hero typically tends to be a North Indian figure. Scriptwriter Javed Akhtar sees Hindi cinema as "another state within India" that does not need to be located or defined specifically as a region (cited in Kabir, 53). He does, however, acknowledge that the "usual Hindi screen hero is a North Indian, perhaps a Delhi Haryana U.P mixture" (cited in Kabir, 53). At the same time, Akhtar reiterates that the hero is "from everywhere and from nowhere" (cited in Kabir, 54). This contradiction in Akhtar's perception about the Bombay film hero is revealing. Whatever the different inflections may be, Hindi cinema has by and large retained the visual, emotional, and cultural iconography of a broad-based North Indian experience. It would be difficult to try and establish this as otherwise. What I propose to show in this chapter is a "field of tension" within Bombay that provokes us to think through the image of the tapori—a figure whose performance has the potential to destabilize the "North Indianness" of the hero—as an ensemble of sounds, signs, phrases, and gestures. Performativity and style operate here to create a rebellious figure of the street. This is a formulation based on the different ways in which the tapori's imagination has emerged out of a complex web of linguistic, spatial, and imaginary journeys.

Language, the Film Industry, and the Rise of *Bambayya*

Popular wisdom has it that it is the film industry that has kept Hindustani alive. This perception exists despite the gradual "purification" of Hindi in postcolonial India, the historical origin of which can be traced to the Hindi movement of the nineteenth century.[2] The film industry's use of Hindustani, in an official climate in which the national state language was gradually becoming Sanskritized, has been a remarkable achievement. The cinema's contribution toward ensuring the survival of Hindustani in the backdrop of an increasing linguistic warfare enabled the cinema to create space for other forms of experimentation. The location of the film industry in a non-Hindi-speaking region allowed the industry to both preserve and experiment with its spoken language. This, in turn, resulted in new kinds of performances through figures who embodied the specificity of the "Bombay experience."

The Bombay film industry was born in the shadow of linguistic conflict that carried on well into the twentieth century. The silent era did not have to deal with the language issue. It was only with the birth of the talkies in 1931 that language became central to the imagination of the Bombay film industry.[3] While catering to large sections of the population in North India, the industry was located in the capital city (Bombay) of a non-Hindi-speaking region (the state of Maharashtra). What is interesting is the decision of the film industry to use Urdu/Hindustani as the language of Bombay cinema. This is all the more remarkable in the face of the entrenched position taken by Hindi-language elites, who advocated a Sanskritized rendering in opposition to Urdu.

Alok Rai suggests a rural-urban division in the language debate. The Persian stream was represented by urban Muslims, professionals, and *Kayasths*. The *Nagari* stream was more rural, but it represented a significant proportion of upper-caste Hindus, including *Brahmins, Banias,* and *Thakurs* (Rai, 255). This rural-urban split may have been decisive in the industry's decision to favor Urdu. Urdu was the language favored by urban poets and writers, many of whom joined the film industry. The predominance of Urdu/Hindustani in the industry is now an undisputed and acknowledged fact and can be traced to a number of reasons aside from the rural-urban split. In an interesting foray into the linguistic roots of Hindi cinema, Mukul Kesavan suggests that the melodramatic nature of the Hindi film form could best be captured through "Urdu's ability to find sonorous words for inflated emotion" (249). Javed Akhtar traces the connection between Urdu and the film industry to the precinematic urban cultural form of Urdu Parsi Theater. These theaters were owned by Parsis living in Bombay. The early Parsi theater created a certain style that combined drama, comedy, and song (Kabir, 50). Akhtar says:

> The Indian Talkie inherited its basic structure from Urdu Parsi Theatre and so the talkies started with Urdu. Even the New Theatres in Calcutta, used Urdu writers. You see, Urdu was *the* lingua franca of urban northern India before partition, and was understood by most people. And it was—and—still is—an extremely sophisticated language capable of portraying all kinds of emotion and drama. (cited in Kabir, 50)

Urdu was definitely the most important language for the Hindi film industry. Urdu's accessibility for a huge mass of the North Indian urban population made it appropriate for the film industry to adopt it. The presence of many writers who wrote in Urdu was the other reason for the popularity of the language in the industry.[4] The use of a poetic, highly cultivated and developed language was thus accepted by the industry and by the audiences that patronized the cinema. Even when filmmakers made the effort to address the streets of the city, the characters retained this poetic language (as in the film *Kismet,* 1943). Urdu's survival in the film industry is not only remarkable but was possible because of the industry's location. It is this very location that has allowed for significant innovations in the image of the tapori, who speaks a peculiar, hybrid Hindi called *Bambayya.*

In a city of migrants, where new migrants meet old ones, language tends to acquire a life of its own. The context of a powerful Hindi film industry that emerged in a Marathi-speaking state has made Bombay's relationship to language fascinating. In the image of the tapori, we see both the performativity of a hybrid city and the language of its multilingual rough streets. In his use of the *Bambayya* language, the tapori represents both the specificity of and the conflictual nature of the city. Through his linguistic performance, the tapori shifts the course of a well-defined language system. What is interesting is that the tapori's language embodies a polyglot culture that does not fix itself within a traditional Hindi-Urdu conflict, but rather enters a space where a multilingual street culture inflected with diverse regional accents can be captured. The first film to popularize the *Bambayya* language was *Amar Akbar Anthony* (popularly known as *AAA,* Manmohan Desai, 1977),[5] which featured Amitabh Bachchan in the role of a small-time (Christian) bootlegger.

The spoken language of Bombay cinema has over the years been considered dynamic and cosmopolitan, speaking as it does to a wide audience in a multilingual country like India. As stated earlier, the arrival of the talkies first put pressure on the film industry to evolve a language (Hindi) for a wide audience. Amrit Ganghar says:

> The question to be resolved was: what kind of Hindi? Sanskritized? Persianized? Or low-brow Hindi? In the event the cinema developed a Bazaar Hindi of its own called *Bambayya,* which is widely understood throughout the country. (233)

The reference to the *Bambayya* language here seems a little out of place. In the early years, the film industry used a cultivated Urdu. *Bambayya* as a language inflected with the resonance of multiple tongues was clearly identified with the Bombay streets. It was used neither by the elite nor by the middle class. The bulk of the people who used this language belonged to the working classes. It was not a language that could be easily heard in cinema. Sometimes comedians and other peripheral figures would use this language (for example, Johny Walker as Abdul Sattar in *Pyasa,* 1957); the hero, however, continued to speak the more "civilized" Hindustani.

In films made prior to the 1970s, the presence of migration from rural India into the city was marked explicitly by dress codes and speech. Depictions of rural presence in urban life had to rely on the use of dialects like *Brajbhasha* and *Avadhi,* which not only marked the figure as a rural migrant in the city, but also metaphorically presented "rurality" as the imagination of the street (for example, in the films *Ram Aur Shyam,* 1967, and *Don,* 1978). Rural dialects could be contrasted with the more cultivated and sophisticated Hindustani. The everyday space of the street was therefore clearly seen as the imagined space of the village. In Raj Kapoor's *Shri 420* (1955), the song "Ramayya Vasta Vayya" generates an imagined universe of the village as a counterspace to the harshness of the city. The community of rural people singing collectively represents the "good city" as they invite the protagonist Raj to join them and identify with their communitarian spirit. The tapori is, however, marked as an ordinary man of Bombay whose language emerges out of a polyglot city-street culture that is entirely urban. The lack of sophistication and street speech is not introduced through village dialects as in earlier films, but through a combination of English, Gujarati, Marathi, Hindi, Tamil, and various other linguistic resonances. While retaining an overall Hindustani speech, the tapori's linguistic turns and phrases evoke a new imagination of the street, wherein the urban identity of a multilingual Bombay street culture gets constituted and reinfused with cinematic iconicity.

It is difficult to trace how the *Bambayya* language actually emerged. Scriptwriter Sanjay Chel, who coauthored the script for *Rangeela,* offers an explanation based on a sense of the street and the nature of Bombay's hybridity. Chel says:

> People come here from all over India with their languages like Gujarati, Marathi, Bengali. All these languages merge to form a unique language of survival in the city, to stubbornly fight for existence in the city. This language is understood by all. This is a language of the street with its own texture. It may not be grammatical, but this *Bambayya* language

is hard hitting and satirical. (interviewed in Mazumdar and Jhingan, "The *Tapori* as Street Rebel")

Chel's assertion about *Bambayya*'s ability to contest the power of a unitary language, drawing on the experiences of the city, has interesting possibilities.

Mikhail Bakhtin has argued that language is densely saturated with the concrete experiences of history. Language is a contested site, a space within which "differently oriented social accents as diverse 'sociolinguistic consciousness' fight it out on the terrain of language" (Stam, 8). Since language exists within an unequal regime of power, its uni-accentual drive is constantly challenged by the multiaccentual presence of the oppressed. Language is deeply implicated in a politics of the everyday, whereby it becomes imperative to recognize the different ways in which "Politics and language intersect in the form of attitudes, of talking down to or looking up to, of patronizing, respecting, ignoring, supporting, misinterpreting" (Stam, 9). Clearly, attitudes, expressions, and gestures have a unique relationship to language. It is in this combined terrain that power is both constituted and challenged.

Like Bakhtin, Michel de Certeau invokes the image of the "ordinary man" as a figure through whom the "vanity" of writing encounters the "vulgarity" of language (1988, 2). Both Bakhtin and de Certeau are interested in the tensions that enable the anonymous figure or ordinary man the possibility of dislodging the vanity of elite linguistic formations. In aural terms, this tension becomes striking when one deals with the spoken language of ordinary people in a communicative and visual medium like the cinema. The tapori is the cinematic figure whose language defies the pure and moral absolutism of other heroes. Emerging in a city that is crisscrossed not only by the differences of class and caste but also by that of region and language, the tapori's *Bambayya* speech becomes a nonlanguage, defying linguistic purity through a performatively charged acknowledgment of the everyday.[6] To trace the specifically local dimension of the image, we need to understand the cultural imagination of the "Bombay experience."

The "Bombay Experience" and the Street

Writers, architects, and poets have tried to represent Bombay's diversity and its brutal contrasts in imaginative ways. The most persistent image of Bombay is the cheek-by-jowl coexistence of skyscrapers and slums, each inhabiting a different experience and world (Kudchedkar, 127). Bombay exists "in one long line of array, as if on parade before the spectator" (Evenson, 168). Roshan Shahani looks at the representation of Bombay in the fiction of many writers to suggest the textual evolution of a multifaceted Bombay. Says Shahani, "to locate the narrative text in Bombay, is to textualize the complexity of its realities and to problematize the unrepresentative quality of a 'typical' Bombay Experience" (105). Bombay emerges here as an "imagined topos," a fictionalized landscape of history and experience wherein the city's diversity, contradictions, and paradoxes "defy any easy definition" (Shahani, 105). Bombay is also a city that showcases the world of glamour and glitter—a "seductive trap that seems to offer much to the upward bound but actually gives very little" (Alice Thorner, xxiii). At one level, the city appears like a "three-dimensional palimpsest" articulating the ambitious drives of a succession of builders; at another level, it presents the city as a sea of slums belonging to the endless migrants in the city.

This narrative of contrasts and compressed spaces has been central to the way Bombay has been imagined in literature and cinema and has informed the city's cultural imagination throughout the twentieth century. The portrayal of Bombay's affluence is exaggerated to highlight its darker and uglier side. For poet Nissim Ezekeil, Bombay "flowers into slums and skyscrapers" (cited in Patel and Thorner 1995, xix). For Marathi poet Patte Bapurao, the city appears like a stage of oppositions, such as the Taj Mahal Hotel and the workers' chawls,[7] speeding modern cars and helpless pedestrians (cited in Alice Thorner, xix). The popular song "Ye Hai Bombay Meri Jaan" (This is Bombay, my love) from the film CID (Raj Khosla, 1956) evokes a phenomenology of the city in which, in the midst of buildings, trains, factory mills, and the ubiquitous crowd, there exists a subculture of gambling, crime, and claustrophobia. This is a space purged of humanity; the crowd moves mercilessly, pushing aside those who cannot keep up with its pace. This diversity and plurality of experience, language, and class produces an acute sense of the city's hybridity. To this, one can now add the rapid proliferation of high-tech products, visual images, and the simultaneous aestheticization and decline of the streets.

Yet brutal contrasts combined with hope have also fueled the creative imagination. Referring to Sudhir Mishra's film Dharavi, Amrit Ganghar suggests that the film's objective is to capture the individual dreams of its inhabitants:

> Each individual has a dream of making it rich: a dream fuelled both by the glitz and affluence of actual upperclass life in Bombay, and by popular cinematic fantasies in masala movies. (214)

Bombay has been described by Gillian Tidal as "a mecca for incoming peoples, seeking work, seeking money, seeking life itself" (cited in Conlon, 91). Scriptwriter Khwaja Ahmad Abbas imagined Bombay as the space for constant struggle and hope:

> Some tens of thousands come here to make their future. Some make it, others don't. But the struggle goes on. That struggle is called Bombay. The struggle, the vitality, the hope, the aspiration to be something, anything, is called Bombay. (165)

In a recent essay, Gyan Prakash captures the lure of the dream city as something that has traveled through signs, gestures, and images. The desire to experience the offerings of the city circulates outside of Bombay, contributing profoundly to the creation of an imaginary city (Prakash 2006).

Bombay is also part of a global chain like no other city in India. This is amplified in the visuals and sounds that circulate through the city. The circulation of an intertextual network of visual and aural signs makes contemporary urban landscapes into "culturescapes" (Olalquiaga). In the "culturescape," temporal movement is represented in a pastiche combination of the here and the now, the past and the future, the global and the local. This supposedly nonrational configuration within the "culturescape" points to the city's inability to cater to the requirements of its growing population. Though not about Bombay, Olalquiaga's description is a dynamic aspect of urban life, a chaotic city, its hybridity visible in all aspects of life, its dreams circulating within the "ruins of modernity." This hybridity can be neither romanticized nor rejected, for it creates a uniquely specific topography. To wander in the streets of this diverse city as a "have-not", and yet retain a sense of identity and belonging is to create an imagined landscape of resistance. The space of this resistance belongs to the cinematic tapori.

Writing on the culture of cities, Henri Lefebvre made a distinction between the different levels and dimensions that go into the reading of a city. The buzz of what actually takes place in the streets and squares constitutes the "utterance" of the city. The language of the city, on the other hand, is made of "particularities specific to each city, which are expressed in discourses, gestures, clothing, in the inhabitants" (1996, 115). Seen in this context, the tapori is the cinematic articulation of a "Bombay experience" whose body operates like a text that lends itself to multiple purposes. Sliding from ordinary humor to everyday resistance, the tapori emerges as a rebel who represents the vibrant "culturescape" of the street.

The historical importance of the street in Hindi cinema was discussed in chapter 1. The changing function of the street alludes to different kinds of representational possibilities. In the post-independence period the street in cinema became an extension of the nation because it was the space that could transcend the regional boundaries that actually divided different parts of the country. Madan Gopal Singh offers an interesting connection between the street and homelessness:

> Immediately after Independence, if we look at the popular forms of address, we have *Chacha*, we have *Bapu*, we have *Sardar*. So the idea of nation as extended family is very clearly entrenched. The street is seen as an extension also of home and to the extent the person involved is actually celebrating the state of homelessness in a new order, where he is on one hand part of an extended family, on the other hand there is no specificity of space where he can be located. I think that paradox is very interesting. We are in the process of discovering where we would be at that time. This is a recurring theme in popular cinema in the 1950's and *Awara* is a seminal film. (interviewed in Mazumdar and Jhingan, "*Tapori* as Street Rebel")

Abstracted from location and specificity, the street in *Awara* (Raj Kapoor, 1951) is invested with the power to locate and address anybody in the nation. The well-known 1950s song "Awara Hoon" from *Awara* shows Raj Kapoor (who acted in, as well as directed, the film) walking down a street singing. The location of the street is not specified as the song invokes a universe of images, transcending into an imagined space of the "national." During the decade of the 1950s, cinema deployed different methods and metaphors to condense the nation in its images; the use of the street in *Awara* is clear evidence of that.[8] In the tapori films (*Rangeela*, 1995; *Ghulam*, 1998), the metaphor of the "street" as "nation" transforms into the "street" as Bombay. The modern tapori emerges from the maze of Bombay's streets using a unique language and gestures wherein performance becomes his sole identity.

In an evocative look at Bombay through the eyes of a wandering passerby, Marathi poet Narayan Surve writes:

We wander in your streets,
squares and Bazaars;
Sometimes as citizens, householders
at times as *loafers*

These streets carry the festival of lights
into the heart of the night;
Balancing two separate worlds
with all their splendor

These crowds move ahead
but where?
A traveler amongst them
I too move, but where? (cited in Kudchedkar, 149)

The "loafer" in Surve's poem sees the magical, seductive appeal of neon lights and rich neighborhoods set against the expanse of slums. While desiring the pleasures of this elite world, the "loafer" rejects its authority, power, and hierarchy—these are the qualities of the cinematic tapori. The city may present itself as a glitzy, panoramic, seductive place, but for the ordinary man in the street, the panorama is a fiction. The walkers/ pedestrians in the street are people whose "bodies follow the thicks and thins of an urban 'text', they write without being able to read it" (de Certeau 1988, 93). These men pick up fragments from the sea of signifiers available to them in order to create their own stories. As the rebellious urban figure/body in the street, the tapori is a visual ensemble of floating gestures, movements, and expressions, both cinematic and non-cinematic.

Cinematic Intertextuality and Performance

The creation of the tapori brought together many character types from both national and international cinema. There is a peculiar hybridity in the performance, the dress codes, and the character's intentionality, which suggests that the tapori exists as a layered articulation of different character types. In a reflexive gesture, director Ram Gopal Varma[9] alludes to this cinematic creation in his title sequence of *Rangeela*. Images of well-known film stars are placed alongside the credit track, combined with a sound track of chaotic city traffic. What we witness is a brief history of the iconic figures of Bombay cinema. The nature of the sound track reveals an effort to make connections between the image and the city. The film's opening is significant in its evocation of a cinematic world within the city. We are invited to participate and engage with another city icon of the cinema—the tapori.

The tapori emerged, like the "city boys" of Hollywood cinema, from the confluence of "performance, genre and ideology transmuted into popular entertainment." (Sklar, xii). Robert Sklar's exhaustive study of three actors (Humphrey Bogart, James Cagney, and John Garfield) presents them as characters who represented "the teeming ethnic polyglot of the modern industrial city—especially New York" (xii). There are popular references to Bombay as the "New York of India," which make the analogy with the tapori relevant. Film director Aziz Mirza describes the tapori as a highly urban phenomenon whose combined projection of cynicism and innocence makes the character attractive to audiences, thereby leading to the tapori's emergence as an established figure in recent years. Mirza says:

> The term *tapori* by itself is urban and *tapori* is a character you can only get in Bombay beacause the very nature of the city, its cosmopolitanism makes the *tapori* use a language of his own, which is very *Bambayya*. Bombay is the only city besides New York, where you can get so many people of different cultures, different races from all areas of India who live together. So Bombay has developed a language of its own and the *tapori* is street smart. (interviewed in Mazumdar and Jhingan, "The *Tapori* as Street Rebel," 1998)

The polyglot culture of New York City obviously resembles the multi-lingual diversity of Bombay. The intertextual current of signs can be seen in other visual characteristics of the tapori: the swagger; the attitude; the use of leather jackets, boots, jeans, and bikes; the leaning posture against the wall; and the forms of greeting in the street. These "borrowed" signs evoke the sensibility of many famous Hollywood rebel-male figures. Three well-known Hollywood actors—Montgomery Clift, Marlon Brando, and James Dean—have been described as "rebel males . . . torn between traditional and novel images of masculinity" (McCann, 28). The rebel male is seen as a figure whose "body is not unhinged from the mind as in the brute, it is the expression of self-hood, of the ability to originate ones actions" (28). Further "It is the democratic equivalent of Baudelaire's dandy/flâneur.[10] Its guiding myth is the myth of youth itself" (28).

The tapori most certainly appears like the democratic equivalent of Baudelaire's dandy. He shuns class, but desires and knows the elite world. Moving through spectacular city spaces and the city's seamy underside, the tapori's gaze is not that of distraction (a privilege of the dandy). Rather, the tapori masters his gaze to retain and assert his power and performative agency. Scriptwriter Sanjay Chel draws attention to this gaze of the tapori within the context of a new culture of globalization, wherein the experience of facing the humiliating aspects of inequality makes the returned gaze a defiant one:

> In the 1990s after liberalization, new desires have arisen for this whole group of people. With the entry of multinationals, we see neon lights, parlors selling ice cream for 100 rupees. There are many in the city who sometimes cannot afford even a bus ticket. This social difference is a very real and felt experience for many and results in anger. This anger is displayed in their language and gesture, in the comments they make: "*Kya Bare Log.*" They cannot change the system; they can only laugh it off. (interviewed in Mazumdar and Jhingan, "The *Tapori* as Street Rebel," 1998)

Chel is referring to a ubiquitous group of people in the city, urban young men on the margins of the "good life" who find a place in the image of the tapori, whose performative stance helps negotiate the alienation of urban life. The intertextuality evident in the uninhibited appropriation of cinematic signs popularized by Hollywood makes the tapori's performative iconography particularly striking. To counter the powerful lifestyle myth of the city, the male body acquires a new identity through a rebellious gaze and performance that is both humorous and hard-hitting.

If the city is a theater of seamless narratives, then de Certeau has most vividly captured the conflict between the spectacular and the mundane:

> Advertising, for example multiplies the myths of our desires and our memories by recounting them with the vocabulary of objects of consumption. It unfurls through the streets and the underground of the subway, the interminable discourses of our epics. Its posters open up dreamscapes in the walls. Perhaps never has one society benefited from as rich a mythology. But the city is the stage for a war of narratives, as the Greek city was the arena for a war among gods. For us, the grand narratives from television or advertising stamp out or atomize the small narratives of streets or neighborhoods. (1998, 143)

De Certeau's narrative on the city is echoed in Chel's perceptions about transformations in Bombay. If the city unfolds as an "empire of signs," then how do we understand the presence of counternarratives or "small narratives" that emerge from the same streets on which the world of consumption unfolds as both a seductive and an alienating experience? In the performance of the tapori, there exists a counternarrative to the lifestyle myth of the city. The tapori's counternarrative, unlike that of the "angry man" or other urban vigilante heroes, is playful. His style is individual and his resistance relies on an ambiguous relationship to issues of lifestyle and consumption. It is this ambivalence that enables such an interesting performance, "a space within which youth can play with itself, a space in which youth can construct its own identities, untouched by the soiled and compromised imaginaries of the parent culture" (Hebdige 1997, 401). Performance here is located within the performative space of the cinema. As copied, mimicked, or circulating gestures and style cohere around the figure of the tapori, the essential self of the character on-screen is dislodged to present the body as a site where gestures turn into allusions. Dick Hebdige writes that the posture of youth in subcultures is "auto-erotic, the self becomes the fetish" (1997, 401). This reference to the self is narrated primarily through performative gesture and symbol. The gaze or defiant look, the gestures, and the tapori's overall performativity also recall de Certeau's observation that "gestures are the true archives of the city"(1998, 141). Within the landscape of the cinematic city, the tapori's performance becomes the key to understanding the specificity of the "Bombay experience" and to drawing attention to the idea of performance within performance. While there are many well-known tapori films, Ram Gopal Varma's *Rangeela* and Vikram Bhatt's *Ghulam* are two films that present us with vivid portraits of Bombay's hybrid street-culture.

Rangeela: The Ordinariness of Resistance

Rangeela (Carefree) is the story of three characters: Munna, Milli, and Kamal. Munna (played by Aamir Khan), a Bombay tapori who grew up an orphan on the streets, is a carefree but irritable youth who loves Milli (played by Urmila Matondkar), a junior artist[11] in the Bombay film industry. One day, Milli lands a big role, and Kamal (played by Jackie Shroff), her costar, falls in love with her. The film weaves in a tale of everyday conflict and tension among the three characters, linked primarily to the differences in social class and aspirations for a changed life. Munna sees himself becoming increasingly distant from Milli's world. After a series of twists and turns, *Rangeela* ends with Milli finally getting together with Munna. This simple story is energized through Munna's role, performance, and playful resistance to the seductive world of the commodity. By weaving in interesting plot situations, *Rangeela* seeks to create a series of seemingly superficial conflicts that speak to a larger experience of the city.

For Munna, the street serves *as* his home, his life, and his place of entertainment and is the place where he encounters both the everyday and the spectacular. The street is the stage where a certain freedom enables Munna the chance to perform for his public. Munna's supposed confidence in the street rests on an absence of inner conflict.[12] His personality combines cynicism with audacity, and he retains a sense of humor in his performance. In *Rangeela*, certain encounters are planned within the narrative that will enable such a performance. These encounters serve to create a conflictual space where the most ordinary and routine aspects of life turn into political performances, like street theater where the actors dialogue with the audience. These encounters produce bitingly sharp, sarcastic dialogues that are meant to convey both the

Urmila Matondkar and Aamir Khan in *Rangeela* (1995). Courtesy Ram Gopal Varma's Factory.

tapori's agency and his live relationship to the "public" in the street. Writing on the modernism of Baudelaire and Dostoyevsky, Marshall Berman observes how both writers created a form in which "everyday encounters in the city street" assume an intensity to "express fundamental possibilities and pitfalls, allures and impasses of modern life" (229). While such encounters are common in Hindi films, in *Rangeela,* these everyday encounters are presented as theatrical events, establishing Munna's live relationship to the crowd, or the "public."

Munna is first introduced in *Rangeela* as a black marketer of film tickets at a sold-out show. The sequence begins with a low-angle shot of a film poster featuring a well-known actor. Munna enters the frame wearing a hat and smoking a cigarette in an exaggeratedly relaxed style. He pauses in front of the poster for a second and then moves away as the shot changes to reveal the crowd of people waiting outside the movie theater. Munna's first entry in the film, using a film hoarding (billboard) as a backdrop, again draws attention to the specifically cinematic iconicity of the tapori. In the next shot, we see Munna softly muttering "Dus Ka Tees" (30 rupees for a 10-rupee ticket) as he swaggers through the crowd. Munna is trying to sell tickets at a higher price than they are worth. Munna's friend Pakhiya is doing the same thing. The dialogue, the mise-en-scène, and the performativity in this sequence require some detailed analysis, for these elements introduce the idea of the casual encounter acquiring a larger-than-life, sometimes-political dimension.

Munna saunters through the crowd, cigarette in hand, exhibiting confidence. His ticket sale to a man is laced with one-liners, cocky comments, and underlying humor. Next, Munna turns to face a policeman. Munna tries to retreat, but the policeman calls him back. The policeman questions Munna about his illegal ticket sales, but Munna denies doing anything illegal. The policeman starts searching Munna, who removes the tickets from his rolled shirt sleeve and tucks them into the fold of the policeman's cap. Throughout the search, Munna performs loudly for the public. The dialogue is significant here:

टपोरी

अरे देखो भाइयों, बम्बई में दंगा-फ़साद करने वालों को छोड़ देते है। शेयर बाज़ार में करोड़ों का घपला हुआ है। किसी को पकड़ा क्या? और अपुन सीधा-सादा आदमी पिक्चर देखने को आया, अपुन को पकड़ता है। पकड़ो भाई पकड़ो, तुम्हारा राज है पकड़ो....। अरे क्या होगा इस कंट्री का यार!

Aamir Khan selling tickets in *Rangeela*. Courtesy Ram Gopal Varma's Factory.

Amir's public outburst

Hey brothers, look! The perpetrators of the Bombay riots were never convicted. Millions were embezzled in the stock market. But did they arrest anybody? And me, a simple man who comes to see a film, is harassed! It's your rule anyway.... What will happen to this country yaar [buddy]! (Laughs)

This encounter reveals the centrality of performance in the sequence. Munna's loaferlike clothes are contrasted with the police constable's uniform. The appeal to the public is made through references to well-known incidents like the Bombay riots of 1992–93 and the share market conspiracy of the early 1990s.[13] By contrasting Munna's petty crime with the larger world of intrigue, violence, and corruption invoked in the dialogue with the public, a certain character development is made. Munna's style, performance, and posture are presented as a critical strategy, while at the same time his charm is introduced to the audience. Actor Aamir Khan says about the tapori:

Generally the taporis shown on screen have a very good sense of humor. They do exciting stuff, they are very attractive as characters, so they play to the gallery most of the time. As a result the audiences end up liking them. They speak well, they are funny, their one-liners make you laugh, they have a sense of humor and generally they do crazy things. (interviewed in Mazumdar and Jhingan, "The *Tapori* as Street Rebel," 1998)

The theatricality of the movie-theater sequence in *Rangeela* resembles the spatial organization of street theater, for which audiences usually sit

Aamir Khan facing the policeman in *Rangeela*. Courtesy Ram Gopal Varma's Factory.

all around the performance space. The use of stereotypes and direct visual contrasts also closely resemble the traditions of street theater. The encounter in front of a movie-theater crowd becomes the space for the policeman and Munna to act out a larger world of conflict through an everyday encounter or incident. The tapori's street encounter, while introducing the character, also establishes his particular appeal to the public, similar to what happens in agit-prop theater. One is reminded here of Brecht's concept of the social gest. Gest constitutes an ensemble of gestures that can evoke the conflicts and contradictions of society (Brecht, 283–84; Barthes 1977, 73–74). Gest becomes social when the interaction or performance is implicated in a larger space of hierarchical conflict, either in the form of a physical gesture or in the twists and turns of language. By invoking the public during Munna's humorous encounter against a policeman, the movie-theater sequence appears like a "Brechtian tableau," in which Munna's playful one-liners are directed both at the people outside the movie theater, in the frame, and at the spectators watching the film, outside the frame. Munna depends on the crowd in the street for his identity. The crowd heightens Munna's performance and establishes him as different and uncaring of power.

Located at the intersection of a range of forces, the human body either submits to the pressures of authority, coercion, and surveillance or creates "spaces of resistance and freedom" (Foucault). This assumption is based on the ways in which power is exercised within organized spaces of repression such as the prison, the asylum, and the hospital. But it is possible to have a more creative engagement with the notion of space. Despite the disciplinary formations that govern our existence in the city, it is possible to create alternative (spatial) practices within it. It is through these "tricky and stubborn procedures that elude discipline without being outside the field in which they are exercised" that one can see the formation of a "theory of everyday practices, of lived space, of disquieting familiarity of the city" (de Certeau 1984, 96). De Certeau emphasizes everyday practices through the metaphoric use of the pedestrian's walk in the city, as the walker assimilates the fragments that make up the everyday world of existence:

> The walking of passers-by offers a series of turns (tours) and detours that can be compared to "turns of phrase" or "stylistic figures". There is a rhetoric of walking. The art of "turning" phrases finds an equivalent in an art of composing a path. Like ordinary language, this art implies and combines styles and uses. Style specifies "a linguistic structure that manifests on the symbolic level . . . an individual's fundamental way of being in the world. (1984, 100)

This "fundamental way of being in the world" is articulated through gestures and speech acts that are drawn from fragments selected during the pedestrian's walk through the city. Confronting a "forest of gestures" that are manifestly present in the streets, the walker exaggerates some aspects of the city while distorting or fragmenting others (de Certeau 1984, 102).

Sanjay Chel has alluded to the experience of intoxication and alienation in the city's life world. For Munna, the glitzy world of glamour, ice-cream parlors, and neon lights stands in sharp contrast to his everyday world, in which even a bus ticket is unaffordable. Located at the crossroads of these contrasting worlds, Munna creates a performative mask, like a veneer that can protect him from the humiliating experience of facing inequality. His desire for the other world or the "good life" exists, but his body acquires gestures and movements that can help him to produce an alternative regime of resistance and autonomy. In this process, Munna's performance produces a spatial practice of negotiating the city, making his presence felt in the densely saturated street. The modern tapori, a creation of the cinematic imagination, articulates in his performance a network of fragmented and fleeting images.

Following the encounter with the policeman outside the movie theater,

Munna walks into a tea stall with his friend Pakhiya. The two friends are established as drifting personalities in the city, with no real commitments or responsibilities. Suddenly Milli walks in. She talks to them about her frustrations at the film set where she works as a dancer. During the conversation, Munna tells her that his own experience is that of the street, which Milli cannot understand. Milli responds to this in irritation: "The problem with you is that you can't think beyond the footpath! You should try and get a job somewhere." Munna replies emphatically in the negative: "Rather than be a dog living on the crumbs of some rich man, I prefer to be on the street, in control of my life." This exchange is significant and leads up to one of the most important songs of the film ("Yaron Sun Lo Zara"), in which Munna's "footpath" worldview is pitted against Milli's desires and aspirations. Munna gathers with his friends as the song becomes the conflictual space where the world of the commodity confronts both desire and playful rejection. The song, which becomes a dialogue between Milli and Munna, is:

आमिर का गाना

यारो सुन लो ज़रा हाँ,
मेरा भी कहना
जीना हो तो अपुन के जैसे ही जीना
गाड़ी-बंगला नहीं, ना सही, ना सही
बैंक-बैलेंस नहीं, ना सही, ना सही
टीवी-विडियो नहीं, ना सही, ना सही
सूटिंग-शर्टिंग नहीं, ना सही, ना सही
इनकी हमको क्यों हो फिकर
जी लो जैसे मस्त कलंदर

गाड़ी-बंगला अगर हो तो क्या बात है
बैंक-बैलेंस से रंगीन दिन-रात है
टीवी-विडियो अगर हो तो क्या है मज़ा
सूटिंग-शर्टिंग से कुछ और ही ठाठ है

इनकी कर लो कुछ तो कदर

हमको देखो, हम हैं यारा, अपनी मर्जी के राजा
दुनिया बोले, तो मज़ा है, ना कहो खुद को राजा

नाम अपुन का मुन्ना भाई, हम करें वो जो दिल में समाए
अरे धंधा किया ना किया, क्या फिकर
कोई आया, गया हमको क्या खबर

इस दुनिया से जो तुम रहे बेख़बर
कहीं दुनिया तुम्हें ना भुलाए

कल का है किसने देखा, हम तो आज में जीते है

जिनमें हिम्मत है नहीं वो ऐसी बातें करते है

इसकी तो तुम बात न करना, हमको दादा सब कहते है
अरे शेरों के जैसा है अपना जिगर, ऊँचा ही रहा है सदा अपना सर

सर से ज़्यादा ऊँची रहे ये नज़र
आसमाँ भी तो सर को छुपाए

Munna: Friends! Just listen a while
          If you want to live, then live like me!
          No car, no bungalow, it don't matter!
          No money in the bank, it don't matter!
          No video or TV, it don't matter!
          No suiting or shirting, it don't matter!
          Why care for these things
          Live life, fancy free

Milli: Car and bungalow would be great
          Bank balance would light up our days and nights!
          Video and TV, Oh what fun!
          Suiting and shirting, that's called style!
          Watch out for these, mend your ways!

Munna: Look at us, we are the kings of our will

Milli: If the world thought so, it would be fine,
          but don't call yourself a king.

Munna: Munna Bhai is my name
          I do what my heart desires
          Work or no work, doesn't worry me
          Who comes and goes in this world, doesn't bother me

Milli: If you're cut off from this world,
          What if it forgets you?

Munna: Who cares about tomorrow, we live for today.

Milli: So speak those who lack courage.

Munna: Don't you say that, I am called the boss
          With a tiger's heart, my head stands high

Milli: If you try to look above your head
          Your head will be hidden by the sky

The dialogue in the song reveals a split in the way Milli and Munna relate to the world of luxury and lifestyle. Though humorous in its rendition and performance, a sense of freedom, rejection, and irony is found here. The song visualizes the impact of commodity display when, in one section, Munna climbs onto the roof of an expensive car, with his friends heckling the well-dressed car owner. This image appears like a parody of television commercials in which cars are advertised through lifestyle myths of the successful corporate executive. The car glints in the sunlight just as Munna and his shabbily dressed brigade make fun of the lifestyle associated with the car. Munna is opting for a life on the street as a counter to the luxurious world of the commodity. In presenting a counterworld, Munna creates an individualized space, a fantasy world where the rules and surveillance of society do not operate, where the present and the immediate are celebrated, and where Munna is the local *dada* (colloquial term for "boss"). This is also a gendered space, where the commodity and the figure of woman cohere, and the vantage point of critique is occupied quite conventionally by the male figure. Munna's emphasis on a "tigerlike" heart and an arrogant stature draws attention to the specifically performative role of resistance in the tapori's image.

Munna's performance in *Rangeela* is charming, but a deep sense of despair informs the narrative. Munna is not an idealistic figure but someone who would like to make his adjustments with the city without losing his sense of pride and dignity. His desire to settle down with Milli

Aamir Khan with his friends in *Rangeela*. Courtesy Ram Gopal Varma's Factory.

seems difficult, given the world she has become a part of. Munna is not drawn to the world of glamour and showbiz, but he tries to compete with that world. This fact is rendered powerfully in a humorous encounter at a fancy five-star hotel, to which Munna invites Milli for dinner. Dressed in a shocking yellow outfit he thinks is presentable for a hotel, Munna arrives in a borrowed taxi to pick up Milli. At the sight of the yellow outfit, Milli bursts into laughter. Munna, however, thinks he is appropriately dressed for a fancy dinner. The two arrive at the hotel where Munna's incongruity is exaggerated through his speech and body language. When the waiter comes to take their order, Munna demands street food that a five-star hotel would never offer. Milli looks shocked and the waiter is dumbfounded. The hotel's elite space is highlighted by the waiter's posture and use of language (English), while Munna unselfconsciously speaks the *Bambayya* street language.

This restaurant encounter is laced with humor, and while Munna looks completely out of place, he does not look wretched. Munna's arrogance and confident posture appear like a performance that can give him access to the pleasures of an elite world without losing his dignity. Munna is positively dejected and hurt only when Milli sees her costar Kamal and rushes off to meet someone with him. Munna's defeat and hurt in this sequence is given another twist much later in the film, when he chats with Kamal in Milli's hotel room. Kamal asks Munna about his profession. Munna replies defiantly, "Apun Black Karta Hai" (I sell tickets in the black market). Munna's posturing with Kamal is directly related to what Aamir Khan calls an "inferiority complex" which the performance is supposed to mask (interviewed in Mazumdar and Jhingan, "The *Tapori* as Street Rebel" 1998). Munna then sees the necklace that Kamal has presented to Milli. He also sees Milli's delight at receiving the present. Munna, on the other hand, has a small ring that he wants to present as a marriage proposal. The difference in wealth and personal ability is contested by Munna through his arrogant gaze and defiant posturing.

These encounters take place in locations of wealth and luxury—the restaurant at the five-star hotel and a suite in another hotel. Munna's posture and inner conflict in the hotel restaurant and in the hotel room sequences combine the comic with the tragic. This twofold tension imbues the tapori with a sense of power and freedom—even defeat can be survived with dignity and pride. In a sense, Munna's performance creates a "form of empowerment which expresses the fact of 'powerlessness'"

(Gelder and Thornton, 375). As anxieties about class and sexuality get articulated through a defiant performance, certain expressions are deployed to mask this "inferiority" complex. We are again reminded of Chel's emphasis on the tapori's defiant gaze. The role of masculine performativity is central to the production of this defiant gaze, which becomes an important element of subcultural politics. This is evident in the way Munna deploys his body. There is, however, a playful approach to masculinity in *Rangeela*. Specific plot situations are woven into the narrative to draw attention to this playfulness, usually through a series of amusing encounters.

Munna is willing to make fun of his physical strength and masculinity in *Rangeela*. This is highlighted through a drunken conversation between Pakhiya and Munna, which starts with Munna confessing his love for Milli to Pakhiya. Pakhiya does not believe Munna has the guts to tell Milli *(tere me daring nahin hai)*. Pakhiya says he himself had proposed to a woman a while ago and told her he would buy a house and have their children study at a school where the medium of instruction is English. Munna looks at Pakhiya in wonder and asks what happened next. Pakhiya says the woman took off her sandals and hit him! The entire conversation is laced with humorous one-liners in the best tradition of the *Bambayya* language. The conversation is as follows:

आमिर व पकिया के बीच बातचीत

मुन्ना - फटाफट बोल डाला?
पकिया - हाँ बोल डाला
मुन्ना - फिर क्या हुआ?
पकिया - फिर क्या हुआ, उठा के चप्पल मारा!
मुन्ना - क्या चप्पल!
पकिया - हाँ वो अभी भी मेरे पास है।
मुन्ना - साला तेरे को चप्पल पड़ा और तू मेरे को सलाह दे रहा है, उससे डेयरिंग कर!
पकिया - लेकिन बॉस डेयरिंग तो किया अपुनने? तेरे जैसी थोड़ी है फट्‌टास!
मुन्ना - अरे ऐसे तू डेयरिंग करता रहा न, तो बहुत जल्दी तेरे को लेडीज़ चप्पल का दुकान खोलना पड़ेगा!

Munna: I must say this to Milli.

Pakhiya: You will say it? What will you say? You don't have the guts [the word used in the conversation is *daring*] to express your feelings.

Munna: Hell! Why raise the same issue. You will understand if you're in my place.

Pakhiya: Oh, I know! Say you don't have the guts.

Munna: As if you have guts!

Pakhiya: You know what happened two days ago? That fruit seller's woman, Meena.

Munna: Who, Deccan Queen?

Pakhiya: Yes, that woman! Day before yesterday, she walked by Gautam street. I stopped her, took her to my room, and proposed to her. I told her that I would buy a house and our children would study at an English medium school.

Munna: You proposed!

Pakhiya: Yes, I did!

Munna: What happened then?

Pakhiya: She hit me with her sandals.

Munna: She hit you with sandals and you want me to be gutsy?

Pakhiya: But, boss, you must admit I have guts. I'm not wimpy like you.

Munna: If you go on like this, very soon you will have to open a shop for women's sandals!

Pakhiya and Munna's conversation reveals a small world of quotidian dreams and desires. Masculinity here is a combination of innocence and machismo, vulnerability and street-smartness. These characteristics of the tapori's personality are appealing, as they celebrate an ordinariness of existence in the world. Pakhiya wants a little home with children who are educated at elite English medium schools. Pakhiya's little dream is virtually unrealizable. *Rangeela* does not present the tapori in a heroic struggle against a larger-than-life force, but rather destabilizes conventional approaches toward both heroism and masculinity. In this sense, *Rangeela* remains one of the most interesting of the tapori films.

Rangeela's guiding myth is the space of the "footpath," which Munna invokes to legitimize his worldview. It is also the space Pakhiya refers to when he shouts at Milli for not understanding Munna. A youthful spirit, quotidian dreams, and desires within a changing urban context mark the tapori's identity in *Rangeela*. Mediating the encounters of daily life, *Rangeela* does not try to project a sense of spectacular vision or direction; rather, mundane stories are strung together to foreground the tapori's embeddedness within the cultures of contemporary urban life. Munna's ordinariness is ultimately his most appealing quality.

Ghulam: The Tapori as Street Rebel

An adaptation of Elia Kazan's *On the Waterfront, Ghulam* is the story of Sidhu (played by Aamir Khan), a petty criminal who rebels against the *basti*'s (poor neighborhood) local don, Ronnie. Sidhu has been bailed out several times by a young female Muslim lawyer, Fatima (played by Mita Vashisht), who has faith that someday Sidhu will renounce the world of crime. Sidhu's brother Jai (played by Rajat Kapoor) works for Ronnie, helping him collect extortion money from neighborhood residents. Jai is the educated member of Ronnie's gang, and his computer abilities allow him a special status with Ronnie, who is about to become a powerful builder. *Ghulam* builds on the relationship between the two orphan brothers with a deeply traumatic past. While Jai rejects his past by keeping its memory alive, Sidhu represses his memory and has a complicated relationship to the past.

Sidhu falls in love with a girl, Alisha (played by Rani Mukherjee), whose brother works as a social worker in the neighborhood. Sidhu unknowingly allows himself to become part of a conspiracy, planned by Jai and Ronnie, to kill Alisha's brother. The murder is the turning point in the film and creates a wedge between Sidhu and Jai. Alisha's brother's idealism strikes a chord in Sidhu's memory, bringing the past back into his life. The story of the two brothers is situated in an urban context of crime and the illegal operations of builders. This context is grafted onto the city of Bombay through innovative sequences that highlight the spatial contrasts navigated by the tapori, providing the film with a contemporary ambience.

In the course of the film, we learn that Sidhu and Jai grew up on their own after witnessing their father's suicide, following a confrontation between their father and Shyam Sunder, their father's comrade from the freedom struggle, who accused their father of having betrayed five of their comrades. This confrontation is revealed much later in the film in the form of a flashback. It is an incident that is both present and repressed in Sidhu's memory. This significant appropriation and repression of the past is important for Sidhu's identity as a tapori in the city. The narrative fragments the incident by providing us with expressionistic and impressionistic visuals of the father at home, in happy situations, and in flames, falling off the edge of a terrace. The projection of the suicide as a fragmented part of Sidhu's memory is highlighted in the way

Aamir Khan as the tapori in *Ghulam* (1998). Courtesy Studio Links.

the incident is shot. There is rapid cutting between fire, twisting feet, close-up shots of eyeglasses, and sugar falling to the ground. These images are woven together by the sound of a tortured scream. This sequence is repeatedly shown as an enigmatic aspect of Sidhu's memory.

The entire confrontation between the father and Sunder and the ensuing suicide come together at a pivotal moment that will enable Sidhu a second chance to redeem both himself and his father. *Ghulam*'s narrative seems to suggest that Sidhu's aimless loitering in the city as a tapori is possible through a repression of his past. Once his memory returns, Sidhu takes on a heroic persona, elevating the tapori to a new level.

Anjum Rajabali, who wrote *Ghulam*, brought his own perceptions and experiences to the script. Reacting to the rising tide of jingoistic patriotism in several films made in the 1990s, Rajabali consciously chose to evoke in *Ghulam* a jagged history of the national movement. The past is the site of weakness and betrayal. The father (played by Dalip Tahil) is unable to live up to the expectations of the nationalists. In betraying his comrades, he appears cowardly. But he lives with the memory of the past, and his guilt makes him instill a sense of idealism in his children. This is what Sidhu holds on to. Moving away from uncritical and heroic representations of nationalism, Rajabali destabilized the established norms within which nationalist history had been portrayed within popular Indian cinema. By foregrounding the contradictions and conflicts of the past, history's relationship to memory and everyday life is established for a new kind of intervention in the present.[14] The use of the historical past as a haunting memory for the protagonists gives *Ghulam* an unusual texture as the city of contemporary Bombay becomes the stage for working out past conflicts.

Ghulam presents Bombay as a series of compressed spaces, visually exploring the proximity of rich and poor neighborhoods. Sidhu is introduced as a man who harbors dreams of the "good life," precisely because it is inaccessible to him. Like *Rangeela*, *Ghulam* develops a conscious strategy of using performance to foreground inaccessibility without making it tragic. City life is introduced in the film first through a series of fragmented shots woven into a song sequence in which performance goes hand in hand with the spatial unraveling of the city. The sequence is rendered through a combination of panoramic and fragmented shots that introduce us to various aspects of city life—shopping arcades, weddings, lovers on the beach, snack vendors in the middle of traffic, and a discotheque. Sidhu and his gang move through these different spaces, dancing in a disco, trying on clothes at a department store, heckling lovers at the beach, and gate-crashing a wedding party.

Just before the song begins, Sidhu wields a knife at a man in a car and steals his leather jacket. Sidhu ridicules the English speech of the car owner and the Western music playing on the stereo. However, both the leather jacket and the pizza ordered by the car owner fascinate Sidhu, who appears wearing the stolen jacket several times in the film. The jacket functions as a sign of the "good life," a prop that the tapori is fond of, drawing attention to the circulation of signs. In a discussion of Marlon Brando's persona in *On the Waterfront* (1954), James Naremore elaborates on the importance of the short jacket for Brando. The jacket, says Naremore, is not only symbolic of James Dean's red windbreaker in *Rebel without a Cause* (1955), but is also evocative of a fragile masculinity that alternates between vulnerability and a rough persona (1990, 206). The intertextual current of the jacket as a sign of "existential rebellious-ness" also makes it a fetish object, enabling the projection of a style in which display becomes "the most self-absorbing feature of a subculture" (Gelder 1997, 374). Ken Gelder draws particular attention to the diffused spaces such subcultural forms may enter, like the spaces of commodi-fication and fashion (Gelder and Thornton, 374). While Gelder's anxiety is well placed, it is precisely this ambivalent terrain of appropriation and rejection that makes the tapori a significant icon of the cinematic city. In many ways, lifestyle mythology linked to globalization is both rejected and selectively appropriated in *Ghulam*.

The entire aforementioned song is produced through a stylized move-ment of both spatial transitions and rhythmic editing. For instance, when the friends try on outfits at a department store, the scene is edited in fast motion. Comic gestures and gags become part of the performance. Each man emerges from the dressing room to pose before the camera. The last to emerge is Sidhu, who comes out dressed like Zorro. Sidhu shows off his clothing with a mimicked galloping movement. This little performance again draws attention to the intertextual and performative ensemble of the tapori. The irreverence of the song, which suggests a playful and blasé approach to life, is highlighted in the mens' energized body movements, particularly Sidhu's. An occasional wriggle of the hips, a backward glance, a pose before the camera, a leather jacket, and a playful masculinity are all on display. With Bombay as the backdrop, the young men are presented as unemployed youth involved in petty crime. When the gang is seen dancing at a disco, one of them picks the pockets of the dancers. The easy movement from one space to the other is remarkable. Sidhu's gang is comfortable with this diverse spatial land-scape of the city.

Later in the film, when Sidhu drops Alisha at her home, the camera tilts up to reveal her skyscraper apartment. At the sense of wonder on Sidhu's face, Alisha says, "Top floor, flat 22." This reference to a space in the building situates her in terms of both class and power. The entrance-way to Alisha's apartment is dramatized by low-key lighting, low-angle shots, and slow-motion movement. She walks through the apartment, revealing a large, posh, and excessively expensive home. This is followed by a romantic song, as Alisha imagines herself with Sidhu in scenic natural landscapes. The incursion into this fantasyland comes to an end when Alisha, now back from her reverie, walks to her window and sees Sidhu climbing the water pipe that runs from the ground to the terrace of the building. Shocked at the risk he is taking, Alisha starts screaming, begging him to wait until she gets a rope. Undeterred, Sidhu keeps moving. The camera is deployed to highlight both the risk Sidhu is taking and the spatial location of Alisha's apartment. Top-angle shots show cars down below on the road that appear like a line of tiny toy cars. The elite space of the apartment is cinematically enhanced through angular shots of the distant street below, captured from the privileged point of view of the high-rise building. This is constantly contrasted with Sidhu on the pipe, trying to reach the apartment. He finally makes it to Alisha's room and tells her that he was forced to use the pipe because the doorman would not allow him official entry to the building. Sidhu wanted to collect his jacket from Alisha, but his tapori appearance marked him as an outsider to this skyscraper. Class differences and the inaccessibility of elite spaces are highlighted here through a humorous incident that deploys a combination of dazzling aerial views with Sidhu's risky and foolhardy journey up the pipe.

Alisha cannot get over Sidhu's madness. Sidhu casually wanders about Alisha's room, which is scattered with cut-glass bottles, a luxury bed, designer mirrors, and posters on the walls. The mise-en-scène plays on the seductive appeal of glass and light, as diffused lamplights are used to make the objects look pretty, expensive, and appealing. Objects in Alisha's room evoke the lifestyle mythology of the rich. Looking at objects in wonder, but not entirely uncomfortable, Sidhu compliments Alisha on her home. Suddenly, the doorbell rings, and Alisha goes into the living room as her father comes in with a woman. Both are drunk. Sidhu walks into the living room and witnesses a fight between Alisha and her father. When the father sees Sidhu, he demands an explanation. In the heated encounter, he slaps Alisha. Alisha charges out to the terrace in tears. Sidhu walks up to her and says, "Every time I walk by these high-rise buildings, I see the staircase, the windows with their velvet curtains, and the glinting lights. I envy the rich who live in these apartments for their wealth and happiness. But today I have seen what lies beyond the façade."

Sidhu's encounter in Alisha's apartment is reminiscent of the five-star-hotel lobby sequence in *Rangeela*. Alisha's penthouse symbolizes the lifestyle myth of Bombay. Sidhu's entry using the water pipe shows both the inaccessibility of the place and its distance from the street. Like Munna in *Rangeela*, Sidhu displays a fascination for elite spaces, but does not lose his street arrogance or performativity.

Immediately following Sidhu's encounters in Alisha's apartment, the persistence of performance is highlighted through the film's most popular song, "Ati Kya Khandala"(Will you come to Khandala). By showcasing the tapori's body gestures during the song, *Ghulam* attempts to create an alternative spatial landscape of gestures. Despite Alisha's father's rude comments about Sidhu's loaferlike appearance, Sidhu retains his dignity through his subsequent performance. The song is staged at an empty stadium. Sidhu's solo performance, with Alisha as his spectator, is laced with sharp, cutting lines. Sidhu's body discourse and performance reject conventional forms of propriety, to foreground a unique language of

Rani Mukherjee and Aamir Khan in *Ghulam*. Courtesy Studio Links.

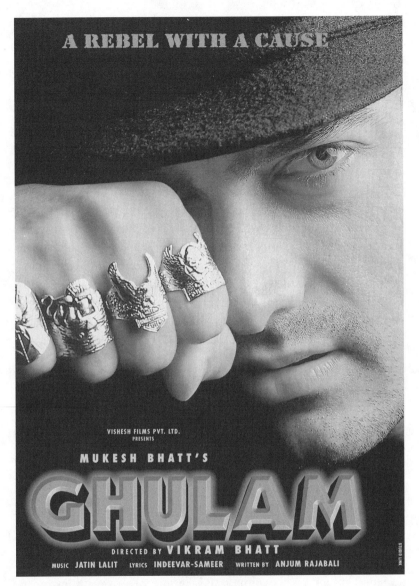

Publicity still for *Ghulam*. Courtesy Studio Links.

survival. The performance combines tricks of the street with the playful use of a red kerchief. The empty stadium becomes a stage for Sidhu's verbal and gestural performance and for the development of his romance with Alisha. The *Bambayya* language used in the song becomes a dialogue between Sidhu and Alisha, with Sidhu inviting Alisha to join him on a holiday in Khandala. Sidhu's swagger, arrogance, and body language are all on display. As in Narayan Surve's poem on Bombay, the "loafer" encounters "two separate worlds," or spaces of the city, and like a member of the city's teeming crowd, his movements remain aimless, but his performative stance provides the necessary strategy for survival.

Ghulam also consciously evokes particularly male anxieties of class and sexuality, explicitly evident in Sidhu's fascination with boxing. Early on in the film, Sidhu runs into a gang of youth on their bikes in the street. A fight breaks out, but is interrupted by the arrival of the police. Sidhu agrees to meet the gang later at a place called the Sangpara Station, to settle the unfinished fight. The Sangpara Station becomes the site for an unusual duel between two gangs. Charlie (played by Deepak Tijori) and his gang arrive on their bikes. Sidhu is waiting there with his friends. Sidhu and Charlie, leaders of their respective gangs, have to compete against each other. They have to race toward an incoming train and jump off the tracks near a flag on the left side of the tracks. Sidhu's friends are hesitant about the act, but Sidhu spots Alisha (who at this point is a member of Charlie's gang) looking at him from behind Charlie's shoulder. There is a relay of silent looks here as the performance of masculinity for the gaze of the woman, the real spectator for this event, becomes important. Sidhu agrees to run toward the train, an act that is visually rendered through a combination of speed, sexual energy, the mystical hue of the night, and the decrepit state of the rail tracks. Performance is central to the identity of all the people gathered at Sangpara Station. Sidhu successfully makes it to the flag in a dramatically shot sequence that creates a montage of the wheels of the train, Sidhu's running feet, the tracks, Alisha's tense expression, and angular shots of the speeding train. Charged with a heightened energy, the sequence combines adventure with sexual power. The fascination with the train becomes the medium through which other anxieties are worked out.

In the Sangpara Station sequence, the anxieties of class, sexuality, deviance, adventure, masculinity, and illegality are woven into the performance. Sidhu not only makes it to the destined spot before the train, but also risks his own life to save Charlie's, when Charlie falls on the tracks while running toward the marked spot. That everyone in this group is part of a defiant space is obvious. There is a visual ensemble of signs used here. The noise of the bikes, the flashy leather jackets, the knuckle-dusters, and the hooting of the gang are all woven into this intensely charged moment. Emerging as a subculture within the city of Bombay, the youth display their own codes, which mark them as different, drawing attention to the economy of gestures and style that are central to subcultures. Subcultural performance relies on a set of codes and practices that mark groups as different.

The station sequence recalls the analysis of deviant youth cultures defined by Dick Hebdige. For Hebdige, it is important to remember that while the politics of youth culture is "a politics of gesture, symbol and metaphor . . . subculture forms emerge at the interface between surveillance and evasion of surveillance" (cited in Gelder and Thornton, 403). The evasion of surveillance that marks the space of both the gangs at the station alludes to another aspect of subcultural politics—the revival of community and solidarity within a new imagination of the street. Therefore, Charlie's gang, indebted to Sidhu, reappears close to the end of the film to return the favor to Sidhu when his life is in danger. These elements of competitiveness, solidarity, youthful exuberance, and spectacular performance make the subcultural politics of *Ghulam* an interesting space for the tapori. The Sangpara Station scene at once recalls *West Side Story* (1961) and *Mere Apne* (1971), as themes of male aggression, frustration, and anxiety are woven into a minor event.

Taking the context of Bombay's linguistic and cultural hybridity amidst a compressed landscape of architectural chaos, *Ghulam* presents the urban crowd not as an abstract force but as a multicultural presence. The crowd is marked by cameo figures, whose dress, speech, and role in the film become significant. The regional and religious identities of several figures in the film are foregrounded. There is Fatima, the Muslim lawyer, who plays an important role in Sidhu's life. Then we have a Tamilian vegetable vendor, and a crippled Muslim man from the northern state of Uttar Pradesh (U.P.). These characters participate in a local meeting to discuss the violence in the neighborhood. Sidhu himself is presented at the meeting as a Maharashtrian identified by his last name (Marathe). The presence of the crowd and urban chaos are relationally structured around the idea of "empty space." By contrasting "real" space (the space of the crowd, the street, and the home) with fetishized "empty space," *Ghulam* creates a conflictual movement between the space of the everyday and "empty space." This is most vividly imagined in what I refer to as the *ghat* sequence.

Sidhu and his brother Jai meet for conversation twice at a *ghat* (steps on the banks of river) that is difficult to establish in terms of locale. This space of the *ghat* is invested with deep emotion. The enclosed walls are bathed in a light-and-shadow pattern reflecting the water at the base of the *ghat*. The use of the *ghat* as a meeting point for the two brothers is deployed to trigger a series of associations linked to the contours of the cinematic city.

It would be useful here to refer to the well-known taxicab sequence in *On the Waterfront* as the obvious pretext for the *ghat* sequence in *Ghulam*. The taxicab sequence, now legendary for its emotional texture and quality of performance, presented two brothers, Terry Malloy (played by Marlon Brando) and Charlie (played by Rod Steiger), inside the space of a cab in conversation about their deep-rooted conflicts. Malloy's childhood memories are woven into his resentful attitude toward his older brother. In the film, the conversation and the nature of the performance dominate the texture of the image (Naremore 1990). In *Ghulam*, however, a similar conversation is located in a stylized space, where the *spatial* dimension becomes equally important for the sequence to make connections with films like *Deewar* (discussed in chapter 1). While the "empty space" of the *ghat* draws attention to the memorable debate between Vijay and Ravi under the bridge in *Deewar*, *Ghulam* redeploys the *Deewar* debate for a different set of ethical dilemmas. The difference is that the conflict between the state and the outlaw central to the narrative of *Deewar* is replaced in *Ghulam* by an ethical conflict between two brothers, both of whom operate outside the law. What is particularly striking here is that the uneducated, rough, street hood questions the educated, urbane brother.

Henri Lefebvre has suggested that to understand the importance and politics of lived space, it is important to make connections between "elaborate representations of space on the one hand and representational spaces (along with their underpinnings) on the other" (1991, 230). This can then explain a subject "in whom lived, perceived and conceived (known) come together within a spatial practice" (230). This philosophical underpinning that guides Lefebvre's understanding of spatial subjectivity provides us with a remarkable entry into the spatial metaphors and symbolic politics deployed by the *ghat* sequence in *Ghulam*. It is from the realm of "empty space" that *Ghulam* moves into the intertextual space of other antiheroes, like the "angry man." Having erased the present and the immediate from this space, the two brothers acquire mythical powers through their confrontation. As familial bonds are put to the test, this "empty space" allows for a complex exploration of morality and justice, a space where memory is evoked and issues of normative action in the face of evil are settled. Jai wants Sidhu to withdraw as a witness against Ronnie. Sidhu not only refuses, but asks his brother why he did not stop him from entering a world of crime. This reversal of *Deewar's* narrative through an intertextual allusion makes the "empty" space of *Ghulam* significant, allowing the tapori the possibility of using his street language as the medium for an empowered critique of the system.[15] In *Ghulam*, time folds back on itself to invest the present with images of the cinematic past *(Deewar)*. This intertextual current of the persistent with the new produces a typical spatial experience of the city, "a particularly acute experience of disconnection and abstraction" (Terdiman, 37).

While the allusion to *Deewar* allows Sidhu entry into a heroic space of conflict, the final fight in the street creates a contemporary, everyday backdrop for Sidhu to specifically address the experience of Bombay. Sidhu's journey climaxes in a fight sequence with Ronnie as the anxious and expectant crowd watches. Before the fight, the entire *basti* looks abandoned; the shutters of shops and apartment windows are down. Sidhu walks through the empty *basti* to his apartment and discovers his belongings on the street. Enraged, he walks to Ronnie's office and challenges him to a fight. The subsequent fight takes place at the center of the *basti*, with the crowd reappearing as spectators. All the cameo figures are now present in the crowd (Fatima, the lawyer; the Tamilian vegetable vendor; the crippled Muslim figure). After defeating Ronnie in an extended fistfight, Sidhu swaggers to a shop. As Sidhu opens the shop's shutter with a brisk movement, the narrative implicitly and symbolically presents a critique of what has become a recurring problem of the Bombay *bandh* (closure).

One of the peculiarities of Bombay in recent years has been the Bombay *bandh*, which is usually instituted by the Hindu fundamentalist Shiv Sena Party.[16] The *bandh* is used to shut down shops and transportation in the city as a form of protest that has become associated with the violent politics of the Shiv Sena. This strategy was an ironic reversal of general strike tactics used by the radical labor movement up until the early 1980s. The *bandh* is essentially an urban form of political protest in India that surfaced during World War II, in the last phase of the anti-colonial struggle. The objective of the *bandh* was to symbolically immobilize the movement of the military and the police by invoking the co-operation of public transport workers and drivers of private vehicles in order to bring the city to a halt. In the post-independence period, the *bandh* was perfected by left-wing parties to symbolize their disillusionment with governments in power, at both the regional and national levels. In the 1990s, however, the *bandh* was often used by Hindu chauvinist groups like the Bharatiya Janata Party (BJP) and the Shiv Sena to coerce and dominate. Shiv Sena tactics focused more on street intimidation of small shop owners and the institutionalization of an elaborate extortion racket in the street run by local party operatives. By evoking the *bandh* as a coercive experience, *Ghulam* imbues the film's narrative with contemporary events of the city while implicitly critiquing the Shiv Sena's role in street intimidation.

Anjum Rajabali recalls how as a Muslim he was having difficulty finding an apartment in Bombay after the 1993 blasts.[17] The frustration from this experience within the larger context of a changing city where Hindu fundamentalism was becoming more and more ubiquitous pushed Rajabali to address these concerns in *Ghulam*. The reference to Shiv Sena politics, the use of cameo figures who become representative of some kind of urban community, and the desire to reclaim the city became essential markers in the script as the film evolved into a textured archive of Bombay. As the crowd celebrates Sidhu's victory over Ronnie and the subsequent opening of the shops, Sidhu suddenly spots a cracked picture of his father. The inspiration to rebel and win is there in the image of the father. While the father may have betrayed his comrades under pressure, he had tried to be an inspirational presence for the children. In an earlier section of the film, the confrontation between Shyam Sundar and Sidhu's father comes back to Sidhu in flashback. As the fragmented memory takes the shape of a complete picture, Sidhu says to himself, "My father was not evil, he was just weak." By redeeming both himself and his father, the tapori in *Ghulam* emerges as the street rebel. *Ghulam* combines the performance of the tapori in the street with a heroic spirit derived from other vigilante films, in which memory becomes central to the journey of the hero. While in *Rangeela* the tapori remains wedded to an ordinariness of survival and being in the world, in *Ghulam* the tapori takes on a bolder, more conscious form of resistance, with the street as the stage for the resolution of several urban Bombay themes.

Challenging Propriety in the Street

At one level, *Rangeela*'s street is a space abstracted from all conflict. The unequal city is rendered as a general problem, rather than being woven into the immediate experience of public conflict. Vikram Bhatt's *Ghulam*, on the other hand, prepares the street as a stage full of contradictions and conflict. *Ghulam*'s tapori mediates the world of crime, underworld dealings, and the specifically Bombay context of builders. Like *Rangeela*, *Ghulam* introduces the tapori's worldview through snatches of conversations and songs right at the beginning of the film. Sidhu in *Ghulam* seems very much like Munna in *Rangeela*.[18] However, if in *Rangeela* the tapori's identity is retained in his ordinariness, in *Ghulam* Sidhu acquires an image that elevates the potential of the tapori to a heroic level, pushing him into a straightforward ethical conflict. The tapori in *Ghulam* acquires a social vision.

The tapori's live engagement with the street and the role of the street in film narratives that continuously evoke the orphaned status of the protagonists are crucial cinematic strategies. Munna in *Rangeela* has no family. In fact, it is difficult to even establish his religion, an ambivalence that was consciously maintained in the film. In *Ghulam*, the protagonist's family is missing. We have images of the father only through fragmented memories. Sidhu in *Ghulam* is a Hindu Maharashtrian. In *Amar Akbar Anthony*, the first film to present the tapori as a hero, Anthony (played by Bachchan) is the adopted child of a priest in a "lost and found" narrative. Anthony is a Christian who speaks the *Bambayya* language. Clearly these fluid identities of the Bombay tapori provide scope for the projection of religious and regional ambiguities in ways that can transcend the "North Indianness" of the Bombay film hero. The orphaned status of the protagonists is central to this fluid identity, for the family in many ways marks people through ritual, habit, custom, and tradition. The lack of family is therefore an important element in the formation of the tapori's hybrid identity, as he becomes the iconic body of the Bombay Street.

De Certeau has suggested that the body in the street is always aware of the represented body. It is through the body that we signal to the world our place within society, within class, and within power. The role of propriety in creating a polite regime of gestures that indicate the body's acceptance of norms and rules within the public sphere is central to our awareness of the street. Propriety on the street is central to the way public spaces maintain discipline and control. For de Certeau, "propriety is the symbolic management of the public facet of each of us as soon as we enter the street" (1998, 17). While propriety ensures a place for us in the public space of the street, it also controls and creates boundaries within which we must function. Propriety on the street can be challenged to create transgressive spaces. The tapori is a figure of transgression who borrows from the world of gestures to create a new space for the performance of a bodily resistance in the public spaces of the city. The actor Aamir Khan attributes this to the performative desires of marginalized groups. Khan refers to African American youth culture in New York City as an analogy wherein street-smart one-liners, swagger, and attitude produce a defiant regime of gestures within New York's multifaceted street culture (interviewed in Mazumdar and Jhingan, "The *Tapori* as Street Rebel" 1998). Similarly, the tapori invents a regime of gestures, made up of fragments gathered from the world of represented gestures, to create an intertextual, hybrid image that can announce rebelliousness in the streets of a cinematic Bombay.

CHAPTER THREE

Desiring Women

Drawing inspiration from the feminist interventions made in the terrain of the cinematic city, this chapter looks at the performance of an urban anxiety about women's sexuality to present the city as a site of deviance and moral anxiety. A conscious attempt to foreground questions of gender in the understanding of urban vision has been a much needed and welcome development in the rising interest on the cinematic city. One of the pioneers in this understanding is Guiliana Bruno (1993), whose feminist analysis of the geography of space as elaborated in the work of Italian filmmaker Elvira Notari significantly pushed the cinematic city debate in new directions. In Bruno's later work on architecture and cinema, she develops new ways of looking at the feminization of urban space. Thus, in Pier Paolo Passolini's *Mamma Roma,* Bruno shows us how the semiotics of prostitution is deployed to explore the landscape of the city. Through techniques like walks, chase sequences, and panoramas, a certain landscape of the city is navigated through the use of motion. In Jean-Luc Godard's *Contempt,* Bruno reveals how the geography of woman's body is mediated via architectural landscaping. In Nanni Moretti's *Caro Diario,* architecture is experienced in motion when the camera is placed on a vehicle in an inventive dream sequence in the film. Alain Resnais's *Hiroshima mon amour* explores a "difficult love for a city and the city as the site of a difficult love," elaborated through an architectural exploration of memory held as a shared space between two people (Bruno 2002, 39).

In a slightly different way, Anne Friedberg, in her book *Window Shopping* (1993), locates the cinema within pre-cinematic forms that profoundly changed our relationship to physical space. Elaborating on the concepts of *flâneur* and *flânerie* within the context of cinema, Friedberg introduces concepts of the "mobilized" and "virtual" gaze, both of which are used to comment on modern and postmodern forms of perception and the subjectivities they engage.

An intriguing figure of Bombay cinema is the westernized vamp,[1] a nightclub cabaret dancer who was pitted against the female protagonist in many films. The vamp occupied a hypersexualized yet illicit space, which, despite all moral discourses, continued to be popular into the 1980s. The 1990s witnessed the dispersal of this original image, when explicit dance sequences associated with the vamp began to be performed by the heroine. These performances, usually shot in spectacular outdoor locations, offer spectators a virtual, novel, and innovative form of "window-shopping" experience that becomes widespread after globalization. This contemporary moment of transformation cannot be comprehended without tracing its genesis in the recent past.

Journeying through the historical formation of a moral discourse on women that sought to divide their existence within the modernist categories of public and private space, this chapter looks at women's relationship to the city and its articulation in Bombay cinema. I trace transformations in screen representations to show how these narratives have related first to nationalism and the city, and second to *speed* and the transnational imaginary. These twin formations are analyzed through a historical debate on women and the city, and a theoretical discussion of the flâneur. What follows is a dialogue between two different moments that seeks to understand the changing relationships between the heroine and the vamp, dance and fashion, and urban space and desire.

Sexual Anxiety, City Space, and the Streetwalker

Elizabeth Wilson has shown how in much of European urban writing, women's presence in the city was seen as a source of both pleasure and danger (1991, 59). This dual-edged relationship produced an anxiety wherein the lure of the city was not only seen as dangerous for women, but women's very presence seemed to make the city a dangerous place. The public-private divide intensified during the industrial period, leading to tremendous anxiety about women's presence in the streets and in other public places of entertainment (1991, 59). Any woman seen loitering and walking the streets could very easily be viewed as a prostitute. The public-private division played a crucial role in harnessing a moral discourse around the "woman of the public," who was more often than not seen as a prostitute.[2] Given the fact that women in large numbers have always been present in the public spaces of Indian cities, it becomes important for us to ask how and why the streetwalker discourse described by Wilson is reproduced in the Indian context.

Academic writing on Indian street culture has been frugal and often uneven. In a rare piece, Arjun Appadurai describes the Indian street as the space where "India eats, works, sleeps, moves, celebrates and worships. The street is a stage that rarely sleeps" (1987, 14). Through a vivid visual anthropology (across different cities of India), Appadurai traces both the historical formation and the function of the street, as well as its present location in the cultural and social life of India. The multiple activities and events of the street are a clear reminder that the "sharp demarcation of public from private spheres is a recent addition to the Indian consciousness" (1987, 14). For Dipesh Chakrabarty, the modernist categories of the public-private divide were challenged by the street in India where "People washed, changed, slept . . . out in the open" (16). But neither Appadurai nor Chakrabarty refers specifically to the presence of women in the street. The Indian street as described by these writers is *ubiquitous* and peopled by all types engaged in different forms of activity in an almost genderless space.

In his study of women's popular culture in nineteenth-century Bengal, Sumanta Bannerjee makes a distinction between two classes of women who occupied different spaces of the city according to their class position. While the elite, including the new middle-class women, were secluded and stayed indoors in *andarmahals* (palace interiors), the majority of working women (mostly self-employed as sweepers, owners of stalls selling vegetables or fish, street singers, dancers, and maidservants) performed different activities in public city spaces (Bannerjee 1997, 129). Despite this overwhelming public presence of working women (who were not always seen as streetwalkers), the outside-inside dichotomy nevertheless seems to get consolidated as a moral discourse. In the Bengali language, the word *Bajar* (bazaar) represents the outside as opposed to the space of the home. Prostitutes are thus called "women of the bazaar" as opposed to "women of the home" (Chakrabarty, 21–23).

This disjunction between the preponderance of workingwomen in public life and the emergence of a powerful moral discourse on sexual practice is indeed intriguing. In what can now be called a paradigmatic text analyzing the "nationalist resolution of the women's question," Partha Chatterjee mounts a provocative critique of Indian nationalism's ambivalent relationship to women providing us perhaps with an "originary" moment of a reformulated public-private construction (*Recasting Women*, 1997, 233–53). While the nationalists fervently hoped and fought for the end of British rule in India, they imported the binary oppositions of nineteenth-century Western social theory into their narrative. Thus, the key Eurocentrist distinctions of the century—the "materiality" of the West as opposed to the "spirituality" of the East; the "historical" nature of the West as opposed to the "eternal" dynamic of the East— were reproduced in the discourses of Indian nationalism. This dichotomy is further condensed into an "analogous, but ideologically far more powerful dichotomy: that between the outer and the inner" (Chatterjee, *Recasting Women*, 1997, 238). When applied to everyday living, social space gets divided into *ghar* and *bahir*, the home and the world. The *world* is the external domain of the material while the *home* remains the spiritual self, with woman as its representation (238).

Like other anticolonial struggles, gender and sexuality became areas of confrontation between nationalism and colonialism in which "women in fact became the site on which tradition was debated and reformulated. What was at stake was not woman but tradition" (Mani, 118). Victorian ideology entered into a comfortable alliance with Indian myths to reinvent the "virtues" and "purity" of the Indian woman (Tharu, 254–68). These negotiations became the process through which the upper castes constituted themselves as the new middle class. Given the symbiotic relationship of Indian nationalism to middle-class cultural production, "the discursive production of public and private spheres occupies literature, popular writing as well as the writing on reform" (Sangari and Vaid, 11). The colonial encounter thus provides the cultural terrain for the formation of a powerful moral discourse around women. The emergence of this discourse was a consequence of both colonial ideology and middle-class nationalism's engagement with colonialism. In this complicated double location, it is not surprising that the metaphor of the streetwalker as the only "public" woman of the nineteenth-century Western city is reproduced in the cultural imagination of India's emerging nationalist and literary elites.

The relationship of the city to the prostitute seems a recurring motif even after independence.[3] Expressing a deep disgust for the city of Bombay, Marathi poet Namdeo Dhasal says, "In this life, carried by a whore, not even the sidewalks are ours. Made so beggarly it is nausea to be human" (cited in Thorner 1996, xxxiv). Filmmaker Satyajit Ray once described Bombay as an "overpainted courtesan" that was "at once seductive and revolting" (cited in Shahani, 103). In a poem titled "On Bellasis Road," Nissim Ezekiel describes the garish dress of a street-walker. Ezekiel tries to give voice to a sense of despair by describing a Bombay street through the overwhelming presence of a prostitute:

> I see her first, as colour only
> poised against the faded red of a post-box:
> purple sari, yellow blouse, green bangles,
> orange flowers in her hair.
>
> A moment later, I sense a woman,
> bare as her feet, beneath the shimmer
> Then I look at her, the colour disappears,
> she's short, thin and dark,
> without a cage to her name,
> as low as she can go.
> She doesn't glance at me,
> waiting for her hawker or mill worker,
> coolie or bird man, fortune-teller,
> pavement man of medicine
> or street barber on the move.
>
> I see her image now as through the telescope,
> without a single desperate moral to keep it in focus,
> remote and closeup. Of what use then to see and think?
> I cannot even say I care or do not care,
> perhaps it is a kind of despair.

Ezekiel's feelings are mediated through the image of the prostitute, whose physicality and body attire foreground a certain presence in the street that is seen as problematic. Ezekiel mentions several urban types in his poem, like the coolie, the barber, the fortune-teller, and the hawker, assuming their male status. While some of these "types," like the hawker, the fortune-teller, or the mill worker, could very well be women, the poem's focus on morality and despair completely erases all these other identities of city women. We are instead presented with a multitude of workingmen, and, amongst them, the prostitute as the only public woman. Not only is she the only workingwoman in this poem, but she represents the "dreadful decadence" and "crisis" of the city.

Sexual Anxiety and the Cinema after Independence

The association of prostitution with decay and collapse in the city was also clearly established in cinema. Popular culture generated by the Bombay film industry in the period after independence was a typical combination of the themes of nationalist modernization and upper-caste cultural fears of female sexual energy and subaltern stirrings. These themes dominated the films of the post-independence era. Guru Dutt's *Pyasa* (The thirsty one, 1957) evokes the metaphor of the prostitute to present a critique of the times. In an emotionally charged sequence, Dutt (who also acts in the film) bemoans the state of independent India by showing the degradation it has brought upon its women. As Dutt wanders through the brothel area of the city, singing the words of the poet Sahir, we encounter a dilemma that is important to trace. Sahir's pathos and troubled relationship to the city is mediated through images of prostitution and a certain disdain for the street at night:

> These fragile bodies, these wan faces
> Where are those who claim to be proud of this land?
> Old men pass through here, young men, too, stop awhile
> Sons, respected fathers and husbands
> These are our sisters, our wives, our mothers
> These daughters of Radha, these daughters of Zulekha, these children
>   of God?
> Summon all the leaders of this land
> These lanes and these auction houses of pleasure
> these caravans of life that are ravaged and looted . . .
> Summon those who claim to be proud of this land.[4]

The song in this poetic sequence evokes monetary transactions, the frivolousness of courtesan dances, and the specter of disease, as we journey into the night with a sense of doom. Referring to Dutt's imagery, Alison Griffith has commented that "as an allegory of social morality, the prostitution narrative articulates discourses of the nation on a visceral level, representing human pain and suffering in both the song lyrics and visual imagery" (180). Though the critique of commodification and decadence of the street at night is powerful, the metaphor of the prostitute here is laden with a certain anxiety that the film later tries to deal with through the prostitute's redemption. Sahir's powerful lyrics seem to bear some relationship to the way Bombay cinema evolved a unique relationship between sexuality and space. As the protagonist traverses the city's labyrinth, the lyrics evoke a darkness of the city, whose harshness and cruelty appear to mask the anxiety that is embedded in the skillful presentation of the sequence.

In the song "Ramayya Vasta Vayya," one of the well-known songs from *Shri 420*, actor/director Raj Kapoor encounters two different parts of the city. He first walks into a nightclub/casino where Maya (played by Nadira), dressed in Western clothes, is dancing with great abandon on a revolving table as people clap and cheer around her. The juxtaposition of Kapoor's pained face with the laughing faces of other men and the dancing Nadira shows Kapoor's disturbed reaction to this space. He walks out of the nightclub and encounters another part of the city's poor neighborhood, where life is symbolic of the village. "Ramayya Vasta Vayya" recounts the lost life in the village as images of motherhood and simplicity dominate the narrative. This juxtaposition of the "bad" city and the "good" city is presented using Nadira's dancing body to feminize the "bad" city. Unlike the prostitute in *Pyasa*, Maya's sexualized imagery evokes no pathos—it is not despair but an open critique of what is perceived as the degenerate westernization of cities, wherein the values of the past, the village, and "Indianness" are lost. In many ways, the anxiety writ large in these seminal films prefigures the emergence of the standard cabaret number in several films of the 1960s and the 1970s—an image that is marked both by fascination and revulsion. The spatial location of the dance and its place within the narrative acquire a formulaic quality of constant repetition. The image of the vamp needs to be analyzed, for it was the result of nationalism's complex relationship to the city.

The Westernized Vamp and the Nightclub

The vamp emerged in cinema sometime during the late 1950s and became common to many films of the 1960s and 1970s (for example, *Caravan*, 1971; *Mere Jeevan Sathi*, 1972; *Sachcha Jhutha*, 1970; *Do Raaste*, 1969; *Anamika*, 1973; and *Zanjeer*, 1973). The vamp was a visible intrusion of the West into the cinematic space of Indian films, signifying an unrestrained sexuality and license, given to vices "unknown" to "Indian" women. The vamp was the outsider, distinct from the iconic woman of the nation. While the heroine was the site of virtue and "Indianness," the vamp's body suggested excess, out-of-control desire, and vices induced by "Western" license.[5] The vamp usually occupied the public spaces of the casino/bar/nightclub, often as a floor-show artist. It is interesting how Helen, an Indian actress born to Burmese and English parents, was used extensively to depict the vamp. Helen's blond hair and blue eyes were highlighted in her vampish image. Later, other actresses performed the role, but by and large they retained a westernized appearance. With the vamp came the invention of the Indian "cabaret," a spectacle of vice and abandon allegedly of Western origin, in which the vamp danced provocatively in front of the audience.

The vamp was always seen as an outsider, a home breaker who dis-played wanton sexuality on the screen. In filmic terms, the display of sexuality was usually restricted to certain spaces like the nightclub, the bar, and the casino.[6] The nightclub is one of Bombay cinema's fascinating creations—an illicit landscape of gambling, gangsters, and smugglers, on the one hand, and the excessive and dangerous display of female sexuality, on the other. The representation of the purity/spirituality of the nation was negotiated through the image of the heroine, and the woman's body became the site of conflicting value systems. Images of the chaste woman and the nightclub vamp continued to inform Indian cinema right up to the early 1980s.

The nightclub emerged as an imagined, placeless, and virtual space of sexual excess, villainy, and underworld negotiations. In the nightclub, a combination of desire and anxiety produced an insecurity about female sexuality in the city. What occurs here is a visual condensation of city space, arising out of the sexual being identified as the marker of urban disorder. As in nineteenth-century cities in the West, the cinematic nar-rative's engagement with the nightclub dancer provided "the conditions for the woman in city space, the public woman, to be used as a sign of urban pathology" (Swanson, 80). In the enclosed space of the nightclub, the vamp could dance provocatively. The popularity of such dances and the iconic stars who played vamps points to an interesting tension. Films of the late 1960s and 1970s had to have at least one cabaret dance; it was considered almost mandatory by distributors. Film posters of the period usually show a cabaret in one corner, so that the audience would

Helen dancing as the vamp in *Caravan* (1971). Courtesy Tahir Hussain, Al Tahir Entertainments, and Kamat Foto Flash.

know of the cabaret's presence. The immense popularity of the cabaret and of the vamps who performed the dances seemed to stand in sharp contrast to the moral coding of this space. Helen became so popular with her dances that a commercial videotape of her well-known dances was released in the late 1980s. The tape is called *Raat Ki Rani* (Queen of the night, 1987). In this compilation, it is difficult to judge where one song ends and the next starts. A distinct pattern can be traced through the similarities in the dance sequences taken from different films. It is difficult to analyze these dances individually, since the elements are constantly repeated. I will try to focus on some of the recurring and distinct features in order to enable a deeper understanding of the image. The prevalence of certain techniques became important in the 1990s as the heroine began to occupy the space of the vamp.

The cabaret is usually presented as a performance that swings between grace and awkwardness. Hands travel over body parts, intent on exploring the anatomy. The body swings about almost in dialogue with something personal. There is no compulsion to present the dance as a harmonious movement. On the contrary, the dancer throws herself onto the floor, but has a dynamic energy and total disregard for identity. Madhava Prasad sees the "mandatory cabaret sequence" as a space where cinematic voyeurism is created by the dancer's direct look into the camera. This violates the recipe of "classical cinema" where voyeurism is mediated through someone else's gaze (102). Perhaps cinematic voyeurism is too sweeping a term to explain a direct look into the camera. A direct address is deployed in many situations.[7] What makes the vamp look different is not just her direct address, but also her deeply erotic performance. It is this act of defiance and deviation that announces danger. A heavy movement of the bosom is usually accompanied by coy and seductive expressions on the face. The dancer's relationship to music is unique. There is a rhythmic combination of sound and body that evokes a hyperreal world of desire.

The architecture of the nightclub usually exudes a gaudy decadence, adding to the heightened anxiety already present in the dance sequence. It also presents us with the hidden life of the city, whose pleasures lay in what Wilson calls the "illicit enjoyment of the forbidden other" (1991, 27). We enter the space of the nightclub without ever getting an exterior view. A large floor area is always present, with tables and chairs for customers. At the center of the club is a ramplike stage for the dancer, designed to provide her easy access to the spectators. She moves from the stage to the customers at the table, blurring the intended separation from the stage. Arches and pillars in the nightclub are foregrounded through tracking and crane shots, a technique that heightens the camera's erotic relationship to the dancer. The dancer's ability to create contact with the customers, and her highly provocative and excessive performance situate her within a moral universe of ungainly femininity.

What is interesting about these dances is that a series of spectators connected to the nightclub are always present. Either the villain, or the hero in search of the villain, or the hero who uses the help of the vamp is present in the nightclub. Violence, intrigue, death, and sex lurk close to the vamp. The nightclub's aura is evoked through a play of light and shadow; cigarette smoke and camera movements establish the place as a den of violence and excess. The dancer's body creates the spectacle necessary to produce both revulsion and fascination. Through the vamp's performance and location within the nightclub, we are presented with a duality that becomes the fertile ground both for the articulation of sexual anxiety and the performance of sexual excess. A critic's sharp remark about Helen betrays the latent anxiety linked to the spectacle of the nightclub dances:

Sensuality and eroticism have always been a part of Indian films but they have been presented with grace and style by filmmakers like Kidar Sharma, MehboobKhan, Zia Sarhadi, Guru Dutt and Vijay Anand. The lesser elements in the film community had correctly gauged the fast deteriorating public taste and inserted into their films titillating song and dance numbers picturized on vamps who, by virtue of their screen role, could get away with a fair amount of mischief. Helen was the most successful of the tribe. (Chatterjee 1995, 214)

The vamp's closeness to a corporeal sexuality made her both fascinating and dangerous, embodying the dialectic that marks urban life. Urban degradation and disorder are presented through a performance of sexual excess, in which it becomes imperative to regulate the "corporeal, in the interest of cultural achievement and civilization" (Swanson, 86). A sexuality bordering on the pathological had to be countered effectively, and in cinematic language this opposition needed to be visually stark. Thus the peculiar tableau framing within the nightclub emerged, in which counterimages of femininity were galvanized to enable a striking opposition between female virtue and "dangerous sexuality."[8]

Kati Patang (Broken kite, Shakti Samant, 1970) had a famous dance by Bindu (a popular vamp) in a nightclub. Here a play of opposites is set up as body attire and movement are contrasted throughout the performance. The film's protagonist, Madhavi (played by Asha Parekh), is sitting with her boyfriend (Rajesh Khanna) at a table. She is clad in a white sari, which signifies widowhood.[9] Although Madhavi is not really a widow in the film but only poses as one, her expression of shock when she sees the dancer Bindu (a woman who knows Madhavi's past) is presented through a series of alternating shots. While the shock on her face is supposed to create a new twist in the narrative, the dance in the club appears to present its own logic. The sequence opens with the camera focusing on the lower part of Bindu's wriggling body as she looks down at a man moving on the floor. This rather explicit movement is then contrasted with Madhavi's static position and shocked expression, signaling both her recognition of the woman and the "decadence" of the performance. Bindu never really looked westernized, but she carries the Western image in films through her body attire, gestures, and performance. Her supposed westernization in *Kati Patang* (as Shabnam) is contrasted with Madhavi's "Indianness" (rendered most explicitly in her white sari). Bindu performs for the people sitting in the nightclub, but also for the film audience who now have an independent relationship to the dance. The entire performance is laced with hyperbolic emotions, exaggerated body gestures, and bizarre costumes. The contrasting images of femininity and the heroine's restraint and control over her own desires and sexuality became the vehicles through which female sexuality was negotiated in the city. This dichotomized narrative of sexuality presented through a tableau framing the "westernized vamp" and the "Indian woman" was common in many films.

The regulation of desire was already undergoing a series of disruptions in the 1970s. The emergence of the actress Zeenat Aman marked a distinct shift, since Zeenat naturalized the Western look (for example, in *Hare Rama Hare Krishna*, 1971, and *Yaadon Ki Barat*, 1974). Zeenat was never the vamp; she always played the heroine. As Rajadhyaksha and Willeman suggest, the actress heralded the "70's look of the westernized 'liberated' young woman in Hindi films. At its best this attempt to represent 'modernity', redefined the love story by violating several moral codes advocated by earlier melodrama to control female sexuality."[10] By the 1990s, the earlier binary oppositions, so dear to the nationalist imaginary, had ceased to hold. The heroine now occupied the space of the vamp, through a process marked by a public display of desire and an entirely new discourse of sexuality that threatened the old boundaries (as in, for example, *Tezaab*, N. Chandra, 1989, and *Khalnayak*, Subhash Ghai, 1993). The space of the nightclub has today lost its earlier iconic status. What happened to the vamp and her space? As the heroine moves into the space of the vamp (or vice versa), desire and space are dispersed. The dances were no longer located in a morally coded space, but moved into multiple locations. These fragments negotiate fashion, the female body, dance, and music, to present a performance through which a "spatial relocation of the metropolis" occurs (Swanson, 80). This relocation is embedded in a novel experience of flânerie generated by the new visual cultures of globalization.

Revisiting the Flâneur as a Figure of Perception

For Walter Benjamin, the flâneur was the nineteenth-century Parisian dandy whose walk through the streets of the city gave him visual access to forms of urban life and spectacle. It is a concept that was part real and part imaginary, seen primarily as a male figure, a product of the new industrial modernity of the nineteenth century. For Benjamin, the flâneur was a "panoramically situated" spectator who observed and absorbed through a random selection of visual impressions of the new commodity space. Feminist scholars have seen the panoramic gaze of the flâneur as inherently gendered, reflecting male control over public space. The other of the male flâneur was the prostitute, the only "public woman" who lacked control over her body and the freedom to enter all parts of the city (Wolf, 34–50; Buck-Morss 1986, 99–140).

This reading has been complicated by several scholars who look at women's entry into public spaces like the department store or another modern space of consumption as enabling a new public identity for women (Wilson 1991; Felski). The activity of consumption, which became generalized in the twentieth century, depended to a large extent on women's ability to desire, to gaze, and to move freely through the new geography of the city. I find this reading useful when trying to understand the emergence of a desiring female subjectivity in the cinema of the 1990s. In India, as I have already shown, there is the formation of a moral discourse on women's movement within the city, despite their large presence in the public spaces of the nineteenth and twentieth centuries. The circulation of this discourse through images of the westernized vamp in cinema was widespread. In the 1990s, however, the vamp virtually disappeared as a result of a changed dialectic between women's sexuality, spectatorship, and the new imperatives of consumption. This process crystallizes around fashion, the female body, dance, and urban travel, to enable a novel experience of flânerie.

The idea of a special gaze (the art of flânerie) that can capture the passing moment, bestowing the fleeting with a heightened visuality, remains an important metaphor for our understanding of vision and perception in modernity. The flâneur's gaze is fragmented and adventurous as s/he confronts the magical world of the commodity displayed in shop windows along city streets. For Baudelaire, the flâneur's passion is complexly urban:

For the perfect *flâneur*, the passionate spectator, it is an immense joy to set up house in the heart of the multitude, amid the ebb and flow of movement, in the midst of the fugitive and the infinite. To be away from home and yet to feel oneself everywhere at home, to see the world, to be at the centre of the world, and yet to remain hidden from the world . . . The spectator is a prince who everywhere rejoices in his incognito. (34)

Flânerie's special quality of a "contemporary disposition" is supported by a gaze that goes beyond "rational insights" to create a perspective that is oriented toward "exterior perception." The flâneur's particular obsession for certain objects and sights makes him a significant "kaleidoscope of his time." Anke Gleber points out:

> The *flâneur* comes into being primarily as a figure of perception, as an epic camera, as a representative of the "pure outside" of aesthetics in his modernity. His function is visual perception per se, as a passer by on the street and a figure in the detective novel of the modern metropolis. (47)

Flânerie is also a perceptual mode that depends on distraction and free movement of subjectivity, wherein the gaze is organized according to a "spontaneous, unmitigated and seemingly unsystematic turn of attention towards the surface phenomena of the exterior world" (Gleber, 26). Flânerie thus lends itself to a form of "unmeasured drifting," but with a distance that allows the gaze to acquire a "receptive disposition, a mode of embracing rather than of excluding external impulses" (26). It is important to understand that this gaze is shaped by a "primacy of space and sight" (48). The cinematic gaze has a special affinity with the gaze of the flâneur, since, as perceptual modes,

> *flânerie* and cinema share the montage of images, the spatio-temporal juxtaposition, the obscuring of the mode of production, and the "physiognomic" impact—the spectatorial reading of bodily signs. The dream web of film reception, with its geographical implantation, embodies *flânerie*'s mode of watching and its public dimension." (Bruno 1993, 48)

Signifying an urban phenomenon that coincided with the reception of movie images, cinematic flânerie becomes an important metaphor only when spectacle, shock, and rupture generate new forms of experience. The cinema's ability to combine the "mobile" with the "virtual" significantly changed our understanding of "the present and the real," introducing us to a new, more virtual form of flânerie (Friedberg, 3).

As a figure, the flâneur has been located primarily within the experience of capitalist modernity in major cities of the West. Some have seen the flâneur as an elite experience that excludes other forms of visual experience not always rooted in the flâneur's privileged and bored disposition. The significance of flânerie as a mode of perception linked to cinematic practice, however, makes the art of cinematic flânerie a more generalized form. Given the worldwide circulation of film technology, cinematic flânerie can be accepted as a more universal experience, as a kind of spectatorial perception uniquely linked to cinema. In cinematic flânerie, the primary issue is access to rapid spatial and temporal changes enabled by the art of editing. In the Indian context, the uniqueness of popular cinema's narrative form and the experience of contemporary globalization have created a novel form of cinematic flânerie.

Globalization and Cinematic Flânerie

The past three decades have witnessed the greatest changes within film narratives because of the new temporal logic of globalization.[11] One of the major areas of change has been in the role of television. Cable television came to India between 1990 and 1991, transforming a two-channel state-run television into a forty-five- to sixty-channel system. Cable offered Hollywood-produced English and American soaps, popular shows like *The X-Files,* talk shows, news channels (including the BBC and CNN), the "generation-oriented" MTV, and more. Threatened by the stark reality of empty cinema halls, the film industry had to gear itself to become one of the major suppliers of content for television. Film-specific music videos, talk shows, and lengthy star interviews proliferated on almost all the cable channels. The presence of programming from different parts of the world introduced a notion of simultaneous time, which promoted a hyperreal viewing experience in India. In the past, simultaneity was a monopoly predominantly of real-time sports telecasts on state television. The current constellation, however, introduced a set of references in cultural production that cinema could not escape. Advertising had played a fairly big role on television, even before cable, but the cable boom expanded the advertising industry. Programs promoting lifestyles and consumer goods joined the bandwagon. The visual register now had to contend with a plethora of images creating experiences of shock and pleasure at a purely phenomenological level. The experience of the metropolis in this new visual landscape is fragmented and dislocated, and it becomes the fertile ground for the emergence of a novel form of electronic/virtual flânerie embedded in a slightly different experience of "arrival" without "departure."

The arrival of new electronic forms of communication introduced significant innovations in screen narratives. Modes of travel within the Hindi film narrative are frequently informed by song and dance sequences. Song sequences disrupt the continuum of film, defying its logical, linear movement of space and time. This disruption of space and time is crucial, since an element of "departure" and "return" is assumed within the narrative.[12] While there were similar disruptions in the past, the current mode embodies an acceleration of narrative disruption with a *speed* not seen in the past. Today, a song sequence can suddenly take characters located in an Indian city to the spectacular cities of Europe and America, with no explanation for this transition. There seems to be a great desire to go beyond the possible, to bring the world of distant spaces into the song sequences. This transition seems to speak to the increasing fragmentation of the narrative.[13] In other words, the logic of *speed* and the fragmented cinematic city seem to go hand in hand. The past decade has witnessed the greatest changes within the narrative as a result of the new logic of *speed*.[14]

Narrative fluidity in the 1990s makes the visual mapping of contemporary cinematic flânerie fascinating. The female spectator is not only taken across the world to different sites and cities, she is bedecked in an array of fashionable adornments and clothes. Unlike the streetwalker (the original *flâneuse*), the contemporary female flâneuse belongs to a diverse urban landscape of multiple identities. Like the gaze of the flâneur, the song sequences allow the spectator a state of "unmeasured drifting," a kind of reverie enabling an exploration of the world of consumption. The narrative's sudden disruption of space/time continuity enables the spectator's gaze to travel, like the classical flâneur's gaze, beyond "rational insights." The transformation from story to song also replicates the flâneur's distracted gaze, where the spectator is driven by a desire to collect fragments of perception through both systematic and surprise discoveries. In this journey we encounter the phantasmagoria of Indian modernity.

Cultures of Display, the Electronic Catalog, and Consumption

In the late nineteenth century, the spectacular introduction of the *displayed* commodity in Western cities created an ongoing "hunger for visual experience." Technological developments like light and architectural splendor presented the displayed commodity as belonging to an infinite cosmos. The combination of mirrors, light, and glass made window displays sparkle brilliantly with a magical aura that was intended to seduce the passerby on the street. Window displays made goods look better, introducing "an additional element of deception" (Schivelbusch, 147). Art and commerce came together to propel the circulation of the commodity form as capitalism entered its highly aestheticized phase in the twentieth century. Department stores in Europe and America used special display techniques to ensure the perception of infinity in the world of the commodity. The technological aestheticization of the commodity through the display of goods in department stores and shop windows made the city-street experience of the West significantly different from that of metropolitan India, where a predominance of bazaar culture prevented display techniques from proliferating. Some organized shopping areas existed in the big cities, but by and large the culture of bazaars and little shops continued to dominate the visual landscape of metropolitan India. The bazaar, a chaotic marketplace crowded with stalls, shops, and hawkers, has been considered the "symbolic image and metaphor for the physical state of the contemporary Indian city" (Mehrotra and Dwivedi, 226).

In this urban landscape of chaos and disorder that marked the physical form of Indian cities, neither the department store, nor the arcade, nor shop windows played the role they did in the West.[15] It was *cinema* that played the crucial role of introducing to its audiences the aestheticized world of the commodity. Cinema became the window for (virtual) global travel, urban exploration, and commodity display. Since the physical spaces of metropolitan India lacked the aestheticization that was so crucial to the transformation of cities like Paris, London, New York, and Berlin, cinema provided its audiences with a modern "window-shopping" experience. Just as Hollywood motion pictures from the second decade of the twentieth century "functioned as living display windows for all that they contained; windows that were occupied by marvellous mannequins and swathed in a fetish inducing ambience of music and emotion" (Eckert, 103), cinema in India emerged as the phantasmagoria of Indian modernity.

In her work on 1930s Hollywood fashion, Sarah Berry describes how techniques of displaying fashion drew on the theatrical tableau, the nightclub revue, beauty contests, and fashion shows (47). Berry relates these forms to film genres like the musical, the costume drama, and the fashion film. What is interesting in the Indian context is that all popular films are musicals, and have been since the coming of sound in 1931. Therefore, the picturization of a new kind of fashion has been able to find easy entry within a narrative structure that has historically allowed for a fluid movement into the world of fantasy. In the 1990s, film songs emerged as one of the most important spaces for an aggressive and sophisticated form of fashion display. These sequences appear like mini fashion shows, offering female spectators the freedom to virtually experience the world of fashion. Fleeting, erotic, and utopian, this experience allows the spectator the possibility of inhabiting two worlds—"Indian" and "global." The periodic incursion into the monumental space of global cities heightens the technique of display made possible in the decade after globalization. Operating like virtual, mobile, clothing catalogs embedded within the narratives, the song sequences offer female spectators the privilege of flânerie.

In an insightful essay, Alexandra Keller looks at the role of mail-order catalogs in engendering a kind of female flânerie at the turn of the twentieth century in America. Focusing on the Sears, Roebuck and Company catalogs issued between 1899 and 1906, Keller suggests that this "uniquely American icon" played the role of "bringing the city to the country and the department store to the shopper . . . the outside world into the home" (158). The catalogs operated as moving marketplaces, "a mall between two covers," embedded in the spectacular world of entertainment and fantasy (Keller, 158). Just as these catalogs targeted a female populace whose desire would be sustained through representations of the absent object, the song and dance sequences operated as display windows offering the spectator a range of clothing/costumes. The analogy between the catalog and the song sequence is made here because film songs are seen on TV regularly, both before and after the release of a film. Songs are used aggressively to market films. This independent circulation through television enables the songs to function like electronic catalogs, created as they are through a combination of travel, fashion photography, and the rhythmic movement of dancing. The sheer phantasmagoria of contemporary consumption brings about the demise of the former westernized vamp, whose gestures and performances are now required for the erotic display of women's fashion.

What is interesting here is the disruption of accepted codes of femininity within the narrative of the "formula." Since fashion-display techniques use the performative gestures of the former vamp, screen women in recent years have seen the possibility of transgression. As filmic taboos imposed on the former heroine are fractured, contemporary public discourse displays a latent anxiety. Responding to the new on-screen image, a media critic said, "In the era of pre-fabricated clothes, pre-digested food, and pre-conceived ideas, underdressed models become overpriced icons as Indians look for quick fixes in cheap cinema halls. The bimbo-babble of movie magazines invades public discourse as starlets kiss toy-boys while prancing around trees" (Bamzai, 14). While some critics call the new song and dance routine of cinema "MTV mania," others feel the heroine has entered the "immoral body of the designated vamp" (usually Helen).[16] Morality issues around the sexualizing of the female body have become an everyday part of public discourse in the media. The other feature of this discourse has been a constant reference to earlier films, a golden age of cinema, a "classical" past untainted by the rhythms of the cable boom.

This lamentation over a loss of quality in contemporary cinema clearly reveals an anxiety about the sexualizing of the visual public sphere in the 1990s. Part of this anxiety is linked to the feminized identity of the post globalization period. Feminist scholars have shown how the language of seduction was regularly used to refer to the marketing techniques that developed within the consumption culture of early twentieth-century Europe. Recognizing this, some have argued for an interrogation of consumption practices, in which women are located neither as victims of ideology nor as objectified images of mass culture. Instead, consumption practices need to be seen as both enabling and restricting women's desires (Felski, 62–63). Along a similar vein, some Indian feminists have attempted to understand the growing culture of paranoia associated with the media landscape of contemporary India. Through a narrative that maps the sequence of events that led up to the debate over the Miss World contest held in Bangalore in 1996,[17] Shohini Ghosh suggests that the "spiral of moral panics" blurred the different voices of protest against media images of women. As critics from both the Right and the Left appeared to use the same language, it became clear that the anxiety was expressed primarily around the sexualizing of the female body within a new space of consumption (Ghosh, 233–59). Is it not, therefore, a situation in which consumption practices and the eroticization of the visual sphere created a fluidity of performance and expression for women? Certainly the discourse in the Indian media on the image of the "new woman," who was now both vamp and heroine, points toward that. The role of dance in this transformation has been crucial.

Dance, Space, and the Display of Fashion

Dance is central to the narratives of Hindi cinema. Its increasing popularity over the years, with some dance teachers acquiring fame for their work, is an important new development in the film industry.[18] Analyzing dance in Bombay cinema is very important, given its presence in almost every film. Dance allows the body to perform and express, since "the substance of the material force of dance is body movement, and movement becomes expression through gesture" (Thomas 1997, 173). Dance thus offers us a kind of "cultural knowledge," creating the possibility of reading a range of meanings, both historical and cultural. Through its choreography and organization of bodies in motion, dance also displays "traces of the forces of contestation that can be found in society at large" (Martin, 6). The recent changes in the representation of dancing space have been a significant development within the Bombay film narrative. The nightclub of the former vamp was an enclosed space, but a public space that a particular kind of woman could occupy. It was the dark side of the city, whose carnival pleasures needed to be controlled through effective counterimages of femininity and "Indianness." The enclosure was significant as a moral code. In contemporary cinema we see a new form of spatial positioning in which the heroines (no longer vamps) display an aggressive sexuality through excessive movement of the body. What seems to be happening here is the operation of an "external reality," in which the heroine transcends the expectations imposed on her and moves from a relatively passive to an aggressive performance, enabling a more "active psychic position" (McRobbie, 45).[19]

The exit of the vamp from the screen has been significant. The collapse of certain boundaries and moral spaces in terms of narrative/filmic constructions and the aggressive display of female sexuality is happening at a speed not seen in the past. As modes of travel are used in many song sequences, the spectacle of fashion recasts the original nightclub. Monuments, streets, and landscapes of national and international cities create the global backdrop for the display of fashion, refashioning the heroine's narrative location as she occupies and destroys the space of the vamp's nightclub. The heroine now changes her costume during the dance and, like a shopper, tries on different identities, engaging in the "pleasures of a temporally and spatially fluid subjectivity" (Friedberg, 184).

Cinema is a place where the old and the new are distinguished not only through the story line and narrative, but also through dress codes and body language. Fashion is therefore an important aspect of cinema, generating dispersed notions of identity and selfhood. Jennifer Craik criticizes assumptions about fashion that identify it as either the ultimate symbol of capitalist consumer culture or as the creative aspirations of the artist community. Departing from this binary opposition, Craik locates fashion as a performance that highlights the "relations between the body and the social habitus" (10). In urban societies, fashion is an "essential ingredient in the rituals of the cityscape" (Wilson, 33). While fashion plays a role throughout the narrative, its most reflexive gesture is available in the song and dance sequences, in which the performance, spectator address, and other cinematic techniques create spectacular display forms for women's clothing. Fashion draws the invisible flâneur's/ female spectator's gaze into a landscape of consumption and desire, mediated through the female protagonist's rapid change of costume, jewelry, shoes, and hairstyle.

Although many scholars have indicated the similarity between the shop window and the screen frame, what becomes interesting in the Indian context is the relationship between the narrative and the song sequences. The heightened window-shopping experience in the 1990s is made possible primarily through the song sequences. The combination of choreography, costumes, and landscapes makes the songs appear like mini fashion shows, as the "shop mannequin is transformed into the live action of film performance" (Friedberg, 141).

The global space of the song and dance sequences creates a utopian world where people feel themselves gliding across different landscapes and nations in a virtual form of travel. In a rather self-reflexive mode, *Dilwale Dulhania Le Jayenge* (*We Will Take the Bride Away*, Aditya Chopra, 1995)[20] draws attention to the reverie of the spectator when Simran (the heroine of the film, played by Kajol), in a drunken state, becomes obsessed with a red dress she spots in a shop window in Switzerland. This scene is followed by a sudden transition as Simran, now wearing the red dress, dances in the snow with her partner, Raj (played by Shahrukh

Khan). During the song, the couple moves across diverse landscapes wearing different clothes. While such fantasy is now common in many films, *Dilwale* foregrounds the fantasy world of the song sequences by allowing a drunken girl to experience her most immediate desires. *Dilwale*'s use of the shop window to propel the fantasy sequence is like a condensed image of cinema's ability to frame and display clothing for its spectators.

The inherent quality of fantasy involved in the song sequences is directly linked to the desire for fashion in the sequence of another successful film. In *Biwi Number One* (The number-one wife, David Dhawan, 1999), Prem Mehra (played by Salman Khan), the wayward husband of Pooja (a settled, traditional housewife who is always dressed in saris; played by Karisma Kapoor), is drawn to a successful model. Karisma's mother-in-law advises Karisma to improve her grooming in order to retain her husband. This scene is followed by a fantasy sequence in which Karisma dreams of herself in provocative attire. The sequence begins with close-up shots of lips, hair, and eyes, followed by a song in a jungle during which Karisma displays a range of designer outfits. The stark contrast between the sari (her usual outfit) and the new clothing in the song sequence points to the role of fashion in mediating women's fantasies and desires. This sequence also points to the cinema's desire to target not just young middle-class women, but also housewives and lower middle-class women, whose lives may be devoid of the pleasures of fashion. Both *Dilwale Dulhania Le Jayenge* and *Biwi Number One* self-consciously acknowledge the role of songs in exploring the relationship between fantasy and consumer desire.

Mimicking the Catwalk

Film theorists have made the analogy between the screen and the shop window (Gaines; Eckert). Ann Friedberg says:

> "Window shopping" implies a mode of consumer contemplation, a speculative regard to the mise-en-scène of the display window without the commitment to enter the store or to make a purchase. Cinema spectatorship relies on an equally distanced contemplation: a tableau, framed and inaccessible, not behind glass, but on the screen. (68)

Friedberg is addressing the new ways in which subjectivity and vision were transformed with the birth of the cinema. She shows how precinematic visual experiences like the panorama, the diorama, city strolling, and window-shopping anticipate and influence the multiple pleasures offered by the cinema. In India, the song sequences enable a heightened window-shopping experience. The combination of choreography, costumes, and landscapes enables the songs to appear like mini fashion shows.

Director Karan Johar and fashion designer Manish Malhotra have each commented on contemporary cinema's ability to function like a "department store," particularly through the song sequences. Malhotra's emergence as a designer is directly linked to his film work. In the fashion world, cinema is now seen as the primary showcase for designer clothes. Johar and Malhotra both claim that fashion designers in the past saw film fashion as "lowbrow" and "cheap." The shift to a designer aesthetic can be seen in the 1990s, soon after Malhotra's entry as a costume designer in the film industry.[21] Dance choreography and art direction have also contributed to the emergence of a new aesthetics of display. Choreographers now plan the mise-en-scène with the art directors, in order to create the perfect form of display. Colors are coordinated with the fashion designer. The display of fashionable clothing is seen as one of the most important features in well-planned and -coordinated song sequences.[22]

The spectacular staging and performance of contemporary songs, as discussed in preceding sections, have been influenced by many things, retaining traces of former cinematic innovations and introducing new ones.[23] The image of the former vamp is obvious. We also have the presence of MTV styles and genres, and fashion and travel photography—all coming together in the contemporary moment of globalization. This process of acculturation makes the image a site wherein "one eternal present," all pasts and futures, are contained (Olalquiaga, xiii). It is to the spectacle of these song sequences, with their adventurous and pleasurable landscapes, that I now turn. Only a detailed analysis of the mise-en-scène will help us grasp the function and role of the song sequences as virtual windows of fashionable clothing performed through the sensuous movements of dancing bodies. In the following section, I will focus on the use of fashion and travel photography, which enable the song sequences to operate as fragments within the narrative. Through these songs, the spectator is able to enjoy a situation of reverie, through which she transports herself to another world for a novel form of window-shopping.

"Shahar Ki Ladki"

The song "Shahar Ki Ladki" (City girl), from the film *Rakshak* (The protector, 1996), opens with the camera focusing on the back of actress Raveena Tandon's legs as she walks away from the camera to reveal her full body. Dressed in a trendy short skirt and top, Raveena turns around to pose for a group of male photographers. The opening here is quite clear in its objective, as Raveena's poses and gestures are commonly associated with modeling techniques. During the course of the song, Raveena changes her costume several times. In one section, she shakes hands with the hero four times in a repetitive gesture, her costume changing with each handshake within the same frame. In the background, we see pillars and columns commonly used in fashion photography. The handshake sequence is performed again outdoors later in the song.

In another section, Raveena enters the frame wearing a fashionable lime-green dress. In a seductive movement, she molds her body to the wall, looking coyly toward the camera. Raveena's slow body movements, her gaze and demeanor, and the use of a blank wall (almost like a studio backdrop) combine to encapsulate the process that goes into the making of a cover-girl photograph. This scene is followed by a tracking shot that moves toward Raveena, who is standing at the door of a tiny enclosed space. As the camera moves in for a better view, Raveena displays a long purple dress. The enclosed space appears like a stage as we move closer to her to get a full view.

The most striking and innovative moment of the song sequence shows Raveena walking like a model along a railway track toward the camera. Male dancers cheer from the platform on both sides of the track as Raveena, in great style, turns the track into a splendid ramp. Moving and walking to the beat of music, Raveena, in a new white gown, shows off her clothing to her spectators. The Railway platform and track are unusual spaces for the display of fashion, adding to the fantasy of the sequence. Here, ordinary sites acquire phantasmagoric significance and offer the spectator the possibility of pleasure. While the track is usually a familiar site for a traveler, walking on the tracks is generally a forbidden act, at least in cities.

Raveena's costume changes are accompanied by different hairstyles. In one section, she wears an orange dress and sports a short haircut and boots. Raveena moves her head and body in a manner designed to display her bouncy hair and her clothes. Her image in this dress appears against both interior and exterior space, using different lighting techniques; skyscrapers, the sea, and the street provide a variety of backdrops. These sections are all regularly intercut with close-ups of Raveena wearing sunglasses—her face fragmented into parts, with the sunglasses gleaming in the sun. These close-ups appear like still images, resembling the techniques deployed by models to advertise sunglasses. Raveena stares into space as the camera captures her face from different angles.

The camera uses several foregrounding techniques in this song sequence, including barbed wires, gates, and steps, to add to the staging quality of the sequence. In the nightclub space of the former vamp, the camera used pillars to foreground an ambivalent relationship with the dancer. The technique of foregrounding the camera's supposed absence and presence enabled a peculiar combination of fear and desire. In "Shahar Ki Ladki," however, the camera's gaze is casual and relaxed, generating the reverie needed for the window-shopping experience. The song shows quite clearly how the vamp's representation has been reinvented for the display of fashion.

"Shahar Ki Ladki" ends with Raveena running up to a tiny round platform. She is now back in the dress she started in. She bows to the camera and to the other dancers on-screen. As the other dancers lift her up in the air, the moment of reverie is over and the film narrative moves on. "Shahar Ki Ladki," while not spectacular in its use of landscape and sites, nevertheless establishes the close relationship between fashion photography and the song sequence in cinema. Instead of travel, *Rakshak* uses the most ordinary sites of the city of Bombay to display fashionable clothing. Raveena's assertive performance for a group of male dancers and spectators is organized around geometrical lines and angles. The appeal of "Shahar Ki Ladki" lies in its use of very few props.

Commenting on different forms that were used in window displays in Weimar, Germany, Janet Lungstrum writes, "the symphony of the windows performance occurred in the wares themselves with few appendages; beauty lay in the geometrical yet musical 'rhythm' of unbroken lines and curves, and in the clarity of form" (137). This is precisely the appeal of "Shahar Ki Ladki." The brilliant colors of Raveena's dresses are contrasted with the sameness of colors in the men's attire, for it is the woman's clothing that is on display here. The railway platform/track, the street, the sea, and the skyscrapers become ordinary props for a heightened display technique. There is no effort to turn the street and buildings into fetishized images of modernity. On the contrary, the ordinariness and tactile quality of the images heightens the form of display. The greatest quality of "Shahar Ki Ladki" remains its reflexive gesture, clearly indicating the event of fashion in its song sequence. What makes this film doubly interesting is the use of a heroine (Raveena) in the film for only one song; she plays no other role in the film. Flânerie in "Shahar Ki Ladki" is limited in travel but adventurous in style.

"Sundara Sundara"

In the song "Sundara, Sundara" (The beautiful one), also from the film *Rakshak*, Karisma Kapoor (the heroine of the film) performs like Raveena in the earlier song. However, the presentation of the song is quite different from "Shahar Ki Ladki" in that the landscape is limited to the sea and rocks. Karisma's relationship to the camera is charged with a different kind of eroticism, addressing another order of fashion photography. There is a greater focus on the body, as Karisma looks seductively at the camera. Her relationship to the camera recalls Norman Parkinson's musings on the relationship between the photographer and the model. For Parkinson:

> It is important for the photographer to ensure that the camera and the object maintain both an intimate and disinterested relationship. It is the photographer's job to coax, persuade and manipulate the model to shamelessly perform for the lens through the right poses and gestures. This is achieved through a manipulation of the space between the model and the lens "to create an illusion of sensuality". The space around the model is thus "accentuated by the experimental priorities of fashion photography." (cited in Craik, 111)

In "Sundara, Sundara," Karisma enters the frame in a succession of quick cuts. She is introduced through different frames, dressed in a white skirt and top and a pair of sunglasses. She walks the classic catwalk, looks seductively at the camera, swings her hair, and turns to face the camera in what can only be described as classic modeling gestures. The song then introduces the male singers, who describe Karisma's beauty. Karisma is then seen dancing on the beach in a lime-green minidress, with a flagpole as her only prop. The camera focuses first on her back, as she swings her hips to the music, and then the camera fragments a series of different poses of Karisma alone and with Sunil Shetty (the hero of the film). These fragmented shots are like still images as a door and the frame of a door provide interesting additional backdrops to the already existent beach. The succession of still images, along with Karisma's swinging, allows the spectator the pleasure of absorbing the dress and the figure in the dress. The different stills appear like cover-girl shots, but, unlike a magazine advertisement, on film the spectator is allowed to see several stills within the song sequence. The use of indoor props against the beach heightens the experimental quality of the sequence. Also visible here is the loss of the tableau format, in which formalized settings are usually combined with the semblance of a narrative (Barthes 1977, 69–78). Contemporary fashion techniques instead use moving images to disrupt the "reality effect," for a heightened exploration of fantasy and desire. All these elements are available in the "Sundara, Sundara" sequence, as Karisma's alluring poses with Shetty are followed by vigorous dance movements in a different costume. With the rocks and the waves forming the backdrop, Karisma's performance becomes a solo dialogue with the camera, which returns us to the earlier point made by Parkinson. The sensuality of the sequence is again heightened as the camera fragments Karisma's body and travels up to her face in a slow movement.

Karisma's performance is reminiscent of American designer Abel Rootstein's "Body Gossip" collection, in which the mannequins display "a self aware almost narcissistic expression" (Schneider, 99). Yet unlike "Body Gossip," in which the mannequins were placed in groups and exhibited in their body language the notion of a shared secret, like "a little scandal, a little weakness" (Schneider, 99), the "Sundara, Sundara" sequence is totally devoid of narrative elements. Instead, Karisma's provocative and coquettish gaze is directed at the spectator, inviting and alluring as she swings to the rhythm of music. What emerges is not the fetishization of the body (Mulvey), but a spectacle in which "the female spectator can reject identification with the totalising image and engage with the 'impossible network of gazes' inscribed in the image" (Craik, 110). Karisma here is both "looked at" and "looking," in relation to the other dancers as well as to the camera, thus throwing up a series of conflicting positions.

"Telephone Dhun"

"Telephone Dhun" (Telephone music) is a song in the film *Hindustani* (Indian, 1996). The song is based in Australia, even though the film's narrative has almost no mention of Australia, except at the end. Using

Kamala Hassan and Manisha Koirala dancing to "Telephone Dhun" in
Hindustani (1996).

motifs of both tourist photography and the energy of the city, "Telephone
Dhun" is a clear example of the new ways in which fantasy is articulated
through the exploration of vast landscapes and nostalgic references to
absorb the costumes on display. Like the aesthetics of the department
stores of the West, the song creates an adventurous landscape, traveling
across time and space, the past and the present, to create an infinite
form of display. The song opens with slow-motion shots of kangaroos—
symbolic of Australia—as the two stars (actress Manisha Koirala and
actor Kamala Hassan) run through a grassy landscape. This scene is fol-

lowed by shots of the two stars playing with birds and animals. The song then makes an abrupt cut to the street, where Manisha, in a gray outfit, dances with the hero and with other dancers. Modern, spectacular skyscrapers can be seen in the background. The dance is presented through a combination of long and medium shots intercut with close-ups of Manisha's face in interesting still-like images. We see her face from different angles in much the same way as Raveena's face was portrayed in "Shahar Ki Ladki." The use of these still-like close-ups again foregrounds the techniques of fashion photography. "Telephone Dhun" also showcases a range of period costumes, as the two actors appear in an old ship, dancing and moving through a grassy rural landscape, and riding in a horse-drawn carriage.

The song's combination of city streets and Australian rural landscape; of modern, contemporary clothing and Edwardian costumes; of highways/bridges and old ships, again makes it a reflexive text whose artificiality is overtly articulated in the sequence. The transitoriness of fashion is visible as the characters display period costumes. The movement from the past to the present is spatialized through juxtapositions of different landscapes. Shots of grasslands, cattle, and tranquil village roads are cut to shots of highway traffic, bridges, and spectacular highrise buildings. The character's clothing changes with the location. The images evoke both untamed landscapes and industrialized modernity to create an unusual form of display. The spectacular staging of "Telephone Dhun" generates a visual splendor and eroticism, taking us on a virtual journey of "spatial and temporal indulgence" (Kracauer, 68). The "spatial experience" of display, whose location was once phenomenological (Lungstrum) in the sense that the display was seen on the street, loses its tactility in "geographic reality" and enters a new space of virtuality generated by the "ecstasy of communication" (Virilio 1986; Baudrillard).

Postscript

The journey from the time period of the vamp to the contemporary moment has witnessed a number of changes. The first is a new narrative of female sexuality, which has sublated the old vamp-heroine distinction. By functioning as mobile electronic catalogs of the post-globalization commodity experience, the song and dance sequences have mapped out a certain desiring yet consuming subject. The symbolic association of the commodity with fashion, globalization, and spectacular travel gestures to an image of a sexualized middle-class female consumer. By affirming the abstract equality of spectator flâneurs, these fragments opened up a fleeting performative space for women's desires. The aggressive sexual dancing by female stars, once only acceptable for the vamp, speaks directly to a new generation of female youth culture.

It is difficult to state clearly which class of women is targeted by these images, but there is no doubt that both lower-middle- and middle-class urban women popularly engage with these songs. This is not to suggest that the new song and dance routine can be uncritically celebrated as a radical space for the expression of female sexuality. Rather, I have questioned the idea of the "modern" as either liberating or repressing women (Felski, 62–63). Focusing instead on urban modernity's contradictory manifestations, I have tried to trace the multiple intersections that enabled not just the creation of the former vamp, but also her subsequent demise during the 1990s. There is little doubt that the new image of a consuming and desiring female subject is a fragment of public display that coexists with film narratives that also affirm the hierarchical upper and middle-class families. However, this affirmation neglects to recognize the different ways in which consumption practices can sometimes challenge patriarchal assumptions.

The other challenge is to the way nationalist iconography framed the image of the "Indian woman." The new songs cinematically undermine nationalist discourse by placing the heroine in the globalized location of consumption, fashion, and dance. Today, the initial critical energies that the song sequences unleashed seem to have been dispersed. The hyper-real mobilizations of new images and the increasingly spectacular high-cost locations display a nervous instability in contemporary Bombay cinema. The production of an eternal myth about the power of the commodity and sexuality, which informs the song sequences, television, and advertising triad in a country of sharp inequalities, is the other face of globalization.

CHAPTER FOUR

The Panoramic Interior

If consumption played the decisive role in challenging certain gendered moral codes, it also triggered an intriguing dislocation of the "real" and the virtual city in the family films produced after globalization.[1] The new family films focus on consumer-oriented families, speaking to "tradition" yet geared to global mobility. A hallmark of the family film is the play with lavish interior spaces. The new panoramic interior[2] combines design techniques with architectural space to create a "virtual city" in which the contemporary "global" family could reinvent "Indianness" and modernity. In this scenario, the space of the Bombay street, the *chawl,* the train, and the crowds, which were all central to the narratives of popular cinema, are consistently marginalized. Instead, a changed perceptual experience emerges, one that is linked to the emergence of a new kind of "surface culture." *Surface* here refers to the expressive forms of architecture, advertising, print, television, film, and fashion (Ward 2001). The new *sensorium* of urban life, triggered by an explosion in the surface culture of recent years, needs to be situated in the larger context of urban modernity and the display of the commodity form as it historically emerged in India.

Modernity, the Aestheticization of the Commodity, and Television

Western modernity ushered in a maelstrom of change in the nineteenth century. The dramatic effects of this transformation were evident in the compression of space and time, as electricity, world standard time, the telephone, wireless telegraphs, X-rays, cinema, bicycles, automobiles, and airplanes established the material foundation for a new experience. A concentrated form of this transformation was experienced in metropolitan centers, where technological changes and the flush of commodity culture turned city centers into spaces of rapid and accelerated forms of sensory stimuli. The mythic dream of a future utopia was created through architectural forms and advertising methods that enabled the circulation of the commodity form as a visual sign. Ross King suggests that a systematic study of architectural and design techniques would reveal the representational pattern of how human experiences of time and space, nature and the self have been shaped by rapid transformation (1996). Visual intoxication, seduction, desire for the good life, and fantasy have been powerful themes in the new experience of space and time felt by many after globalization in South Asia. Architecture and design have together provided the expressive vehicle for this transformation which is captured both in the physical transformation of cities and in cinema.

The link between consumption and the aestheticization of urban space has been explored by several scholars (Ward 2001; Friedberg). In India, the recent rise of multiplexes and refurbished movie theaters, the emergence of shopping malls, coffee shops, ATMs, and electric advertisements/billboards across the prime districts of many big cities has introduced a different regime of aestheticized "surfaces." The proliferation of visual surfaces linked primarily to consumerist display has transformed the nature of street interaction in some parts of the city, even as the coexistence with older forms of display continues to be present in other parts of the city. Despite the varying nature and extent of the transformation, there can be little dispute about the emergence of a distinctly different regime of visual culture that constantly generates a fascination for visual spectacle. This is what I refer to as a new kind of urban delirium, in which commodity display, the crisis of space, new kinds of architecture, the spectacle of film, and television converge.

The aestheticization of the streets through the spread of visual signage and surfaces is simultaneously a story of decline. This decline is vividly captured in the prose of Naresh Fernandes, who looks at the transformations in the textile-mill area of Bombay's Girangaon:

> As the city's real estate prices soar ever higher and encourage mill owners to the realization that cotton textiles aren't profitable anymore, glass-and-chrome towers are springing up where factory sheds once stood.

Wooden-beamed *chawls*—residential arrangement for mill workers unique to Bombay—are being replaced by new office blocks. Senapati Bapat Marg, dotted with sooty chimneys, is being transformed into the city's Madison Avenue. (205)

What then is the fate of the people who occupied the space that is being transformed by the logic of global capital? Surely this debris of modernity will circulate in some form within the architectural landscape that seeks to erase it through aestheticization? As the expansion of slums, homelessness, and increased migration constantly exert pressure on the built environment, the city of debris overlaps with the city of spectacle in Bombay. The proximity of the two worlds has become the dominant visual trope to describe life in the city.[3] The existence of two worlds is not new to either Bombay or other cities in India. What is different about the contemporary situation is the flush of consumption, in which global mobility and visual signage have introduced an expansive world of networks and connections, creating new desires and aspirations. The role of television in the new landscape of the city has been a particularly significant development.

One of the major additions to the built environment of the city is the entry of television in the dynamic rhythms of public life and space in seemingly unobtrusive ways. While the public presence of television is a much older phenomenon in the West,[4] in India, television entered public spaces soon after the cable boom, around 1993. As coffee shops, restaurants, airports, department stores, bars, shops, fast food chains, and other public spaces generate the visual culture of "ambient television," the urban dweller's distracted gaze experiences the visual dynamics of the electronic media.[5] Even in the midst of the density and dirt of slum clusters and crowded bazaars, television, with its global visualscape, beams out a world that is fluid, geographically mobile, and seductive. While it is hard to pin down the exact nature of spectatorship, the pressure of an electromagnetic screen with its range of images would surely affect the urban dweller's optical consciousness.

Television's presence in the banal and everyday routine of life, both in public and in domestic spaces, shapes the ways in which we experience *place*. Our eyes wander in a distracted fashion across spaces of vast public terrain and domestic interiors. As we go about the banal routine of moving through the city, waiting at a cafeteria, standing in line at a bank, or buying cigarettes at a corner kiosk, the public presence of television is hard to escape. In the context of Indian cities, particularly Bombay, where physical space is so conflictual and concentrated, television's seductive visuality offers an experience of reverie in which the spectator becomes a traveler, enjoying the exploration of vistas—the "elsewhere" seems close by. Television as a "window on to another world" is a complicated spatial technology, global in its scope and local at the point of reception (McCarthy, 10). The television screen spans geographical scales, which in the context of India is unprecedented, given the "newness" of the cable boom. This pervasive and continuous interaction with the rapid movement of images—whether MTV or news, film songs or cricket, advertising or soaps—both at home and in public (in small towns and in big cities) propels the desire for a smooth "new" aesthetic, since technology has already enacted ineradicable perceptual shifts on the spectacle. The surface culture generated by television is one of the forms that shapes the projection of an urban desire for scale and spectacle, seamless landscape, and high consumption. The sense of connectivity and vista generated by television is, however, in conflict with the topography of public space in cities, leading to an anxiety about physical city space, particularly in Bombay.[6]

Negotiating the City of Two Worlds

Bombay has historically been seen as the quintessentially modern city of India, the country's commercial display window. Yet the question that constantly begs clarification is: How do we look at a city where more than half the population lives in slums or on the streets because they are homeless? The crisis of housing and the topography of squalor that shape the landscape of Bombay have been the topic of much discussion (Appadurai 2000, 627–51). Academics and poets, journalists and architects have all written about Bombay's spatial map. Rahul Mehrotra, a well-known architect and writer from Bombay, notes:

> In contemporary Bombay, the existence of parallel cities is a very striking phenomenon. Until a few decades ago, the many worlds in the city occupied different spaces, but have now coalesced into a singular but multi-faceted entity. Today, the city's image comprises of strange yet familiar juxtapositions—a roadside Hindu shrine abuts St Thomas' Cathedral, chimney stacks are dwarfed by skyscrapers, fishing villages and slums nestle at the foot of luxury apartments, and bazaars occupy the Victorian arcades! (cited in Mehrotra and Dwivedi, 309)

Another description of the city conveys the same evocation of city space as claustrophobic, chaotic, and unpleasing to the eye:

> The cityscape encompasses islands of cohesive aspects amid a vast sea of disparate structures. In the central district, monumental public buildings alternate with office blocks, shopping streets and bazaar lanes. Elsewhere residential quarters—smart, middling or shabby—nestle close to docks, railway lines, hospitals, shops, workshops and the ubiquitous cotton mills. Elevations rise dramatically from the ground-hugging shantytowns to the soaring factory smoke-stacks, now for the most part cold, and the post 1947 twenty or more storey apartment towers. Here and there a bit of greenery remains. Parks are few and, except in the outer suburbs, small Hindu shrines, Parsi fire temples, mosques and churches open directly on to the street. (Patel, xxvii)

The cityscape of Bombay becomes fodder for the continuous production of a discourse on urban claustrophobia, chaos, filth, and dirt. Churned out in the daily papers and magazines, as well as in the documents of planners, this discourse dovetails with a popular everyday perception of the city's landscape. The context of this discourse is the existence of two worlds in the city, which includes the juxtaposition of lifestyles, habits, and transportation. The proximity of the two worlds makes it virtually impossible to transform the public representation of the city as a thriving, global metropolis, except through excessively authoritarian, politically risky, and unpopular methods. The density and chaotic nature of the city has produced for some of its residents a desire for transcendence from the specificity of space, without abandoning the imaginary space of India. This is articulated most profoundly in the creation of new residential enclaves, away from the main city, that mimic the built environment of U.S. and European residential areas.

The other movement is the transformation of the interiors of cafes, banks, office spaces, and residences. Despite the coexistence of wealth and poverty, cheek by jowl throughout Bombay's physical topography, the redesigning of interiors provides an escape from the chaotic experience of the street just outside. Capitalist modernity has historically required a regime of spatial aesthetics that can house and generate the magic of the commodity. But public space in a city like Bombay, despite the pressure of the new delirium of consumer spectacle, interrupts the aestheticized journey of the commodity. There are but few sanitized public realms, which can hide inequality, something that shocks international visitors used to segregated Third World cities. In this situation, the *transformation of the interior* provides the fleeting imaginary possibility of transcending the physical geography of the cityscape.

A common experience in the city is the visual shock of the two worlds, a shock that can manifest itself during a walk through a slum into a tall building manned by security guards. Inside the building we have elevators that take us to well-designed apartments with large windows. If we go high up in the building, then the slums down below do not catch the eye. Rather, the expanse of a sprawling city provides a picturesque view. Those who live lower down in the high-rise can see the squalor just outside their apartments.[7] The movement of the eye and the desire to look out can never ensure the perfectly sanitized and ordered vision of the city that many of the city's middle- and upper-class residents desire. As designers gear up to create enclaves of urban interiors, we see the desire for new styles and modern living performed through a transformation of private space. Histories of consumer cultures have shown how a withdrawal of the middle classes into their domestic interiors, electrical kitchens, and private automobiles was required to enhance the experience of consumption. The withdrawal was made possible through the creation of a privatized and depoliticized subjectivity.[8] In India after globalization, particularly in Bombay, the physical topography of public space has accelerated the stylization of the interior both in literal (through the redesigning of homes, offices, banks, and cafes) and imaginative (through film) terms.

Design and the Rise of Scenic Interiors

The materiality of the world and its relationship to the human habitus involves a serial transference of signs that results in a psychological semiosis. The home interior and its many fragmented spaces—cellars, corners, rooms, closets, drawers, etc.—provide insight into the psychological domain of intimacy, habit, the everyday, and sensuousness (Bachelard). The interior is a locus of pleasure, desire, anxiety, and eroticism. The close attachment to interior space is a major preoccupation within modernity, most spectacularly articulated in the architectural landscape of city spaces. The interior as a place we inhabit every day, our own private world, is the space best suited for daydreaming, and daydreaming "undoubtedly feeds on all kinds of sights, but through a sort of natural inclination, it contemplates grandeur" (Bachelard, 183). Daydreaming transports us to the space of elsewhere, far away from the objects that exist nearby. What is curbed and controlled by life is expanded in day-dreaming as an experience of immensity. Thus the dream house must possess the right combination of intimacy and spatial immensity (184). This charting-out of an unconscious built on our relationship to the interior may be a little romanticized, but there is little doubt that the projection of dreamscapes acquires a powerful dimension when it has something to do with intimacy.

The desire for intimacy creates an aspiration for a shared domain, to create a narrative or story about oneself and about others. These stories are usually located within spaces of comfort and familiarity, particularly friendship and the family (Berlant, 1). In the architectural forms that surround us, the intimate and the immense continue to play a very important role. The spatial dimensions, the use of walls, windows, doors, and passages to mediate space, help us create distinctions between private and public space. This distinction can in certain instances create the desire for a mise-en-scène of infinity, expanse, and scale.

In domestic architecture, the relationship between the indoor and the outdoor has been a much debated and complex issue. Space needed to be privatized, but the connections with the outdoors had to be maintained to enhance the experience of visual expanse. Thus "the central design element used to create an illusion of the outside world was the picture window or 'window wall'" (Spiegel, 187). This spatial ambiguity, where our gaze can move freely between indoor and outdoor space, was central to the home and design magazines of the postwar period in the West (187).[9] The intention was to establish a continuity of interior and exterior worlds. The window backdrop, or the ability to connect with the street from the window, which offered us a perspective and a distracted gaze at modernity's different offerings, has been central to the architectural design of domestic spaces in the West. The use of the window wall is an indication of how interior space can be made expansive and seamless. This continuity of space found in the elite neighborhoods of Paris, London, and New York cannot be easily found in South Asia. It is not continuity but the discontinuity between what lies outside in the street and what we imagine to be the space of the interior that pushes the wedge between these two spaces even further as design takes over the space of the interior.

Interior design is central to the space of the familial and the private. Design techniques not only relate the interior to cultural forms; they also mark the space within a hierarchical chain of taste. Interior design also helps negotiate personal identity, because it is the visible expression of values and attitudes. Through design techniques the interior becomes a miniature *landscape* where photographs, paintings, artifacts, furniture, and people create both a physical and a symbolic world. *Landscape,* as Sharon Zukin says, is "at once a panorama, a composition, a palimpsest, a microcosm" (16). To understand the semiotics of the interior, it is important to think of this space as a *landscape* that emits a complicated set of cultural and social signs.

Landscapes of Fear and the Production of "Indianness"

The interior extravaganza of the family films is rooted in landscapes of fear and anxiety. While fear is not a new phenomenon, contemporary transformations linked to globalization, geographic mobility, the virtual takeover of the public realm, the shift to flexible accumulation, the increasing gap between the rich and the poor, and the rise of information technologies have increased the "fear factor" (Ellin 1997, 25–26). This is evident in the increase in public surveillance, housing security technologies, and car-locking systems. Making a distinction between modern fear and postmodern fear, Nan Ellin suggests that while the former led to an understanding of cause and effect in order to ensure a safe future, postmodern fear has "incited a series of closely related and overlapping responses including retribalization, nostalgia, escapism, and spiritual (re)turn" (1997, 26). Likewise, the movement of architecture in the family films—including *Hum Apke Hain Kaun* (Who am I to you, 1994), *Kuch Kuch Hota Hai* (Something is happening, 1999), and *Kabhie Khushi Kabhie Gham* (Sometimes happy, sometimes sad, 2001)— combines scenic interiorization through design with neotraditionalist nostalgia for "family values." Inside these projected dreamworlds, we see the performance of tradition, religious and cultural rituals, romance, and familial devotion. Created as perfectly designed and landscaped sets, the new interiors have emerged as the space of the "virtual city," where the Bombay of claustrophobia is made to physically disappear. When familial rituals do not play a substantial role, as in the films *Dil To Pagal Hai* (The heart is crazy, 1997) and *Dil Chahta Hai* (The heart desires, 2001), we are made to transcend all specificity of place and culture, resulting in a form that seeks to escape both tradition and location. The narratives move seamlessly between national and global locations while retaining a typically urban feel. Urban spaces are created as spaces of consumption and desire, with affluent global families as reference points. The family is the link that binds national and global space and provides access to new notions of lifestyle. The family is also the organizer of a detailed practice of rituals around marriage. In the context of new insecurities and anxieties thrown up by globalization, the family is seen as the marker of cultural stability and ritual, a space where the idea of "Indianness" is constantly played out.[10]

Writer Gita Mehta, commenting on the upheavals unleashed by globalization, says, "as the pace of India's exchanges with the outside world accelerates, there is a growing demand both inside India and abroad for some comprehensible definition of what India actually is" (cited in Mazzarella, 150). This search for "Indianness" and also the desire to be part of the global landscape shapes the production of popular culture in unprecedented ways. Cultural difference is seen as an essential marker of identity, something that needs to be asserted and "redeemed in a higher global unity" (184). This duality embodies a desire for access to a lifestyle mythology that is seen as global, while at the same time it assuages anxieties about this access through a constant reassertion of "Indianness."[11] The cinematic form mediates this anxiety through a retreat away from the specificity of urban space, particularly Bombay, into an imaginary world of architectural design where the "Indianness" of tradition and modernity are played out. Cinema mobilizes the fantasy of a lifestyle unblemished by the chaos and poverty that exists all around. Cinema is perhaps the medium that can best enable the harmony that has historically been possible in some parts of the Western world. Carefully constructed, abiding by international standards of design and fashion, these cinematic interiors become the display window for an urban lifestyle myth that can never fully exist in the physical spaces of the city. Interior design becomes the map for the charting-out of a spatial unconscious that desires an urban dreamworld of contemporary consumption. The panoramic interior is not just an expression of the sensorium of surface culture, but becomes an essential aspect of the delirium of urban consumption. Its ubiquitous presence in everyday life makes it a reservoir of the delirium, which in turn accelerates the frenzy of the delirium.[12]

Art Direction and the New Political Economy of Design

The spectacular retreat into interior spaces as an expression of crisis was first witnessed in the lavish set-design strategies of Hollywood musicals. For spectators who were tired of the hardships of the Depression years, the musical offered an escape route, a journey into a fantasyland where the play of romance, comedy, music, and dancing inhabited the architectural extravaganza of an imaginary world. The arresting decors; the geometric organization of dancers on stairs, spiraling skyward; moving stages; and fancy costumes and rooms were all created to dazzle the spectator's eye. The set design for this period became so well known, specialized, and distinctive that it acquired a name—"The Big White Set" (Affron and Affron, 140–41). Size and whiteness came to symbolize class and wealth. Donald Albrecht notes the importance of dazzling light in the representation of luxury:

> While as a visual device, large quantities of lighting added to the beauty of film sets, they also suggested the abundance and the luxurious sheen of the high life. Light heightened virtually every element of décor in movie nightclubs, making objects highly reflective, and stressing smooth surface over texture and mass. (133–34)

The musical not only reveled in lavish sets, it also explored the texture of the sets through dancing bodies that moved, traveled, and inhabited space:

> Tapping feet, swinging arms, jumping and bending, they inhabit space with greater intensity than mere talkers and walkers. Dancers endow hotel rooms and piazzas with their rhythms and postures; the high style of the hotel rooms and the piazzas is a congenial setting for the high style of dance and the types of narrative it engenders, stories in which identity is a function of dance. (Affron and Affron, 146)

This relationship of the body to space as mediated through dance is important for our understanding of spatial exploration. The interior panorama of Bombay's family films is also explored through song and dance sequences that seek to navigate and illustrate the power of architectural splendor and design. Like the "Big White Set" of Hollywood musicals, the designed interior of the family-film genre moves away from the physical form of urban space through a mise-en-scène that seeks to enchant.

The production of the panoramic interior is not new to Bombay cinema. The grand staircase or the frontal glance at a large living room was common in many earlier films. Issues of class and power were linked to the use of these spaces. Also, the narratives were punctuated with spaces representing the less privileged. Yet there is a clear distinction between the panoramic vision of earlier films and the ones produced in the 1990s. Today, the production of the interior has acquired a systematic approach enabled by the coming together of art directors, the advertising world, fashion designers, and the film industry. While a relationship of this sort has been prevalent in Hollywood for years, in India the advertising world had never been directly linked to the film industry. Art directors today draw from the work of well-known interior designers to create interior spaces where the mise-en-scène is deployed for the popularization and marketing of lifestyle cultures. Much of this is inspired by an expanding magazine culture and print advertising, where the predominance of the home and other interior spaces seem to have systematically erased outside space. While city space in the family films is virtually created to erase/reinvent the physical city of streets and public spaces, it is also produced through enclosed indoor spaces or spectacular global locations. New networks and alliances are being created both nationally and globally, with the entry of Hollywood-style marketing campaigns, global releases, a tribe of publicists, and syndicated film–based talk shows that not only feature stars and directors, but also art directors, dress designers, and dance choreographers.[13] These new networks produce a distinctly new regime of global "surface culture" that can incorporate the contemporary texture of consumption.

One of the major shifts in the whole area of art direction in the Bombay film industry has been the entry of professionally trained interior designers who are now creating sets for the most expensive films. Sharmishtha Roy, one of the highest paid art directors in the industry, is a trained interior designer who first worked in the advertising world. Branded as an upmarket art director because of her lavish sets, Roy is reflexive about her role in the industry. She refers to her sets as "aspirational" because they emulate Western culture in design and lifestyle.

In her work, Roy recognizes that she is re-creating a lifestyle that is not "Indian."[14]

In the early years of cinema, location shooting was privileged over studio sets. The arrival of sound changed the dynamic, as the use of sets seemed to provide greater quality control over sound and light. By the 1950s, shooting on sets became the norm, though outdoor scenes were also usually incorporated. The arrival of color film rekindled the desire for location shooting, as filmmakers wanted to explore the attractiveness and exotica of real locations in full color.[15] From the 1960s to the mid 1980s, location shooting became the norm, as Bombay became a city explored by filmmakers. From railway tracks to docks, train stations to *chawls,* location shooting helped bring city spaces alive. A retreat toward carefully designed sets began in the 1990s with the family films. Roy says the heavy reliance on sets become necessary because of the "virtual" nature of the interior, which is impossible to replicate on location. Most films have about six to eight sets, but the big family films can have up to eighteen or more sets.[16] According to Roy, art directors in the past were only asked to prepare a set with certain props brought in from specific rental companies that the film industry patronized. Today, Roy insists on a decoration budget, which many of the new art directors see as necessary to create a designer aesthetic that will counter what they perceive to be the flashy aesthetic of the 1960s and 1970s.[17] Roy now rents furniture and other accessories, including small decorative items from well-known home furnishing shops.

The emergence after globalization of a new global market for Hindi cinema has also played a significant role in the construction of the designed interior. The overseas market of the Indian diaspora is today the largest distribution territory for the film industry.[18] The success of the film *Hum Apke Hain Kaun,* directed by Sooraj Barjatya, revealed the importance of the Indian diaspora in the marketing of a film, as a quarter of the total revenue generated by the film was brought in from the overseas market.[19] The narrative place of the diasporic family is important both as a reference point for a second-generation South Asian film public in the West and as a new category in Bombay cinema. The movement between the diaspora and the industry has reoriented both the spatial and temporal coordinates of Bombay film through a *transformation of cinema itself.* In fact, the rise of a sanitized aesthetic has become

associated with directors who are extremely popular in the Indian diaspora. These directors were born in the industry (sons of film directors
and producers), studied abroad, and assumed a global lifestyle. The
release of the film *Kuch Kuch Hota Hai,* directed by Karan Johar, sharply
foregrounded the importance of international travel, lifestyle, and television in its construction of the interior. The film evokes a series of spatial coordinates that link with representations from comic books, international designer manuals, television advertising, and Hollywood teen
films. A journey through particular sequences from a cluster of films
reveals the complex role of the panoramic interior in contemporary
Bombay cinema.

Hum Apke Hain Kaun: Tradition as Commodity

Sooraj Barjatya's[20] *Hum Apke Hain Kaun (HAHK)* is the first in a series
of family films made in the 1990s. Although the film boasts of no international visual travel during the course of the narrative, *HAHK* is spectacular in its deployment of vast interiors, relating space and the commodity to issues of cultural identity and the family. The story of Nisha
(played by Madhuri Dixit), a computer engineer, and her romance with
Prem (played by Salman Khan), *HAHK* has often been described as a
giant marriage video that showcases the rituals and traditions of rich
North Indian families. The film develops a spectacle of ritual consumption and religiosity, as songs become the pivotal driving force of the
narrative, taking us through a series of traditional practices. Presented
in a happy and familial landscape, *HAHK* unabashedly constructs vast
panoramic interiors that are lavish and ornate, spectacular and garish.
Within this space, the romantic narrative is played out as a vehicle for
the coming together of two large families. Familial values of devotion,
Hindu rituals, traditional costumes, and the moral universe of the joint
family saturate the rather thin story line of the film. The film is dotted
with innumerable characters that help construct the carnivalesque utopia
of the great Indian family, in which conflict is minimal and the desire to
be united is powerful. Thus, servants and dogs, friends and foes, Muslims and Hindus, men and women, children and adults are all enjoined
in a carnival of traditional values.

   Amit Khanna, a scriptwriter and producer in Bombay, makes a distinction between the early family films and the ones that emerged in the

1990s. Khanna believes the main difference lies in the spectacularization of rituals.[21] What matters here is not just the relationships within and outside the family, but the fact that family life can be articulated only through a performance of rituals, to lay claim on something that is seen as lost. In that sense, *HAHK* was the first major expression of an anxiety about globalization, in which the path to the global world had to be followed without abandoning the "Indianness" of everyday life.

Hum Apke Hain Kaun's central thematic of the great Indian family in a globalized world is systematically articulated through a mise-en-scène of hybrid architectural and design techniques where both the image of an earlier era of films and the new aesthetics of global consumption coexist in a peculiar harmony. While much has been written about *Hum Apke Hain Kaun*'s cultural politics and its negotiation of anxiety (Ghosh 2000), few critical works have focused specifically on the architectural landscape of the film. One of the first films to mount the grandeur of the interior in a new vision of post-globalized India, *HAHK* combines a vernacular modernity of the mise-en-scène with contemporary design techniques that are currently circulating in the world today.

Prem Niwas is the house where most of the narrative is located. From the outside, it looks like a large, white, two-story villa surrounded by lush gardens. The interior looks more like a medieval palace, with stairs that lead to an open gallery surrounding the living room. Curved pillars, glass chandeliers, ornate furniture, and an air of religiosity mark the interior space. Statues of gods; flowers hanging from the railings, symbolic of Hindu religious ceremonies; and an ambience of the large joint family is consistently placed in the film, to play out tradition through ritual practice. The inside courtyard/veranda has a large private swimming pool and a fountain. The wealthy interiors are made obvious through a style of aesthetics that harks back to the lavish interiors of wealthy family homes in films like *Ram Aur Shyam* (Chanakya, 1967), *Bobby* (Randhir Kapoor, 1973), and *Kal Aaj Aur Kal* (Raj Kapoor, 1971). Spatial expanse, the stairs, and ornate furniture are crucial to the depiction of wealth in Hindi cinema. However, in *HAHK*, spatial expanse is saturated with Hindu iconography, and palatial architecture is enhanced by the presence of many people. The interior, particularly the living room, is cluttered with objects and people. The living room is where servants and maids; Tuffy, the white dog; a Muslim doctor, who is a friend of the family, and his wife; and another family friend and his sharp-tongued wife intermingle. The living room is the space of the community, of family love and devotion.

The most noticeable aspect of *HAHK* is its seamless movement from one palatial interior to another, each interior spectacularly shot using cranes and tracks to enhance both spatial mobility and panoramic angles. Songs play the pivotal role in navigating the hybrid interiors and they also convey the different traditions of the North Indian marriage. *HAHK* has often been called a giant marriage video because of the role played by songs in the film. Most of the songs deal with different marriage rituals, religious festivals, and romance. All the indoor songs are shot with a frontal perspective to enhance the expansive mise-en-scène of the interiors. In "Joote Le Lo," a song describing a very popular ritual dealing with the carnivalesque of the North Indian marriage, the main characters move rapidly through different spaces in the home. The domestic architecture reveals pillars, grand staircases, and a palatial ceiling, tracked by the camera for its entire expanse. During the song, Nisha runs into her room, followed by Prem. A moment of attraction between the two is situated within a designer bedroom scattered with commodities and objects. The singing and dancing acquires a larger-than-life presence through the choreography. Rituals, palatial spaces, and the private bedroom—all edited to the rhythm of the song—allow the camera the possibility of simultaneously situating tradition, love, architectural grandeur, and the commodity. The coming together of all these elements in a moment of intense cultural identity and the phantasmic powers of the commodity make the family films truly unique, for their clever manipulation of the mise-en-scène is geared to relay a multiplicity of signs. The extravaganza of the commodity is matched by intense feelings of attraction, love, romance, and family values. The particular use of the crane to swoop down on the dancers, a movement that reveals the glittering chandelier and ornate architecture, is a common technique used in the film.

The song "Didi Tera Devar Diwana," which is the film's most popular song, is perhaps the most lavishly mounted song in the film. Foregrounding the world of women, "Didi Tera" is ostensibly a post-wedding celebration for Nisha's pregnant sister. Throughout the song we see the lavishness of the home. Prem, who is not part of the song, makes his

Madhuri Dixit and Salman Khan dancing to "Didi Tera Devar Diwana" in *Hum Apke Hain Kaun* (1994).

entry by somersaulting to the gallery floor and then jumping to hang from the chandelier. This body movement and navigation of the mise-en-scène makes the interior appear more expansive, while at the same time creating depth through various foregrounding and perspective shots. The presence of a crowd of people creates not a claustrophobic interior, but one that makes familial rituals expand the terrain of space. People are standing on the gallery of the upper story, just as they crowd the staircases that flank both sides of the room. This overwhelming presence of people dressed in traditional Indian clothes is further enhanced by the use of tracking shots twice during the song. All the other camera angles expand the spectator's field of vision by providing a range of perspectives. A closer look reveals archways and temple architecture. This is not a modern designer space, rather a lavish palatial interior that suggests wealth. In this wealthy interior, the values of the traditional Indian joint family are kept alive. Nothing in this space, except for the music and style of dancing, reveals the present. Instead, we are provided with a nostalgic vignette of an architectural landscape that is supposed to be timeless because it comfortably accepts the eternal performance of tradition. *HAHK*'s ability to create "eternal" architectural spaces while using contemporary design techniques makes architecture central to the relationship mounted between tradition and modernity in the film. The panoramic architectural landscape substantiates and enhances the story line of the film. This carefully worked out relationship between modernity's offerings and the persistence of tradition made *HAHK* a much-cited film in debates about tradition and modernity.

Dil To Pagal Hai: Love, Eroticism, and the Performer's World

The perfect example of a completely set-driven designer film is Yash Chopra's *Dil To Pagal Hai*. It is the story of a theater troupe training for a gala performance. Woven into this tale is the love story between a theater director, Rahul (played by Shahrukh Khan), and an actress, Pooja (played by Madhuri Dixit). There is also another actress, Nisha (played by Karisma Kapoor), whose love for Rahul is unrequited. This simple, fairly well-trodden narrative is soaked in dance, fashionable clothing, and carefully constructed sets. Sharmishtha Roy, the art director for this film, was given a brief by Yash Chopra to create the ambience for a group of creative people.[22] Barring one song abroad and a few nature sequences, the entire film is shot indoors.

The most often used space in the film, where the group rehearses, is a loftlike modernist space with large windows. The rehearsal space is divided into different levels without the separation of walls. The eye can therefore freely gaze across the room. One corner of the room, where the group meets to discuss scripts, is at a slightly lower level, with cushioned benches and a hammock in the corner. Scattered throughout the room are steel pipes, black pillars, wooden floors, a band ensemble, a treadmill, and a red car against a brick wall. There is some graffiti on the wall designed to mimic the look of a New York City loft. Roy says she was asked to create a Broadway-theater feel for her sets.[23] During the song "Bholi is Surat" (The innocent face), Rahul plays the guitar while sitting on a red ladder, his back to a window through which we can see the hint of a skyline. Subsequently, the entire troupe joins in the singing. In the course of the song, Nisha changes her outfit three times—from casual to sporty to dressy. During the song, the dancers move across the room, occupying and navigating different levels and spaces. The camera reveals art on the wall, expansive floors, and Nisha on the treadmill in sports clothing. Brands like Pepsi are prominently displayed as wall decorations. The modernist architectural interior is combined with cool colors and mood lighting. Everyone in the cast is dressed in

The rehearsal space in *Dil To Pagal Hai* (1997). Courtesy Yashraj Films.

trendy clothes, particularly Nisha. This is a zone for individuals who are professional, creative, lifestyle-oriented, and "cool." None of them seem to have any real family attachments.

The first meeting between Pooja and Rahul is staged in a big department store where Rahul has come with Nisha to shop. The camera moves through the store to the dressing room and back. We get a sense of the architectural layout of the store as Rahul moves back and forth. The trial-room area displays brand names of jeans on the corridor wall. This "dream house" of the commodity looks very similar to the loft space of the troupe. The department-store sequence takes place after the song "Bholi is Surat" in the loft, enabling movement from one interior to another while retaining the look of a flashy, fashionable, and aestheticized modernity. *Dil To Pagal Hai* relies overwhelmingly on interiors that are strategically organized to evoke a spatial flattening and timelessness. Here, lighting, mood, product placement, gym activity, perfect bodies, and musical energy come together. The interiors are combined with dances choreographed for the first time in Hindi cinema by Shyamak Dhavar, a modern dancer. Lyotards, gymnastic movements, modern-dance gestures, sexual energy, modernist architecture, and a designer's spatial coordinates combine in *Dil To Pagal Hai* to produce a regime of virtual space that is quite different from *HAHK*. Here, it is not within "tradition" or the play of "vernacular architecture" but within a pure abstraction of space that the characters play out their emotional anxieties.

Nisha's personal room is designed to evoke a single workingwoman's lifestyle. We don't know if it's part of a larger house or just a single-room apartment. The bed is placed right in front of glass windows that flank three sides of the room. Through the blinds we can see the hint of a skyline. The blinds work as a filter that prevents us from actually locating the skyline, while at the same time they create a generic-skyline window view for the room. Scattered through the room are floor cushions made with tartan checks, a white bedspread, a wooden stand that holds bags, a range of artifacts, a hammock, and dolls. One side of the wall has space for a music system and books. Early on in the film, a little tussle between Rahul and Nisha is staged to enable the camera to capture a range of angles in order to establish the design aesthetics of the room. Clearly, the idea is to convey a very "modern look." Straight lines, art on the wall, and contemporary furniture mark this space as distinctly different from the space in *HAHK*.

The department store visited by Pooja and her friend on Valentine's Day is slightly different from the other department stores seen in the film. First revealed through a high-angle long shot, the space is neatly organized with pine shelves dotted with accessories. Leather bags, candles, little gifts, lots of balloons, and satin evoke a fluffy mise-en-scène. The naive conversation between Pooja and her friend on love is placed within the pink-and-lilac hue of the store. We never enter the store from outside, but are always already inside. This strategy of movement through a series of interior spaces renders the street and the city of Bombay superfluous. The outdoor has to be erased, for it is where the specificity of the city lies. The interior, then, is not just an escape, but also conveys a state of mind in which lifestyle mythology finds its complete visual articulation. The spatial topography of public spaces is a reminder that the city is conflictual—the street is a site of contradiction, inequality, and violence. The interior counters this perception through a hyperstylization of space and light, objects and furnishings, mood and mise-en-scène.

Dil To Pagal Hai revels in the spatial exploration of the department store, the gym, the designer bedrooms of the two main protagonists, and the theatrical performance space. Coke, BPL television, and beer adver-

Shahrukh Khan and Karisma Kapoor in *Dil To Pagal Hai.* Courtesy Yashraj Films.

tisements are now strategically placed in a mise-en-scène that is seam-less in its movement. The characters may be Indian, but their location in space is virtual. In this private haven, the fantasy of a global lifestyle is played out, and it is in this haven that one can detect the anxieties and dis-comfort of an urban elite wanting to transcend the specificity of physical space, while at the same time wanting to hold on to a strong sense of cultural identity. The erasure of outside space becomes crucial to this strategy. Unlike *HAHK*, *Dil To Pagal Hai* transcends both tradition and geographical specificity. In its carefully mounted choreography of erasure, we see the imaginary expression of an architectural mise-en-scène that conveys what Nan Ellin refers to as a "landscape of fear" (25–26).

Kuch Kuch Hota Hai: Comic Culture and the Performance of Popular Fantasy

Karan Johar's[24] first film, *Kuch Kuch Hota Hai (KKHH)*, became the biggest hit of that year. *KKHH* opens with a funeral for Tina (played by Rani Mukherjee), as her husband Rahul (played by Shahrukh Khan) stands by the pyre. Memories of his wife, who died soon after giving birth to their daughter, flash past as Rahul stares at the flames of the pyre. In one of the flashbacks, Tina asks Rahul to name their daughter Anjali (the reason is soon revealed in the film). Tina leaves a set of letters to her daughter with her mother-in-law (played by Farida Jalal), with the instructions that her daughter should read them on her eighth birthday. In the letters, Tina describes her college life with Rahul and their friend Anjali (played by Kajol). The letters reveal that Anjali and Rahul were best friends until Anjali realized she was in love with Rahul. Rahul's involvement with Tina proves to be devastating for Anjali, who suddenly packs her bags and leaves to be with her mother. Since that day, Rahul and Anjali have not seen one another. Tina is convinced that Rahul and Anjali loved each other, and she requests that her daughter ensure the two meet again. The story of college life in the letter is recounted through a long flashback sequence. The subsequent hunt for Anjali and the ensuing romance between Rahul and Anjali form the second half of the narrative. The movement from college life to the present is mounted through lavish sets—from school grounds, classrooms, auditoriums, and children's camps, to the interiors of the characters' homes and of hotel lobbies. Barring one shot right at the beginning of the film of the Gateway of India, with a caption that reads "Bombay 8 years later," we have absolutely no reason to believe in the existence of any specific location. Instead, a dazzling display of interiors and natural landscapes is deployed to depict teen life, adult romance, and marriage rituals.

Spectators are first introduced to Rahul and Anjali's friendship at a basketball court. The movement of the ball, the energy of the two play-

Rani Mukherjee in *Kuch Kuch Hota Hai* (1999). Courtesy Dharma Productions.

ers, and the rise and fall of the ball through the basket provide the camera with a range of angles that help to create the sense of an expansive court. One side of the court wall has colorful graffiti—very similar to that found in New York City and in *Dil To Pagal Hai*. Much as the rehearsal space was used to create ambience in *Dil To Pagal Hai*, *KKHH* uses the basketball court to create ambience for the display of teen fashion. All around the indoor stadium we see brand names on billboards and banners. Cars, sportswear, shoes, and the like are all advertised throughout this sequence. Anjali, for example, is wearing a DKNY shirt.

The basketball game is quickly followed by a song, which begins outdoors and then moves inside, and then to Goa and back to the college campus. As the two protagonists change costumes, we are shown a range of teen-sport and casual-wear attire. The outdoor shots are landscaped in front of buildings that stand out as generic architectural ensembles with no specificity of place. Immediately after the song, we are introduced to the girls' dorm—a large color-coordinated space with luxury beds, wall paintings, shelves with decorative items, Venetian blinds, and large windows. Several pillars in the room add depth, with the floor space split into two or three levels.

Rahul's home, navigated several times in the first part of the film, is a largely modernist interior that displays several artifacts and furniture

Publicity still of *Kuch Kuch Hota Hai.* Courtesy Dharma Productions.

strewn with cushions. The living room is first introduced as Rahul's mother tries to sing the "Gayatri mantra" with a group of women friends. Suddenly, Anjali (the granddaughter) arrives, and the camera pulls out into a circular tracking shot, capturing the expanse of the room. Black stone pillars and a staircase dissect the middle of the room. What is striking here is the large window in the far corner of the room, which simulates a skyline unavailable in any Indian city. The simulated skyline is a slightly faded image of neo-Gothic architecture displayed through the window. Sharmishtha Roy says the Gothic form was simulated because the characters supposedly represented people from South Bombay.[25] In a sense, the simulation expresses a nostalgic desire for an upper-class experience of South Bombay, an area that many city residents today see as having declined. The simulated skyline, which provides an interior-exterior connection that is physically unavailable, creates imagined possibilities of travel and makes the home's interior and window an appropriate metaphor for the politics of public erasure. This simulated skyline emerges again, in a slightly different form, a little later in the film. Simulation ensures that the physical topography of public space does not impinge on the design aesthetics of the interior.

The interior of the college provides one of the most striking images in *KKHH*. We see a corridor that has a sparkling black-and-white floor reminiscent of teen television shows in the United States. One corner of the set has a DJ with his equipment. A bright yellow pay phone, a Pepsi machine, and colorful lockers are also in the corridor. Karan Johar's own vision of the school space was highly influenced by American popular culture:

> I used to love Archie comics. If you see *Kuch Kuch Hota Hai*, it's really that. It's Riverdale High with all the colours for no reason. When I used to see *Beverly Hills 90210*, I liked those corridors and those lockers. None of that exists in Indian colleges. Our colleges look like public bathrooms, excuse my saying so. I was 25–26 and I was influenced by things I saw and things I read about and basically I was a huge Archie fan. If you see *KKHH*, Shahrukh plays Archie, Rani Mukherjee plays Veronica and Kajol plays Bettie. It was exactly that. And the principal looked like Weatherbee and Ms. Grundee was Archana Puran Singh.[26]

Roy recalls Johar's brief: "Give me the classroom of Archie's Riverdale High and the Locker room corridor of *Beverly Hills 90210*."[27] In the classroom where all the protagonists meet, we are offered a visual array of color, sleek furniture, and teen fashion donned by all the students. The back wall has a huge painting of Shakespeare, and on the left we see what apparently looks like a highly detailed Renaissance painting. The reproduction of the architectural space of comic books and television shows immediately draws attention to the role of the film set in the creation of imaginary worlds. Cable television's circulation in the last ten years in India, with U.S. shows and MTV programming, has only added to the proliferation of international signs.

Kuch Kuch Hota Hai evokes a series of spatial coordinates that link with representations from comic books, international design manuals, television advertising, and Hollywood teen films. The outside space of the world at large is completely erased, as in *Dil To Pagal Hai*. Designer wear, brand names, and product placement add to the panorama of the interior, reinforcing what Hal Foster refers to as the permeability of design in contemporary capitalism. The terrain of romance and desire works through the circulation of commodity signs and design, expressing

Kajol and Shahrukh Khan in *Kuch Kuch Hota Hai.* Courtesy Dharma Productions.

the cultural values and attitudes of the youth. Design in *KKHH* is a direct product of popular cultures of consumption, and the role of advertising is one of the most significant influences.

In Guy Debord's original definition, *spectacle* was defined as "capital accumulated to the point where it becomes an image" (24). Reversing this original thesis, Foster suggests that contemporary spectacle needs to be seen "as an image accumulated to the point where it becomes capital" (41). In the new world of signs, speed, and surface, design forms circulate to entice and affect the urban dweller's gaze of distraction. The inflation or all-pervasive power of design has increased in the era of digitization and television's expanding presence. Design techniques lie at the heart of both production and consumption. The constant mediation of the commodity through design strategies makes the category and role of design central to our understanding of the signage that defines contemporary urban landscapes. Perhaps, as Foster suggests, we now need to speak of a "political economy of design" (22). The landscape of *KKHH* in many ways expresses the euphoric language of design that is so central to contemporary capitalism.

In the second half of the film, *KKHH* creates another order of experience. All the characters are older. They look and dress differently and thus inhabit different kinds of homes and other spaces. While Rahul's house displays a semi-modernist aesthetic, Anjali's house is constructed as the generic Hindi film set—a palatial house with a grand staircase dissecting the middle of the living room. Chandeliers, carpet on the stairs, traditional costumes, and Rajputana architecture saturate the mise-en-scène when Anjali is introduced in this space. Gold brocades, jewelry, and music add to the opulence of the interior. This part of the film reminds us of *HAHK,* as *KKHH* displays a range of architecture that helps the spectator negotiate the complicated experience of tradition and modernity. So while the first half of *KKHH* revels in the performance of high consumption and simulated spaces of modernity, in the second half, the adult romance of the two protagonists is reinvested with an older narrative of Hindi cinema. Here, the freewheeling playfulness of youth is replaced by the play of family values, tradition, and ritual. Again, architectural texture evokes a longing for what is seen as lost.

In *KKHH*'s second half, the romance between Rahul and Anjali, rekindled after many years, is abruptly halted because of Anjali's engagement and impending marriage to Aman (played by Salman Khan). Anjali's withdrawl from Rahul results from a sense of duty, and only Aman can really make the decision to withdraw and leave the road open for Rahul and Anjali's marriage. The climax of the film is situated in the palatial interior of Anjali's house. The staircase, the railings, and the columns are used to foreground and add depth. Rahul's meeting with Anjali in her room is reminiscent of a miniature painting from the medieval era, expressing nostalgia for an imagined architectural classicism. The only difference here is that Rahul is wearing a suit. Nothing else in the room conveys the texture of the present. This scene could easily be a historical image. Like a snapshot, the mise-en-scène conveys yearnings and desires born from anxiety. The imaginary construction of a past through this sequence is a form of architectural withdrawal and nostalgia, or a return to a pristine past that is uncontaminated by the contemporary speed of change. Small wonder that patriarchal culture is reinforced here, with Aman as the heroic figure of sacrifice.

Aman's final withdrawal and Rahul and Anjali's marriage are saturated in wealth, rituals, traditional lamps, flowers, and marriage costumes. The marriage is the climax of the film; duty has been restored and romance has been made possible in this world of family loyalty and duty. The fact that Anjali is always dressed in a sari in the second half of the film, as opposed to Western clothes in the first half, only adds to the point I am trying to make. Romance and the incursion into global modernity must necessarily recognize the specificity of the traditional, which is performed as a visual marker of "Indianness." This relationship, as in *HAHK*, adds to the storytelling strategy and also enables the spectacular performance of the climax in interiors that express wealth and tradition. Through the exploration of architectural interiors, *KKHH* expresses both the desire and the anxiety that marks the cultural politics of globalization today. In its virtual spaces, we see the powerful play of the commodity as a simulated sign where both nostalgia for an older architecture and the desire for the hypermodern get structured around a tale of love, grief, and reunion.

Kabhie Khushi Kabhie Gham: The Hypervirtual

Kabhie Khushi Kabhie Gham (K3G) is Karan Johar's second film, boasting a huge cast of superstars from yesterday and today. Like *HAHK*, *K3G* can be described as a nostalgia film that creates a spectacular stage that moves across global locations to create a theater of family and moral values. The story of a patriarch, Yash Harshwardhan (played by Amitabh Bachchan), and his two sons, one adopted and the other biological, *K3G* mounts a classic melodramatic tale, albeit with interesting twists and turns. The adopted brother, Rahul (played by Shahrukh Khan), is estranged from the family because he chooses to marry outside of his class to a girl, Anjali (played by Kajol), from Chandni Chowk[28] in Delhi. After ten years of separation, the younger brother, Rohan (played by Hritik Roshan), decides to go in search of his older, adopted brother, who now lives in London with his wife and sister-in-law, Pooja (played by Kareena Kapoor). The story takes place at three major locations in the film: the home of the father, Yash Harshwardhan; Rahul's home in London, including the public spaces of the city; and Anjali's home in Chandni Chowk. A simple drama about a large family, its subsequent conflicts, and a final reunion, *K3G* is mounted through lavish sets and costumes within the urban space of London.

The film opens with a series of black-and-white snapshots of a mother with her child. The photographs spill onto the screen like snapshots from a family album. They evoke moments in the life of Rahul, combining both motion and stillness. In the photographs, the palatial surroundings are obvious, as the camera focuses particularly on angles that help create depth. The stairs on each side of the living room, the heavy architectural work on the railings, and the light shining in from distant windows are all deployed to articulate expanse, wealth, and power. Black-and-white images also convey a sense of nostalgia. The mother-and-child imagery is about tenderness in a world of nobility and grandeur. Even the publicity campaign for the film used the iconography and aesthetics of the family photograph. The main poster for the film has the entire family of six placed facing the camera, much like an album photo. All the women are wearing maroon, which is offset against the black background. The men, in black suits, stand next to the women. The uniformity of the colors seems to signify some form of evenness and a shared world. The byline of the poster and all the television trailers say, "It's all about loving your parents." While much of the film is shot in London, the posters do not divulge any locations. Instead, the aesthetics of the family portrait becomes the clever device deployed to evoke a certain thematic of the Indian joint family.[29] The history of the family album as a concept works to situate a world that is seamless and eternal. The family album is a universal phenomenon that creates an "imaginary cohesion," while also evoking self-representations that many families are unable to uphold (Hirsch, 7). The spectacularization of the family-album concept on the main poster for *K3G* presents the idea of an "ideal family" situation, which became the main marketing strategy

The family in *Kabhie Khushi Kabhie Gham* (2001). Courtesy Dharma Productions.

for the film. The style of the family portrait clearly evokes notions of royalty and grandeur, with everyone dressed formally. The family portrait is a recurring theme even in the mise-en-scène of the film, creating a link between generations and between past and present. Its constant recurrence in the narrative is evoked like a trace of what is lost and needs to be recuperated. The grandeur of the family is situated in interiors that are deliberately made to look larger than life, spectacularized by the obsessive use of a wide-angle lens for many of the long shots.

The credits fade in and out over the opening black-and-white track of snapshots, suddenly moving out to provide us with shots of a building's exterior. With the camera placed in a helicopter, we glide across the expanse of the front lawns of a castle-like structure—"Woodstock International." A cricket match is being played here, with the camera angles providing the speed, energy, and perspective usually associated with televization of the game. The college building is framed using dramatic crane and tracking shots, evoking the wealthy grandeur of this space. The batsman at the center of the field is Rohan, the younger son of the Harshwardhan family.

The Harshwardhan family home is first introduced as a space ten years in the past, as Rohan hears from his grandmother the story of Rahul's departure. The camera literally glides over expansive lawns and then enters the interiors of a giant castle-like structure. It is Diwali night and the house is lit up with traditional lights.[30] Women are shown praying in large numbers as the camera moves from plates with *diyas* and flowers to the statues of gods inside a shrine. The religious chant of "Om Bhu Bhawa Swaha" is playing on the soundtrack as the sequence conveys Rajput palace interiors,[31] glass chandeliers, and a heavy air of religiosity. Women are dancing to music, expressing a sense of gaiety. The space of this interior is constantly alternated with shots of Rahul, who has just arrived in a helicopter, making his way to the house. The energy of the helicopter blades alternating with the feverish religiosity of the women provides an interesting narrative theme of multiple temporalities: a combination of technological speed and the eternal play of "tradition."

The film's story then builds to the conflict between the father and Rahul. This buildup is narrated through a visual backdrop of two contrasting spaces—the home of Yash Harshwardhan and the neighborhood of Chandni Chowk. The Harshwardhan house is expansive, almost like a museum, displaying artifacts and paintings, satin and net curtains,

Amitabh Bachchan and Jaya Bachchan in *Kabhie Khushi Kabhie Gham*. Courtesy
Dharma Productions.

lamps with different color hues, and glass chandeliers. The camera landscapes the house to create a mythical fantasyland where art and commerce converge in a spectacular architectural ensemble. The camera
angles are largely frontal, moving up and down, horizontally and verti-
cally, as if to ensure the spectator's eye travels throughout the interior
expanse. There is a great desire to show everything in each shot. Thus
the camera perspective is centered from both low and high angles, as
well as from frontal shots. Each frame conveys expanse, with designer
furniture, gold-framed paintings, lamplights, wallpaper, and highly
ornate chandeliers on display, as if to create a grand semiotics of artistic
and technological objects, evoking both a sense of "classical" tradition
and modernity.

Albumlike photographs, in the form of portraits on the wall, are used
throughout the film. The desire to make the portraits' imagined cohesion
come alive is a recurring theme. The portraits provide the link to the
ancestral home and to tradition. In one of the early conversations
between the father and Rahul, we see three television monitors placed
like an installation piece on one wall, with the other wall covered with a
giant-sized painting of Yash and his father, framed like the portrait of
an aristocratic family. Yash talks with his son about tradition *(param-
para)*. The men are surrounded by a virtual interior in which public

and private worlds, nostalgia and the futuristic panorama of high consumption converge. Later, in Rahul's home in London, a portrait of
Yash and his wife plays a similar role. Johar's strategy of using the language of grandeur and tradition associated with traditional portrait
photography is cleverly played out in the film, with the portraits surrounded by hypermodern objects.

The Harshwardhan home interior is constantly juxtaposed with what
can only be described as a sanitized Chandni Chowk—a world of crowds
and spatial density, little shops and alleys, public festivals and chaos.
Chandni Chowk's spatial relationship to the Harshwardhan castle is
never revealed in the film. The narrative movement instead conveys a
seamless transition in which Chandni Chowk seems just a breath away
from the castle. Chandni Chowk's upmarket look is part of the aesthetics
deployed by Johar. While the question of class is played out in the film in
a classic melodramatic plot of love as the greatest challenge to class differences, Chandni Chowk's sanitized space helps create a seamless visual
and virtual world. When Rahul falls in love with and marries Anjali, father and son part company. The loss and conflict in the family becomes
the space that has to be renegotiated in order to bring about the family's
final reunion. For this reunion, the narrative traverses the cityscape of
London, creating a hypermodern landscape of commodity excess.

The film now shifts gear and moves to London. Rohan has arrived
here in search of his brother. His entry into London is presented with
the song "Bande Mataram,"[32] as postcard images of London's technological and architectural expanse dominate the screen. Brand names,
cafes, public transportation, and the ubiquitous urban crowd saturate
every frame. The nationalist refrain of the sound track seems rather
ridiculous, saturating the narrative of the film from this point on. The
desire to come home, evoking the Indian diaspora's nostalgia for cultural legitimation in the nation, is played out against a wealthy interior
and public world.

Rahul's home is a hypermodern space. Each room offers a range of
architectural designs and home interiors. Pooja is first introduced in
this space in her bedroom, dancing to the song "It's Raining Men." We
see the expanse of the room, split into two levels, with light fixtures,
flat-screen television monitors, a sea of colors, and designer magazines
strewn about. A spiral glass staircase connects the two levels at the center of the room. Hanging lamps, floor lamps, and neon light fixtures

add to the room's ambience. One side of the room displays a line of clothing hanging in open closets. Pooja is dancing on her bed to the energetic tempo of the song. On the left of the staircase is a curved table with a high-tech computer. The upper level of the room is a sitting area with a different lighting texture that enhances the separation of the two levels, adding more depth and expanse to the room. Pooja's frenetic dancing moves, her body fragmented in parts (much like in advertising), creates a space for the display of women's fashion. The room operates like a miniature department store. The spectator's gaze travels with the energetic movement of the camera, taking in the wealthy interior at an unforeseen speed. A sense of style, wealth, and technology all combine here with the lighting to create the design extravaganza of a shopping mall—a space the entire family will encounter later in the film.

The divided family's first reunion after many years is staged at the Blue Water Mall in London. The glass facades, postmodern architecture, flow of colors, and commodities, all saturated with brilliant light, form the texture of the mise-en-scène. Bodies flow in and out of this commodity cosmos. The mall becomes the space that can enable the possibility of reunion. Unknown to each other, all the members of the family are present in this space. Mother and son suddenly meet after ten years of separation. Tears of loss and reunion are embedded in the dance of commodities all around. The mall provides the dream of the "good life" and also the moral universe of family bonds. The mall is then staged in the film as the space where the hypermodern can coexist with the deeply familial.

Commenting on the mobilized gaze of contemporary film, Ann Friedberg traces the cinema's perceptual experience to that of the shopping mall. For Friedberg, the mall entices us to travel through its many levels, enjoying the displays with no immediate pressure to buy:

> The mall is not a completely public space. Like the arcade before it, the street is made safely distant inside the mall. Like the department store—with shared pedestrian areas between various departments—the mall becomes a realm for consumption, effectively exiling the realm of production from sight . . . The mall is a contemporary phantasmagoria, enforcing a blindness to a range of urban blights—the homeless, beggars, crime, traffic, even weather. (113)

The cinematic ambience of *K3G* works to create the shopping-mall experience, something that is possible through cinema. Given the physical texture of urban space in South Asia, the desire for a seamless world is made possible through simulation. Television's role in the production of other spaces and worlds creates this desire, but the physical spaces of the city stand in contradiction to it. Like the experience of the shopping mall, cinematic spectatorship relies on a perceptual displacement of external reality, offering instead a "controlled, commodified, and pleasurable substitution" (Friedberg, 122). Cinema's ability to do this creates the possibility for imaginary worlds, which, in the current context of urban transformation after globalization, is tapped into in spectacular ways by K3G. The homes in this film are not ordinary spaces but are designed to entice the spectator's desire for a seamless commodity world. K3G emerges as the most virtual of all the big interior panoramas of recent years, a feat achieved through particular design techniques and a highly charged melodramatic narrative. The desire for family reunion, maternal love, and patriarchal authority is played out through spectacular interiors, using the wide-angle lens to convey breadth, depth, and grandeur. Even Roy admits that watching K3G today makes her feel claustrophobic.[33]

Dil Chahta Hai: The Design Catalog and the "Cool Dude"

Dil Chahta Hai (DCH), directed by Farhan Akhtar,[34] is the story of Akash (played by Aamir Khan), Siddharth (played by Akshay Khanna), and Sameer (played by Saif Ali Khan), three young men from Bombay, and their personal and interpersonal relationships. Maintaining a cool narrative style, DCH ponders and dwells on the everyday anxieties, desires, and associations of upper-class urban youth. While clearly the landscape of DCH is that of privileged urbanites, the story, the emotional structure, and the thematic concerns encompass a larger, urban middle-class youth as it looks at different kinds of love, something new to Hindi cinema. This ability to tap into a broad audience with the stories of a small elite makes DCH a significant film. Style, color, minimalism, and the aura of being part of a "happening" moment mark the space of the interiors that this film explores. The bourgeois individual is the center of this universe of style that this film creates.

While the first half of the film is located in Bombay and in Goa, the second half explores the adventurous urban landscape of Sydney, Australia. Air travel, car travel, leisure, art, discos, music, fashion, style, attitude, grace, love, and desire—DCH is a combination of all these, perfected through a play with the interior that is very different from the other films discussed in this chapter. In a significant departure, the film steers clear of the family and the related traditions associated with the family film. We are provided no access to the deeper family relationships of the protagonists. Rather than fix itself within a dramatic structure that often shapes the melodrama of Bombay cinema, *DCH* can be seen as a film that creates a novel space shaped by a deliberate strategy of moving against the grain of films like *K3G* and *HAHK*.

Critics responded quite well to *DCH* upon its release. Most saw the film as representing the current generation of youth and their everyday desires. Others saw the film as elitist, but most recognized that there was something different in this film. Nikhat Kazmi referred to the film as one meant for a "cool" generation.[35] The first striking difference in the film is the complete absence of family traditions and rituals. The family exists only in the background; they do not play any role in the narrative development of the film. Barring the brief focus on Shalini's marriage (Shalini is played by Preity Zinta), the film almost consciously steers away from melodrama. Instead, the attempt is to present a new way of being in the world that is based on a set of codes in which friendship and love need to be tested through individual personalities and their struggle against the weight of cultural tradition. Lifestyle is situated as an individualized space where taboos can be broken to explore new realms of human interaction. Lifestyle in *DCH* represents the values of a generation that has encountered wealth and is sophisticated enough to handle that wealth. This sophistication can only be posed by taking the level of interactions so steeply located within melodramatic structures to a level of cool contemplation and reverie. This is precisely what *DCH* manages to achieve through its innovative play with the interiors.

Dil Chahta Hai presents the spectator with the experiences of three young men from privileged backgrounds who live a lifestyle surrounded by architectural landscapes that belong in a design catalog. All three characters have cars, cell phones, flat-screen TVs, fashionable clothes, and high-end computers. Instead of focusing on the plot, Akhtar develops each character through his distinct personality traits. The combination of architectural forms and characterizations of style makes *DCH* a film that seems to convey the aesthetics of the design catalog. Well-designed sets are mounted in the film to provide consistency to the characters' individual personalities. In that sense, the mise-en-scène in the film makes an attempt to connect with an interior world of the protagonists.

The interiors are shot not in the classic panoramic style of Hindi cinema, but through angular shots that convey an almost modernist and
minimalist framing. This is established through the individual spaces
that the protagonists inhabit, along with their shared public spaces.[36]

Dil Chahta Hai opens with night shots of Bombay. Siddharth has
rushed Tara Jaiswal (played by Dimple Kapadia) to the hospital. He calls
Sameer from the hospital, and Sameer in turn calls Akash. Akash refuses
to come to the hospital, thus revealing to the audience a conflict that
will slowly unravel over the course of the film. The hospital becomes
the "present" of the film, constantly moving backward in time, a transition that also moves across vast geographical terrain. Interestingly, when
Farhan Akhtar was asked why the film explored urban space only in
Sydney and not in Bombay, the director replied candidly that he did not
know Bombay very well.[37] He explored the Bombay that was familiar to
him, which, in the course of the film, emerged as a series of carefully
crafted interiors. The range of apartment interiors displayed in *DCH* in
a sense conveyed a spectrum of the different kinds of Bombay interiors
one sees in upper-class dwellings.

Projecting a cosmopolitan world, Akash is positioned as a man who
is mobile, free, and confident of his place in the world. Akash's interiors

Saif Ali Khan, Aamir Khan, and Akshay Khanna in *Dil Chahta Hai* (2001).
Courtesy Excel Entertainment.

convey a cool selection, very orderly and stylish, minimalist and detached. The actor Aamir Khan himself saw his personality in the film as that of a slightly detached, cool, and insensitive person.[38] Akash's surroundings throughout the film—whether he is in his apartment or in his parents' house or even in Sydney—convey a great sense of wealth, but mounted with the objective of playing out the cultural location of his class. In Sydney, Akash inhabits the public spaces of the opera house, the amusement park, the subway station, his corporate office, and his apartment.

Siddharth, who is a painter, lives with his mother. He is drawn to an older woman, Tara Jaiswal, an interior designer also living on her own in the neighborhood. The outdoor space that Siddharth traverses during his casual walks is one part of Bandra, the neighborhood where he lives. We hardly see any traffic, let alone people. Unlike Akash's space, Siddharth's apartment exudes an ethnic identity. The house is dotted with Parsi benches, artifacts, and paintings; earthy colors; and several cushions and carpets. There is a sense of comfort in this apartment, and also an old-worldliness. There are many old pieces of furniture and antiques in the living room. Unlike the minimalist aesthetics of Akash's bachelor apartment, Siddharth's apartment expresses a desire to project an ethnic style reminiscent of the Parsi world in Bombay. The desire to project an artistic sensibility, since Siddharth is a painter, is established through the mise-en-scène, making his world different from Akash's corporate landscape.

Sameer is usually associated with his bedroom, which is again a minimalist modern space. At no point do we see the panoramic sweep of the bedroom; only a fragmented view is available to the spectators.

Suzanne Meherwanji, who did the sets for *DCH*, has a background in art history and worked in advertising for many years. She started her career as a decorator. Meherwanji felt that even though not all the props are noticed in a set, in a subliminal way they contribute to the characterization of the people who inhabit these sets.[39] For example, Akash is not an intellectual, so his room has no books. Akash is conceived as a cold and self-centered character, so Meherwanji decided to use a neutral blue for his room. Siddharth's house, on the other hand, has a lot of pictures, which suggests a cultured artistic life. This is how Siddharth's mother was characterized, and she made Siddharth the kind of person he is in the film. Meherwanji cluttered Siddharth's place with paintbrushes and

Sameer's (Saif Ali Khan's) bedroom in *Dil Chahta Hai*. Courtesy Excel Entertainment.

other things he had collected, in opposition to the minimalist décor used in Sameer's space. Sameer, who comes from a middle-class background, is concerned most with all the women who keep coming to see him. So the privacy of his bedroom seemed a more appropriate space to quietly meet a girl without interruptions from his parents.

Tara Jaiswal is an older woman, a designer who has entered the design field a little later in life. Her design instincts are projected as traditional. Meherwanji thus used a more old-fashioned Bombay style of heavy drape curtains and rich upholstery to decorate Jaiswal's room, which contrasts with Akash's Spartan elegance. Since Jaiswal is older, warmer woods and richer fabrics with jade-green and gold colors seemed more appropriate to Meherwanji.

Dil Chahta Hai makes a conscious effort to project private worlds through interior spaces. Unlike most Hindi films, in which the private spaces of the individual characters hardly play a role, since all conflict and drama is structured around the spatial expanse of the panoramic living room, *DCH*'s desire to create a highly individualized private semiotics of the interior is unusual and works to enhance the "selves" of the characters. None of the characters want to relinquish their personal futures to the dictates of either the family or tradition. Marriage is important, but more important is love and romance and a way of being in the world that is not "traditional." This cool, upper-class, individual identity can be mounted only through an erasure of social tension. Even the presence of domestic helpers would complicate the sophisticated play of interior space. The interpersonal conflict between the characters is not linked to issues of class hierarchy or to family bonds; rather, it is based on differences about the idea of love. Siddharth's declaration of love for a woman who is fifteen years older than he, is the trigger point for the tension that develops between him and Akash. All the characters believe in living life on their own terms. This strategy of exploring the homes of the protagonists, along with the protagonists' location within other kinds of public spaces such as the disco, restaurants, and an art gallery, presents us with a lifestyle that is different from the lives of other film characters we are used to in Hindi cinema.

The presence of not just *public* conflicts related to class but also family conflicts are completely missing in the film. What emerges instead is a series of designer living spaces, conveying a lifestyle mythology of the urban elite. In that sense, the range of interiors and their wealthy but aesthetic diversity operate almost like pages out of an interior-design catalog. Design catalogs enhance lifestyle mythology through a spectacular performance of the interior. Detailed interior landscaping with furniture, artifacts, wall paintings, and color schemes works through a series

Akash (Aamir Khan) at his parents' house in *Dil Chahta Hai*. Courtesy Excel Entertainment.

of cultural codes, which in turn become markers of taste and class. This process finds an innovative space in *DCH*, a process that requires certain kinds of erasure. The city of Bombay is therefore completely wiped out, almost suggesting that, for a particular class of people, Bombay is experienced primarily through its interiors. But what makes *DCH* unusual is its sharp and overt withdrawal from the iconography and aesthetics associated with the family film. Farhan Akhtar wanted to explore the Bombay that was familiar to him—an exclusive world where restrictions of tradition could be transcended.[40] This thematic unfolds in the film through the mythology of the urban "cool dude" who occupies a range of interior spaces, emerging as the quintessential statement on lifestyle.

The saturation of signs in the form of designer wears, interior design, and commodities in the family films creates a world that mimics the experience we have in shopping malls. The vision of malls, for instance, is to attract the shopper and draw her/him into its designed spaces. The shopper walking through the mall, moving up and down the escalators, is dazzled by the commercial, aesthetic, and architectural splendor of interior spaces. Given the physical topography of urban space in South Asia, particularly Bombay, the desire for a seamless, commodified world can perhaps be made possible *only* through simulation. Television's role in the production of other spaces and worlds creates the desire, but the physical space of cities stands in contradiction to that desire. Cinema's ability to displace external reality creates the possibility for imaginary worlds, which the new family genre taps into, in the current context of urban transformation after globalization. *The panoramic interior expresses a crisis of belonging, fear of the street, and the desire for the good life—all at once.* In this architectural spectacle of light space, the absence of dark space is significant. The shadows of the uncanny, the fear of the street corner, the overwhelming crowd, the chaos of the marketplace, the violence in the street, and the city of strangers remain just outside, threatening to invade but prevented by the new architectural and design aesthetics of the panoramic interior.

CHAPTER FIVE

Gangland Bombay

In his unusual book *Maximum City,* Suketu Mehta presents the reader with an assortment of characters, including film personalities, bar girls, gangsters, and rioters, to create a labyrinthine psychological world, which, according to Mehta, defines the culture of Bombay. *Maximum City's* landscape carves out a world of greed, fear, violence, and riots. While these experiences are certainly not unique to Bombay, Mehta nevertheless manages to capture a certain sensibility and everyday world of stories and legends as they float in the city's density. In so doing, *Maximum City* became the first major attempt in nonfiction writing to take seriously certain aspects of city life considered outside the jurisdiction of serious scholarship. The power of this book, however, resides in its tactile sensationalism, its sense of immediacy, and its vivid sense of the city as a visual palimpsest of dreams and nightmares. Like the cinematic form itself, the writer cannot help but draw on the language of cinema to access worlds crisscrossed by forces that make them virtually unreadable. Mehta reads these urban worlds with an essayistic and passionate force, to tear open and draw out the murky side of the city.

One of the most interesting sections of the book is on the Bombay underworld, which offers the writer a powerful method of reading the city. In so doing, Mehta follows the cinematic landscape of the underworld elaborated in the gangster films of recent years. If the drama of global consumption unfolds in a city where the majority continues to live in very difficult conditions, gangster cinema provides a counternarrative to the designed interior city by drawing on the mythology of the underworld. These films do not adopt a simple form of classical realism to narrate the decline of a city, but rather move into the heart of the urban labyrinth like an allegorical journey, through which the city of *ruin* emerges to express catastrophe, despair, and permanent crisis.

Bombay's underworld has produced many well-known gangsters, some of whom have been represented as heroic outlaws in films. The more current production of gangster films addresses the accelerated activity of the underworld from the mid 1980s. While journalists have written about the underworld, the underworld's linguistic, cultural, and performative styles have been most vividly captured in film. There are two reasons for this. First, gang life and the gangster's world are classic ingredients for a thriller genre and noir cinema. Second, the close connection between the underworld and the film industry has been solidified and consolidated in the last fifteen to twenty years. Suketu Mehta, for instance, speaks about this symbiotic relationship as a system of signs that moves from the underworld to the film industry and vice versa: "There is a curious symbiosis between the underworld and the movies. The Hindi filmmakers are fascinated by the lives of the gangsters, and draw upon them for material. The gangsters, from the shooter on the ground to the don-in-exile at the top, watch Hindi movies keenly, and model themselves—their dialogue, the way they carry themselves—on their screen equivalents" (cited in Tripathi). This mutual fascination and referencing has also found expression in film financing. The underworld's ties to the film industry function largely through a culture of secrecy that makes it difficult to determine the extent of their hold over the industry. Since the 1990s, however, this secret cover has been ripped away by bloody events, controversies, and the arrests of well-known producers and actors in police raids.[1]

Three films stand out for their gritty and psychological explorations of Bombay. What makes these films significant is their desire to present the main protagonists as people who belong to the underworld. All three films deploy the classic features of the gangster genre to explore issues of masculinity and the idea of a new urban community. Vidhu Vinod Chopra's *Parinda,* made in 1989, is an early response to the gangland experience. Ram Gopal Varma's *Satya* (Truth, 1998) and *Company* (2002) are films that present a distinct shift in the journey of the gangster. While each film negotiates the city through emotional and spatial registers that mark it as distinct, together they provide a glimpse into the hidden recesses of the city.

Parinda explores the relationship between space and the uncanny through a ritualistic fascination with death that seems to constantly stand in the way of happiness. Unlike the two later films, *Parinda* struggles with the idea of a better future. *Satya* poses a radical shift from earlier crime narratives. The protagonists of *Satya* do not have a past. Situated as a story that unfolds within an accelerated flow of random events in a decrepit landscape, *Satya* produces the idea of the *residual* city. *Company* moves yet further, to locate crime within an international syndicate. The exploration of space in *Company* is fluid and almost virtual. It produces the networked city and the culture of technological surveillance that mark both the experience of the contemporary city and the gangster world. All three films evoke Bombay as a city marked by violence, terror, claustrophobia, and the uncanny. Bombay becomes a gangland, a disenchanted city haunted by death, darkness, and *ruin*.

The Topography of the Gangster Form and the Bombay Underworld

Historically, the gangster film as a subgenre of crime films is of particular interest in the context of the urban, because gangster films present us with an alternative topography, an alternative community, and an alternative urban consciousness. Fran Mason sees the gangster as a seminal figure "in the history of twentieth century culture, forming the focus for a range of tensions that have dominated the discourses of industrialized society" (vii). These tensions range from an exploration of tradition and modernity, to a politics of urban space, to the individual's role and struggle in the modern world.[2] The street is usually the primary site of narrative action in gangster films because it symbolizes freedom from home and it enables constant movement and liberation from the claustrophobia of restricted and controlled urban space. The street evokes a sense of power when gangs control it. The control of space is also an expression of masculinity, as gangsters fluidly traverse treacherous parts of the city—often, gambling and leisure joints—both at night and during the day. Gangster films are also about transgressing spatial boundaries and social hierarchies.

The "travelogue aspect" of gangster films is drawn from a number of important features. The underworld is a space of fascination because it gives the outsider access to a world that is felt and seen at the street level, but whose inner workings are not understood. The performative gestures of the street and a tough demeanor are recognizable and appealing to audiences. The paraphernalia that accompanies the mise-en-scène of a gangster film—guns, cars, spectacular action, city spaces—capture the visible and material seduction of the underworld. Yet these are only surface features of the genre. At a deeper level, the genre reveals the contradictions of urban life in ways that go beyond rational exposition. Jack Shaodian suggests that in the gangster genre:

> Meanings emerge whether deliberately or not about the nature of the society and the kind of individual it creates. By definition, the genre must shed light on either the society or the outcasts who oppose it, and by definition the gangster is outside, or anti, the legitimate social order. The gangster/crime film is therefore a way of gaining a perspective on society by creating worlds and figures that are outside it. Its basic situation holds that distinction, and the meanings it continues to produce rest on that distinction. In the thirties, the distinction is clear cut, unquestionable, visible. As the genre evolves, it becomes less so. As a culture becomes more complex, so do its products. (5)

Despite differences and variations, the core configuration of the gangster genre is easy to see—an urban backdrop, the play of criminality within a community of men, a performative masculinity, the impossibility of romance, the crisis of the family, and the experience of everyday fear and terror. We recognize the visual codes of the gangster film easily, given its wide international circulation during the past seventy years. As cities tackle their criminal underbellies, the gangster genre becomes one of the forms through which urban legends and myths around crime are created. It is not surprising that gangster films are usually located in specific cities—New York, Chicago, Los Angeles, Tokyo, Hong Kong, London, Mexico, Bombay, and Paris. These are global cities where monetary transactions move through circuits outside of the law. Gangster films therefore play an important role in bringing to the fore an urban life that remains hidden from the urban dweller's distracted gaze.

Organized crime—operating through gangs engaged in smuggling, prostitution, extortion, land grabbing, contract killing, and corporate crime—emerged in Bombay during the 1960s. Bombay, with its commercial enterprises and a prolific film industry, has been the center of underworld operations. Gangs that were initially involved in bootlegging soon expanded their operations to include gold smuggling, gambling, extortion, drug peddling, and contract killing. In the 1980s, the underworld expanded its base, intensifying its activities with the rise of the gangster Dawood Ibrahim. The extortion racket became a much bigger phenomenon, encompassing all walks of life, from the hawker in the street to the businessman, movie stars, and film producers. Dawood fled to Dubai in the mid 1980s, when the police cracked down on the mob after a series of highly publicized killings, but he continued to operate in Bombay through his gang (D Company). Under Dawood, the underworld's connections to the film industry expanded, through financial networks and extortion threats. The underworld became a dreaded presence after the Bombay bomb blasts of 1993.[3] Suspected of masterminding the blasts as retaliation for both the demolition of the Babri Mosque by Hindu nationalists and the subsequent pogroms of Muslims in Bombay, Dawood became a household name in the city. The blasts changed Dawood's status from a mob leader to that of an international terrorist, because of his suspected connections with both the Gulf and Pakistan.[4]

Access to the culture of the underworld comes to us primarily through cinema. In gangster films, overlapping themes of masculinity and brotherhood, identity and aspiration are played out in rich performances where excess in every way becomes the driving force of the narrative. The cinematic mise-en-scène and narrative world of these films provide us with clues and myths that link social space with cinematic space. This exchange is not a simple transfer of a "realistic" world, but rather a process that expresses *crisis* through a narrative of urban disintegration. In the gangster films, the banality of everyday life unleashes a torrential force of excess, whose imaginary relationship to Bombay's contemporary social topography is crucial. It is therefore important to briefly negotiate Bombay's contemporary history, which, in the following section, will be a narrative of urban crisis. Only through this historical contextualization is it possible to make sense of the zones of indeterminacy within which the gangster myth mobilizes its central theme of a Bombay lost in the present performance of violence. As I argue, the genre of gangster films taps into the anxiety, confusion, despair, and fear emerging in city life during the 1980s and 1990s.

Banality and the Crisis of Everyday Life

The spatial crisis of Bombay, as I have indicated in the previous chapter, is not new. The acceleration of the crisis linked to criminal activity, however, is a more recent phenomenon. Journalists and academics alike have traced the rise in criminal activity to the decline of Bombay's textile mills, which once provided employment to almost two-thirds of the city's industrial workers.[5] The decline was accelerated by a strike that lasted for almost eighteen months (1982–83).[6] The textile strike has been the subject of much debate.[7] Journalistic accounts of the time, and rumors about the union leadership's role, continue to circulate, even twenty years after the strike. Stories abound of adventurism, behind-the-door deals, and self-interest within the union leadership. There is little dispute, however, that the strike gave rise to an entirely new situation of despair for many workers in the city. In retrospect, the textile strike had all the makings of a "suicidal death wish" (Bakshi, 232–33).[8] Driven by their circumstances, but unable to see what they were up against, ordinary workers were caught in a "morass of impotence vis-à-vis the world" (Bakshi, 233). While many saw the vast multitude of unemployed men as the reason for an increase in crime, others saw an element of nihilism and self-destruction emerging from the workers' inability to sustain the force of the strike. For most workers, in the end, the defeat was a personal tragedy (Bakshi 1986).

The textile strike and its aftermath have functioned as a turning point for describing the transformation of Bombay from a manufacturing city to a global city with an expanding service economy. The dream to change the city into a financial center like Singapore or Hong Kong was often expressed in newspapers, even as retrenched workers continued to battle for survival in the city. The despair of the workers has inspired urban poetry, short stories, and even films.[9] The factory sites and the residential areas where the workers lived during the post-strike period have been depicted as spaces where the pressure of local time, global imaginaries (through television), and spatial claustrophobia collide to create a new urban landscape.[10]

Thomas Blom Hansen provides an exploration of Bombay's heartland in the aftermath of the textile strike. Blom Hansen's vivid exploration of Central Bombay reveals how working-class despair became evident in the spatial topography of the neighborhood. Most of the adult population in this neighborhood was once employed in the textile mills. Today, Central Bombay is known as an area of crime, prostitution, and gang wars. The loss of a cultural and moral fiber is spatially visible, particularly in the Muslim *Mohalla* (neighborhood). Extra floors have been added to preexisting buildings and rooftop workshops have been added to high-rise buildings, creating both noise and air pollution. The presence of hawkers and pavement dwellers has only added to congestion in the streets. The visible impact of this spatial density is overwhelming (Blom Hansen, 164). This is the urban landscape of spatial disenchantment, where despair shapes architectural texture and density.

In addition, large-scale migration to the Gulf beginning in the late 1970s has led to the emergence of many travel agencies and subcontractors for larger agencies who handle employment and visa facilities. Fierce competition to relocate to the Gulf, in order to earn more money than was possible at home, gave rise to groups of men taking bribes to ensure a trip to the Middle East. Hansen suggests that the gradual proliferation of money through circuits of illegality created an extremely volatile situation with the Gulf, providing an imaginary space for upward mobility and a better life (Blom Hansen, 164).

Paralleling the spatial decline of the city is the increasing presence of the Hindu nationalist Shiv Sena party. Responsible for the renaming of Bombay to Mumbai, the Shiv Sena has been active in many political, economic, and cultural zones of the city since the 1970s. The support base of the Sena is largely composed of unemployed youth, industrial workers, and office employees, along with some petty gangsters. The organization has long had a habitual relationship with violence, often using emotional themes for its mobilization strategy. Initially presenting a strong regional (Marathi) identity as a basis for attacking "outsiders" in the city (particularly South Indians), the Sena reinvented itself as a Hindu organization in the mid 1980s.[11] Driven primarily by a culture of brotherhood, self-assertion, and street action, the Sena has tried to present a coherent utopian vision to restless and frustrated unemployed urban youth. The Shiv Sena has also been involved in an elaborate extortion racket demanding protection fees from builders, exporters, smugglers, and drug pushers. The organization also promotes a *dada* (hood) culture, created through its work with neighborhood associations of men (*mitramandals*).

The 1993 bomb blast followed the slaughter of hundreds of Muslims by crowds that included neighbors and former friends. The events of 1992–93 brought into sharp focus the misplaced myth of cosmopolitanism identified with Bombay. As the communities of Hindus and Muslims became polarized, Muslim isolation, gang wars, and urban

decay marked the city after the riots. The Muslim community's negotiation of identity in the aftermath of the riots, says Blom Hansen, has
taken two directions: internal purification through withdrawal from
dependence on the larger society, and a strategy of plebeian assertion
through small business, quick-fix jobs, and strongmen tactics, whereby
men can accrue money within a short period of time (Blom Hansen,
179–85). The emergence of the local street *dada* in these Muslim neighborhoods needs to be understood in this context of plebeian assertion.

> The local *dadas* provide effective role models and often material access
> to signs of the good life displayed in the maze of commercials and TV
> serials pumped out around the clock by enterprising cable operators
> here and in other parts of the city. These signifiers range from cellular
> phones, Maruti Gypsy jeeps, air conditioning, visits to bars and the
> nearby Kamathipura red light district, and, not least, a measure of
> respect and recognition in the local hierarchies. (Blom Hansen, 180)

The combination of cars, cable television, cell phones, and air condition-
ers points to the new landscape of consumption, a nonrational landscape where the dreams of the "good life" circulate via television within
the ruins of modernity. Furthermore, the prevalence of smuggling, drug
peddling, and a thriving extortion racket provided a strong identity for
many unemployed men.

The rise of gangsters and gangster mythology during the contemporary period needs to be located in this spatial backdrop. Dawood Ibrahim
grew up in Central Bombay, where he became known as a courageous
mystical hero (Blom Hansen, 180). Given the polarization between the
Muslim and Hindu communities, Dawood, even in his absence, is seen
as a *dada* who will protect the people during a crisis. The rise of *dada*
culture in the Muslim *Mohalla,* according to Blom Hansen, has a striking resemblance to the *dada* culture generated by the Shiv Sena in other
neighborhoods. The similarity exists because of the social environment
that makes male honor, action, and violence important vehicles for the
construction of a radical new urban community.[12]

The brief map of contemporary events in Bombay that I have traced
is not to suggest a simple link between the textile strike and the rise of
criminal activity, but to specifically understand the role of spatial density
in the construction of new identities. The city after the strike witnessed
an amorphous situation in which a self-destructive nihilism became
the dominant mood for many who lost their jobs. An "obscure anger"

plagued the workers employed in the informal sector after the mills closed down, as workers battled shrinking living space, accelerated work time, and the constant presence of a crowd (Pendse 1996, 19). The over-crowding of *chawls* with multiple families saw a gradual destruction of privacy and ordinary conversation, making it difficult to have a personal world. The density of construction, which artificially encloses space in the city, created additional problems. "There is a constant, though at most times well hidden and perhaps even unrealized fear that the 'closed-up' space may conceal a danger or a death trap" (Pendse 1996, 14). Endless struggle with no hope of a better future—this is the ultimate counterface to the "Bombay dream." Clearly, the post-strike city of spatial disenchantment revealed how repetition of existence and loss of control over personal time leads to a "banality" of the everyday.

· Banality, it has been argued, is "time off its hinges—no longer passing through the present in a neat linear succession that places the past behind and the future always out in front" (Seigworth, 234). In this inner world of banality, sociological readings are impossible, the past loses its connection to the present, and random events shape the identity of particular sections of the urban crowd. When the banality of everyday life reaches a psychological breaking point, different kinds of performative drives are unleashed. The emergence of criminality and gang activity needs to be located within a complex spatial map, where a series of random events both spectacular and routine has led to the assertion of new identities. The gangland experience needs to be seen as an excessive overflow of the banal that challenges the repetition of daily existence through the construction of a new community.

The Underworld in the Urban Delirium

The Bombay underworld today can be understood as a new community of men signified by the use of the term *Bhai* (brother) to refer to members of the gang. The fee paid to assassins for their contract killings is called *Supari*[13] and the language spoken by the gang is *Bambayya*.[14] Although gang activity includes both Muslims and Hindus, the popular perception is that gangs are overwhelmingly Muslim. This perception is largely due to Dawood Ibrahim's stature as the main figure in the underworld; it also persists because of Dawood's connections with the Gulf and with Pakistan. Dawood's suspected role in the 1993 bomb blasts linked the underworld to international terrorism, thus furthering the myth of

the underworld as predominantly Muslim. After the 1993 blasts, popular urban mythology recounts a split, primarily on religious grounds,
between Chota Rajan (a Hindu gangster) and Dawood. This split has
acquired an enormous mythology in urban retellings of gang activity.
Given the culture of fear and secrecy surrounding gangs, particularly
after the much-publicized killings of well-known industrialists and film
producers, an air of caution is deployed when gang mythology is narrated in film. This caution is evident in the two best-known gangster
films (*Satya* and *Company*), in which gang references are oblique rather
than direct, even though popular perception receives the films as narratives based on Dawood Ibrahim's story.

The film industry is responding to Bombay's contemporary urban
climate, where criminal activity has erupted as nodes of violence within
the city. The sense of a city experiencing disorder and crisis dominates
narratives of contemporary Bombay both in journalistic discourse and
in popular perceptions of the city. There are many variations of this narrative. For instance, one variation portrays the loss of Bombay's so-called
cosmopolitan imagination after the riots of 1992–93, when the city of
"citizens" turned into a city of strangers. Another narrative deploys the
underworld to chart out the city's overall decline, degradation, decay,
and crisis. A third narrative focuses overwhelmingly on the city's over-
crowding and traffic.

In the multiplicity of narratives that evoke the decline of India's pre-
mier city, it is difficult to trace any single narrative that can explain the
exact nature of contemporary crisis. *Crisis* is then both an intense experience and a metaphor for the contemporary cityscape. For the film
industry, the experience of crisis can be rendered to audiences only
through narratives of despair. The nature of this expression has to negotiate the idea of a "strategic realism" in which a film's relationship to contemporary events is referred to, but never fully explained. The accelerated
activity of the Bombay underworld is thus picked up as the thematic
concern, which in turn becomes the vehicle through which the idea of
disorder and civic crisis can be expressed. Anurag Kashyap, the scriptwriter of *Satya*, claims that the exploration of urban space is central to
his scriptwriting strategy. The events of the underworld were mytholo-
gized to create unforgettable characters in *Satya*. Only the underworld
could provide the possibility of such brutal depictions of city life.
Kashyap's storytelling strategy was based on research on specific events,

without the trappings of a sociological analysis. Kashyap claimed that he never wanted to take a moral position or provide an analytical structure to his stories. On the contrary, inhabiting the experience of Bombay's disorder is more important than charting out the causal reasons for it.[15]

As a force, the Bombay underworld provides the city with an urban legend that links parts of the city to gang activity. Since the extortion of money from shopkeepers is a routine affair that plays out the territorial function of gangs on an everyday basis, the culture of the underworld is seen as ubiquitous and all-encompassing. The mythology of the underworld that is reproduced in the cinema is then a combination of "real" events, a contemporary sensibility about Bombay's spatial crisis, and mythmaking. These connections are crucial to my argument that film is an archive of the city, since crime evades the gaze of the sociologist unless it can be causally explained. The film industry, on the other hand, creates an experiential realm of disorder by drawing on what I would call an urban delirium about the underworld. Unlike the delirium of commodity spectacle discussed in the previous chapter, this urban delirium is a combination of informal knowledge, direct contact, rumor, and journalistic discourse that provides the city with a vibrant mythology of the underworld. The production of contemporary gangster films draws its thematic force from this delirium. As I will argue, gangster films are not only shaped by this delirium of crime, but become firmly entrenched within the delirium. Like a dark shadow, the delirium of the underworld follows the delirium of the commodity evident in the panoramic interior.

In the hub and movement of traffic, drivers and passengers circulate an everyday knowledge of crime in the city. Some of this is reported in the press, but much information circulates only within the domain of conversations. When people arrive for work from different parts of the city, they bring stories of violence in their neighborhoods. This informally circulated news is combined with newspaper headlines—a hyperbolic narration of gang violence in the city. Whether it's the *Midday,* the *Afternoon Dispatch,*[16] or the regional papers, reporting on the city includes substantial coverage of the underworld. In fact, reports on encounter killings and extortions have become regular news items. Commerce in the city must necessarily reckon with the force of the underworld either through negotiated space and activity or through monetary supply, to earn the safety of individuals. Stories of death threats if money is not provided on time circulate as rumor, providing the city with a hidden but violent narrative. In this daily routine of the city, we see the making of an urban delirium of crime—a sophisticated combination of print, sound, speech, and image.

Director Ram Gopal Varma amply demonstrates the transaction between circulating knowledge and film narrative. In an interview, Varma claimed that *Satya* (one of the most successful gangster films of recent times) was "a chance occurrence. I was reading these reports on the underworld and that started off a train of thoughts in my mind. I wondered about these people—who they were, what they did between killings, whether they suffered from viral flu. They are obviously human beings with a sense of commitment. All these things never occur to you otherwise. You think they are evil people who come from the dark, do their job and go back into the dark again."[17] Varma wanted to capture the texture of life that formed the gangster's world inbetween killings. There is a desire here for detail, for an entry into the gangster's psyche. Varma's interest in the time between killings is also important because it draws attention to the everyday texture of the gangster's world. Varma's own relationship to the city of Bombay is that of an outsider who saw the living conditions and claustrophobia visible everywhere as central to Bombay's spatial identity. In this urban landscape, Varma wonders about the strategies people adopt to acquire private lives, forms of intimacy, desires, and aspirations. Spatial claustrophobia combined with deprivation creates psychological worlds that are difficult to comprehend. Varma sees the gangster myth as something that emerges from this psychological urban world.[18]

In the gangster films, shooting is done at real locations—alleys, claustrophobic hutments, and the docks are all explored. The gang's places of meeting and operation sometimes look like abandoned factory sites, sometimes like half-constructed buildings. Chase sequences are deployed to navigate the density of the city's public spaces. In place of the sanitized aesthetics and the bright lights that saturate the mise-en-scène of the domestic interiors of the family films, low-key photography, reminiscent of film noir, is used to enhance the spatial topography of dread, decay, and death. One of the principal features of noir is its ability to destroy urban spectacle. By using low-key photography to evoke shadowy and mysterious spaces, the texture of the city is given a twist directly in opposition to the phantasmagoria of the aerial photography so com-

monly used in tourism and travelogue films. Urban display is countered by dark shadows, panoramic visions with fragmented shots, and
the glitter of daylight with the darkness of the night. Clearly one can
draw a connection between Benjamin's evocation of *ruin* in the city and
the shadowy pursuits of the noir genre. In many ways, the dark textures
of the city have enabled a cinematic exploration of the idea of *ruin* and
spatial disenchantment. There is little doubt that the gangster genre
navigates the city of spatial disenchantment like no other existing form
in Bombay cinema today. In these films, the despair of Bombay is articulated though the gangland experience. The social space of the city
emerges not as an authentic world to be represented realistically, but
through a formal play with mood, mise-en-scène, characterization, and
plot. The city of darkness provides us with a prism through which the
experience of disenchantment can be grasped.

The Uncanny City of *Parinda*

Vidhu Vinod Chopra's[19] *Parinda* weaves an intricate plot that deals with
the underworld's overpowering capacity to destroy ordinary dreams
and pleasures of city residents. Karan (played by Anil Kapoor) returns
from America after completing his education, full of dreams and romantic feelings for his childhood sweetheart Paro (played by Madhuri Dixit).
These dreams are shattered when Anna (played by Nana Patekar), the
eccentric underworld don, gets Prakash, a police officer (Paro's brother,
played by Anupam Kher), killed when he meets Karan at a favorite spot
from their shared childhood. Kishen (played by Jackie Shroff), who
works for Anna, tries to dissuade his brother Karan from appearing as a
witness for the state. Unable to work through the law, Karan gets involved with Anna and strikes a deal with a rival don to kill the three
men responsible for Prakash's death. Subsequently, Karan marries Paro
and decides to leave the city for their village. On their wedding night,
Anna kills Paro and Karan. Unable to save his brother's life, Kishen
finally kills Anna. The ordinariness of *Parinda*'s revenge plot is energized by a complex evocation of space to show urban terror. *Parinda*
does not use many location shots; instead, the limited use of space is
fragmented further through a skillful editing pattern that combines film-
noir cynicism with Eisensteinian montage and Hitchcockian terror.

    Parinda develops the image of the city as *ruin* through a peculiar
articulation of the "architectural uncanny." Anthony Vidler suggests that

the notion of the uncanny as an older private form transforms itself into a public experience in the modern metropolis (1992, 6). The metropolitan uncanny was commonly associated with all the phobias related to spatial fear, particularly claustrophobia. The uncanny therefore works metaphorically to articulate a "fundamentally unliveable modern condition" (Vidler 1992, x). The interpretive force of the uncanny is best captured in film, where the "the traces of its intellectual history have been summoned in the service of an entirely contemporary sensibility" (Vidler 1992, x). In literary and cinematic forms, the uncanny emerges within a tense space where the yearning for a home and a fear of homelessness constantly impinges on desire and freedom. Thus, the homely, the domestic, and the nostalgic are constantly placed under threat (Vidler 1992, 10). Memory, childhood, nostalgia, claustrophobia and primitivism coexist in the uncanny city of the imagination, to produce a distinct form of spatial anxiety. Destroying the myth of the rational planned city from within, "this modern uncanny always returns as the labyrinth to haunt the City of Light" (Donald, 73).

Parinda's Bombay is fragmented into dark, morbid spaces with all the characters framed within a light and shadow zone. Rarely in the film do we see a riot or a spectacular display of color. There is a peculiar obsession with the night and with fragmented, darkly lit interior spaces,

Karan (Anil Kapoor) in *Parinda* (1989). Courtesy Vidhu Vinod Chopra Productions.

as opposed to the panoramic vision one usually sees in Hindi cinema. The city appears decrepit and Spartan, with no directorial gesture toward conventional cinematic spectacle. Modern life, said Jean-Paul Sartre, increasingly appears like a "labyrinth of hallways, doors, and stairways that lead nowhere, innumerable signposts that dot routes and signify nothing" (cited in Polan, 252). *Parinda*'s alleys, closed spaces, ordinary sites, elevators, dark staircases, peeling walls, and streets are ubiquitous. The city is dark, crowded, and ruthless; its human form is Anna. Anna is the center of the city and his social net connects him to the police, other underworld rivals, factories, politicians, and more. Anna's eccentricity or "madness" is central to the way the city's lawlessness and decay are portrayed. He is ordinary and spectacular, human and inhuman, powerful and vulnerable. Like other noir films, *Parinda* offers a combination of the themes of excess, the bizarre, cruelty, madness, innocence, and a fascination with death. Death here acquires a ceremonial quality that is elaborately staged, but it is not associated with martyrdom, as in the case of the classic antihero. Rather, death is the culmination of a series of failures. Central to the narrative of death is the noir-like darkness of the city.

Parinda opens with long shots of the city of Bombay in twilight as the credits appear without the loud, spectacular music usually associated with Hindi film credits. An eerie sense of danger is evident from the staccato music. As twilight turns into night, a sense of expectancy and mystery surrounds the city. The credits end with the director's name appearing on the long shot of a house with light filtering out of the window. Here, the music sound track is mixed to introduce a mechanical sound. In the next shot, the sound is identified as we see a little toy moving on the floor. There is a clear association here with a child, but we see no child as the camera tilts to show Anna standing before a photograph of himself, a woman, and a child. We hear a woman's tortured singing on the sound track as Anna folds his hands to pray before the garlanded portrait. The strangeness of the scene is evident; the portrait on the wall seems to evoke the death wish of a tortured yet powerful man.[20]

This initial introduction is suddenly interrupted by the sound of the phone, and Anna turns to walk toward the sound. He picks up the phone and curtly says, "Anna." We then hear the sound of a scream and the profile of a dead man's face, shot in close-up. In the next cut, we see the face of one of the three men who killed the man whose scream was

Anna's (Nana Patekar's) fear of fire in *Parinda*. Courtesy Vidhu Vinod Chopra Productions.

just heard. The men, close associates of Anna's, wipe the blood off their weapons. The close-up of weapons and faces in low-key lighting give this murder the appearance of a ritual killing. The discontinuity in the editing imbues the killing with a level of grandeur, ritual spectacle, and primitivism. This aesthetic framing of death is repeated several times in the film. As in the classical form of Eisensteinian montage, the act of killing is never shown directly but is instead projected through an effective editing pattern.[21]

Film-noir heroes tend to live in the present, retreating into the past only when they are unsuccessful in the present. Themes of loss, nostalgia, lack of clear priorities. and insecurity are presented primarily through mannerism and style (Schrader, 58). Anna's mannerisms are peculiar and his eccentricity and madness are linked to a traumatic event, the burning of his wife and child. At one point in the film, a cameo character informs Karan that Anna fears fire because he burnt his wife and child alive. This fear of fire is evoked several times in the film through fragmented visual intrusions (bodies enveloped by flames) and always from Anna's point of view. This fear of fire is of Anna's own making, embedded in the recesses of his consciousness. The fear of the "self" is thus his greatest weakness and ultimately consumes him at the end of the film.

Anna's power and complexity, his psychic investment in violence, are established through associations: objects (the toy), memory (the portrait, the singing), and the burning figures of his wife and child. Anna talks about the need to forget, even though his past follows him constantly. He maintains a simmering exterior, a savage control, an ascetic persona and intimacy with the everyday violence of the city. The psychological investment in Anna's character clearly breaks with popular representations of villains in Bombay cinema, villains who are rarely invested with a complex past. Terror in *Parinda* is linked to "madness" and madness has to be located spatially. Anna brings to his performance a sense of both everyday ordinariness and a spectacular and exaggerated form of brutality. Anna's importance lies in his ability to render visible a sense of internal destruction and neurosis that drives the people around him to brutal deaths.

The Uncanny Invasion of Private Worlds

The inability to sustain a personal private world runs throughout *Parinda*. In what is perhaps the film's only romantic moment, Karan and Paro go to her house after a scuffle near a temple with one of the killers. We hear night sounds of the city as Paro cooks inside the apartment. Karan is in the veranda. Paro walks up to him and tries to console him. A romantic song intercut with images of their childhood follows. This happy moment is suddenly interrupted when the lights go off and Paro drops her plate. A disturbed Paro pleads with Karan not to leave her. The song resumes, then ends abruptly again when the phone rings. The juxtaposition of these sounds with the song on the sound track introduces a terrifying invasion of personal space. The song resumes after some time and then ends with Kishen breaking into the house to drag his brother away.

The invasion of personal space is developed again in Karan and Kishen's apartment. When Kishen is shot, Karan brings his injured brother to the apartment. The doctor comes home to treat Kishen, then leaves, promising to send a nurse. Karan uses all the latches to bolt the door. Karan's fear is justified, as in the next shot the killers talk to the doctor in the darkly lit staircase outside the apartment. The doctor is with the underworld.

Paro (Madhuri Dixit) and Karan (Anil Kapoor) romancing in *Parinda*. Courtesy Vidhu Vinod Chopra Productions.

Just as Karan and Kishen start reflecting on their childhood entry into the city, the doorbell rings again. This ominous sound is intercut with close-up shots of Kishen, Karan, the doorbell, and the staircase outside the apartment where the killers stand ringing the bell. The shots are repeatedly cut to music and end in silence, with the staircase now empty. The doorbell rings again after a pause, and this time Karan, gun in hand, walks toward the door, with Kishen begging his brother not to open the door. Again the film uses a montage of shots and sounds as Karan removes all the latches, to reveal a nurse standing outside. Unknown to the brothers, their private space is already invaded by someone whose real self is not visible to them. The night clock chimes and the nurse injects Kishen. Suddenly, the doorbell rings again. The nurse tries to walk to the door but is prevented by Kishen. Karan again moves, gun in hand, toward the door, as Kishen shouts from his bed. All the latches are again removed, and Paro walks in. In a stressed state, Karan tells her he cannot be a witness because Anna's men shot his brother. There is an argument and, ultimately, Karan agrees to be a witness.

The incessant use of the doorbell to trigger tension inside the apartment is cinematically developed through a Hitchcockian montage. Close-ups of faces, door latches, and the gun in Karan's hand are regularly intercut with the sound of the doorbell to create a palpable tension within the apartment. The power of the sequence lies in its very cinematic quality, its ability to create a visual and aural language with which a written narrative cannot compete. While the visual appears like a set of fragmented shots, the sound track combines Kishen's desperate voice with the sound of the doorbell and highly effective music. Fear is now all-inclusive, as terror is omnipresent. The next day at the police station, Karan refuses to be a witness when he learns of the nurse's identity. As Vidler suggests, "the uncanny emerges as a 'frame of reference' that positions the desire for a home and domestic security with its exact opposite" (1992, 12). In *Parinda*, the cycle of terror encircles the city, the home, and the private world of the protagonists. As a result, the desire for peace becomes a nostalgic yearning for a return to childhood.

Childhood Memory and the City: The Form of Remembrance

Childhood impressions and experiences connect all the characters, including Anna, as orphaned children. Childhood images are woven together through songs and a few conversations. Childhood is a state of homelessness. Living on the "footpath" is brutal and cruel, but also full of hope. Images of the children singing on Bombay's Marine Drive are presented against the magical backdrop of the Nariman Point skyline.

Childhood experience of the street in *Parinda*. Courtesy Vidhu Vinod Chopra Productions.

The city is represented here as the city of dreams. This mythology of the city is linked to the idea of childhood and dreaming. The city never appears magical in the adult life of the characters. Karan and Paro's relationship also develops during childhood, at a neighborhood fountain—an image that is recalled in their adult life, only to be destroyed by the violence around the site. The twilight hue of many of the childhood sequences invests the past with a certain beauty, magic, and innocence. Yet *Parinda*'s childhood images are like snapshots, dislocated and unresolved. They do not provide us with a well-developed chain of events. Memory in *Parinda* appears like a series of unfinished moments. Recalling the past of childhood homelessness seems to be the only way to deal with the terror in the city.

Childhood remembrance and perceptions are particularly significant in the development of an urban identity. As an adult, these perceptions turn into nostalgia, remembrance, and yearning. In "A Berlin Chronicle," Walter Benjamin presents us with a series of impressions of the Berlin of his childhood. Contrasting his style of remembering the past with that of autobiographical writing, Benjamin suggests that, while the mapping of time in the classical autobiography tends to be sequential and linear, urban reminiscences are usually discontinuous (1992, 316). The relationship of specific locations to time, and the ways in which the city both shapes and in turn is shaped by memory, become the core of Benjamin's investigations. The space of moments and discontinuities presents the recent past as fragmented, fleeting, and in the form of snapshots. It is this aspect that seems so relevant to the structure of *Parinda*. For unlike other popular film narratives that create a temporal continuum of past/present/future, *Parinda* reproduces the past in flashes, as incomplete and unfinished moments that are relevant only in the adult lives of the protagonists.[22] All the characters remain caught in a battle with fate, their past and their future and all are defeated by life in a poignant loss of innocence in the city. The film, however, goes beyond the everyday sites of memory to question the mythic power of the monument, whose relationship to the city has always been complicated.

Monument and the City

The monument is a deeply contradictory site, often presenting itself as the concentration of a city's historicity. As a spectacular space, the monument renders the city to the world, while at the same time displacing the everyday sites of memory. The monument hides the persistence of barbarism in the present. It presents us with a false history, eternalizing the past as a closed space with an end. However, it is possible to set up a series of counter-monuments that bear witness to a personal history (Benjamin 1992). Drawing on Benjamin's thesis, Graeme Gilloch writes, "While the city's proud monuments most clearly articulate the glorification of history, in their 'afterlife', these same structures come to unmask the modern metropolis as the locus of mythic delusion" (73). In *Parinda*, the space of both the monument and the counter-monument of the individual is shattered by the spectacle of violence. The film uses the Gateway of India, the Babulnath Temple located in Malabar Hill, and a neighborhood fountain as spaces of terror. These display sites, which are central to the cartography of Bombay, are turned into nodes of violence and death. Fragmenting the panoramic vision of tourism photography, which establishes monuments and display sites as beautiful and spectacular markers of the city, the use of montage in *Parinda* creates conflict and introduces the uncanny shock of the urban. In one of the most dramatic scenes of the film, Prakash is murdered at a neighborhood fountain, a site that has traditionally evoked romantic and joyful associations for all the characters, particularly Karan and Paro. The fountain operates here like a counter-monument, a particular site of memory whose use in the film is deployed effectively to show both the yearning for peace and happiness and the impossibility of peace and happiness within the space of the city.

The fountain is the place where Prakash and Karan meet after many years. Just before their meeting, we see them in cars driving through the city's labyrinth, singing a childhood song. During the song, we are taken back to the past to see childhood shots of happiness, anger, destruction, and love. The Nariman Point skyline is often present in the childhood sequences. These visuals are woven into the song and are important for their depiction of innocence, hope, and a child's vision of the city "at first sight." By the time Karan and Prakash finally reach their meeting point, we are aware of their friendship. From here on, the editing and the music change as the car with the killers in it arrives at the site. *Parinda*'s film editor, Renu Saluja, contrasts action and emotion using a rapid back-and-forth structure. We see the glass panes of the car come down three times, intercut with shots of startled pigeons each time a window comes down. The killers are revealed in this montage just before we hear gunshots and see Karan's helpless expression as his friend is shot. The entire action is fragmented into minute parts, with close-up shots of pigeons (startled by the sound of gunshots) providing the bridge for the editing pattern. In Saluja's words, "city films demand a kind of editing where the cutting is visible" (interviewed in Mazumdar and Jhingan, "The Journey from the Village to the City"). Saluja contrasts the editing here with that of a lyrical story line where the cutting is made to look invisible. In *Parinda*, disembodied shots are put together through a stylized editing technique to produce the shock of the urban. The images are cut to the sound of music and gunshots, creating a montage from collision, rather than linkage.[23]

Like the fountain, the Babulnath Temple emerges as a violent space. Karan runs up the steps of the temple to see Paro feeding pigeons. Paro has broken up with Karan, since he refused to be a witness for her murdered brother. Karan walks up and expresses a sense of desperation to Paro, who finally relents, knowing that Karan himself had no role in her brother's death. A romantic song plays on the sound track. Suddenly Karan spots one of the killers and starts chasing him down the steps, followed closely by Paro. The downward descent introduces a dynamic movement. The spectacularly visual conflict of steps, people, lines of force, and the sound of the temple bell are all linked together through the chase. The chase down the steps stands in contrast to the casual climbing of other temple visitors. Moving from the close-up of running legs on the steps to long shots of all three characters, the sequence appears to combine montage based on the mechanical beat of cutting and montage based on the pattern of movement within the shot. As a statement about a sacred site of the city, *Parinda*'s temple sequence envelops the city with crime and violence.

The Gateway of India is similarly implicated in the violence of the city. Throughout the narrative, the Gateway is used as a major backdrop. Kishen is shot by Anna's men near the Gateway, and it is the use of the Gateway during this climactic moment that concretely presents it as a space of terror. Karan and Paro decide to spend their wedding night on a rented boat near the Gateway. The couple want to return to their village. The narrative presents this imagined space of the village as a sign of hope away from the violence of the city. But this is not to be. Anna emerges from the crowds participating in the revelry of New Year's Eve at the Gateway of India. He appears both as a man of the crowd and as a stranger to that crowd. He boards a little boat that ferries him and his companions to Karan and Paro's boat. This entire sequence is presented using a back-and-forth editing structure.

We see the Gateway of India, well lit, surrounded by crowds. Anna on his boat moving toward the other boat is regularly cut with shots of Karan and Paro making love. The erotic energy of this sequence is heightened by its fragmented and expressive quality, which is regularly contrasted with shots of Anna coming closer to the boat. Just as Karan and Paro reach their climax, with Karan whispering the name of their future son, Anna pushes open the door and releases a volley of bullets. The bed is now covered with blood. The power of the monument as a symbol of the beauty of a city is systematically destroyed as Bombay looks dark and terrifying, a city of death.

While there are many characters who die in *Parinda*, the cinematic shock in the erotic and aestheticized killing of the newlywed couple after a sensual lovemaking sequence is the climactic moment of the film. With the volley of bullets, the two fall into each other's arms, united in death but unable to reach their dream. Death here is symbolic at many levels—while a return to the village is no longer possible, a return to childhood is fleetingly posed through a childhood song playing on the sound track. It is this utopian flash combined with deep despair that makes *Parinda* such a fascinating film about the city. Throughout the narrative, we are reminded of the village, but a return to the village is now no longer possible. *Parinda* does not try to project a heroic figure caught in an urban nightmare. Instead, every character except Paro colludes in the making of the nightmare. The film's cynicism is crafted through an uncanny interplay between a constant yearning for happiness and its systematic destruction in the fragmented and dark city of Bombay.

The Residual City of *Satya*

Ram Gopal Varma's *Satya,* released in 1998, a decade after *Parinda,* tells the story of Satya, a recent migrant into the city of Bombay who slowly becomes part of an accelerated flow of sporadic and random events that make him join the underworld. *Satya* retains an existential relationship to all the characters: their location within the city is neither causally nor sociologically explained. The city's wasteland and urban detritus saturate the mise-en-scène of the film almost like a space that forms the heart of the city, not its periphery. Within this urban decay and dereliction, gangsters embark on a journey of survival. As Bombay becomes a gangland, the desire for home, domesticity, and peace continues to elude its citizens. The remarkable feature of *Satya* is its play with space and bodies to craft an urban jungle where the "spectacular global city" is completely erased. The film revels in a landscape of claustrophobic spaces, *chawls*, crowded streets, and traffic. We see neither the dance of fashion, nor the glint of objects and dramatic architecture. Instead, we embark on a spatial journey that moves from private to public worlds, constructing a city of modern *ruin*.

Visuals of the Bombay skyline, the boats, the sea, and the city at night are introduced right at the beginning of the film, followed by visuals of cops arresting people. A narrator tells us in the "objective" voice of a documentary maker that Bombay is a city that does not sleep; it's a city where the underworld is powerful. The narrator moves from the broader context of the city and its current problem of crime, to Satya (played by Chakravarthy), a man whose story the film seeks to narrate. This opening suggests a link with current news and the particular relationship of crime to Bombay in recent years. Crime becomes the imaginary reference point from which to tell the story of a city, with Satya emerging as a man who belongs to the crowd of this huge metropolis.

The interesting quality of this film is that Satya lacks a past. There is absolutely no effort to situate the narrative within a temporal chain of past/present/future. Satya gets involved with the underworld for no apparent reason. An egotistical gangster, Jagga, throws beer at Satya in a sleazy bar during Satya's first day at work as a waiter. Satya winces but does not retaliate. This sequence is followed by another sequence in which Jagga's men demand extortion money from Satya in return for his shelter. Satya responds by knifing one of them on the face. Jagga decides to teach Satya a lesson. On the terrace of the nightclub, several people thrash Satya as Jagga watches. The crowded streets of Bombay are in full view in the background. This moment of violence has a sporadic but everyday quality; it occupies half the screen diagonally while the other half shows people and cars moving about at their usual pace.

Violence is an everyday occurrence and is located within the hub of the city. Negotiating this world of everyday violence, Satya enters the world of Bombay's hitmen. Two men shoot a film producer in his car in broad daylight. While running, one is arrested and the other captured and tortured by the police. This leads to the arrest of the gang's leader, Bhiku Mahatre (played by Manoj Bajpayee).

Jagga's contacts with the police ensure that Satya is sent to prison on false charges of pimping. In prison, Satya meets Bhiku Mahatre, thus setting the stage for an interesting male friendship that forms the heart of the narrative and marks Satya's entry into the underworld. The film plays out gang life as a space where brotherhood, community, death, and defiance coexist. The gang's boss, Bhau Thakarey, kills Mahatre. Satya kills Thakarey, and then gets killed by the police. Intra-gang warfare kills the others, leaving one sole survivor. This cycle of violence is inventively crafted through the mise-en-scène.

The Residue of Urban Detritus and the Aesthetics of Garbage

Cities are built structures that dissect open space with buildings, flyovers, bridges, and streets. In any context, built structures create in their wake a series of spaces on the margins that cannot be incorporated within the master design plan. Such spaces, the leftovers and the discarded, can be called residual space. The residual constitutes "elements of the world that are engulfed by the process of capital, turned into waste or leftovers, even thrown away" (Raqs Media Collective). The discarded space then becomes important for us to understand the nature of contemporary modernity. In a poetic evocation of residual space, the Raqs Media Collective provides the following description:

> What happens to people in the places that fall off the map? Where do they go? They are forced, of course, to go in search of the map that has abandoned them. But when they leave everything behind and venture into a new life they do not do so entirely alone. They go with the networked histories of other voyages and transgressions, and are able at any point to deploy the insistent, ubiquitous insider knowledge of today's networked world. (221)

This description of people who have fallen off the map evokes the space of contemporary Central Bombay described by Blom Hansen (179–85). Blom Hansen's evocation of density and despair provides us with a concentrated vignette of the city's residual spaces and the logic of sustenance and survival that drives the underworld. Residual spaces do not fit into any vision of the planned city because they take a life of their own. It is this space of the residual that is inventively evoked in the mise-en-scène of *Satya*.

Bombay in *Satya* looks almost like a documentary montage of claustrophobic spaces, *chawls*, crowded streets, and traffic. Like *Parinda*, there is a desire to present a counternarrative to tourism photography, but as we discover, this counternarrative is not influenced or coded by the dramatic aesthetics of light and shadow found in *Parinda*. *Satya* moves deliberately with the aesthetics of shabbiness, television reportage, and documentary-style visuals—but these elements are combined with the dramatic use of the steady cam[24] and spectacular editing strategies that provide the film with a remarkably different aesthetic mode. Reviewers responding to *Parinda* immediately after its release expressed a guarded appreciation, but accused the filmmaker of resorting to an open aestheticization of violence.[25] *Satya*, on the other hand, was hailed for its "realism." Gerrard Hooper, the main cameraman for *Satya*, brought his own influences as a documentary filmmaker in the United States. He saw *Satya*'s shooting style as a form that resembled the work of American independent cinema. Hooper used very little light and tried to create a dynamic movement of the camera in claustrophobic situations. Hooper's own vision of Bombay seeped through his cinematography. He was struck by Bombay's extreme congestion, its appearance as a city bursting at the seams and yet bustling and functioning, unkempt and out of bounds. Entering the city from the airport, Hooper was astounded by the packed streets—people sleeping and working in the same place. Bombay didn't appear sprawling, but compacted. Hooper was responsible for the look of the film—an experimental documentary-style look that used very little artificial light to create a mise-en-scène of urban detritus.[26]

Satya is a hard-hitting story of gangsters involved in gang wars, extortion, and encounter killings. The film takes us through the streets of Bombay to narrate a violent and tragic story of everyday survival in the city. In a review of the film, Shobha De wrote, "*Satya* spoke the language of the streets—rough, crude, brutal. And yet, did not offend sensibilities. It perfectly captured the savagery of what has become our daily reality while also uncovering the final futility and pathos of mindless gang wars."[27] Another reviewer referred to *Satya* as a "no punches pulled movie mirroring, authentically, the visage of a sick society."[28] In an interview about the film, Ram Gopal Varma said,

> Actually I decided to make *Satya* as an action film since I had not made one for quite a long time. Mumbai has always attracted me because it is a fascinating city. In the process of making an action film, I bumped into some of the people in the underworld. And I realized that the human side of theirs attracted me much more than what they did. It never occurs to us that anyone who is shot dead in an encounter by the police has a face. To us he is just a name in print to be forgotten the very next day. *Satya* is the story of people who are put in a position that the average man may not be able to identify with.[29]

The reviewers' perceptions and the director's own commentary suggest that what was seen as a situation gripped by the city needed to be creatively portrayed. *Satya* succeeded in presenting a gritty and innovative narrative on the underworld. In this powerful depiction of gangland Bombay, we see a particular vision of the city that is not marked by the uncanny but by the excessive logic of survival that takes place in the residual city. Representing the residual requires an aesthetic mode that evokes disenchantment, without falling into a clichéd sentimentalism of poverty images. What makes *Satya* particularly interesting is its aesthetic strategy, which establishes Bombay as a giant garbage dump.

The underworld in *Satya* is portrayed as a community of men, operating from different parts of the city. As the emblematic spatial symbol of the city, the street becomes a place of violent crime, with gangs seeking to make their home on the margins of the street. This is why *Satya*'s architectural mise-en-scène is so interesting. At no point in the film are we dazzled by light. The flush of commodities so intrinsic to family films is crucially absent. We move instead through the bylanes and dark interiors of slums, half-constructed buildings, dingy rooms, street corners, a car park, and a prison. Varma uses the steady cam creatively to navigate the decrepit landscape of the city. In one of the major chase sequences early in the film, two gang members on a scooter kill a film producer at close range while he sits in his Ambassador car. As the gang members run from the police, the camera follows them moving across spaces of Bombay that look horrifyingly shabby. Crossing walls, train tracks, narrow alleys, and open drains—the camera captures the chase in real locations, providing a fairly detailed account of the city's spatial topography. Hooper recalls that artificial rain was used for the entire chase sequence, because the film was supposed to be set during the monsoons.[30] The rain seemed to add to the documentary effect of the film, enhancing the spatial metaphor of the city as garbage dump.

Satya's little one-room apartment is placed next to a darkly lit corridor with clothes hanging against both walls. The shortage of indoor space forces people out into this shared corridor space. All the apartments convey a shortage of space, and the camera almost always presents the busy street outside as a backdrop. These are the *chawls* in the most crowded parts of Bombay, and *Satya* attempts to make sure our eye connects the outside to the inside, rather than create a wedge between these spaces. The space from which the gang operates is located inside an empty half-constructed building with dark alleys, wooden poles, a little table with a few phones, and old chairs strewn about. This is a space that is hidden from the "public," but it is a space that exists in almost every other corner of the city. Almost like a counterspace to the brightly lit wealthy spaces of the designed city, the gang's interior space is bereft of all commodities.

In a sense, the mise-en-scène of *Satya* also recalls Rahul Mehrotra's elaboration of the "kinetic city." Mehrotra notes that most South Asian cities comprise two elements in the same space. The first is the "static city," or the permanent city, which is immovable. Made of concrete, brick, and steel, this static city is monumental and can be traced on maps. The other city is the kinetic city, which is a city in motion—"a three-dimensional construct of a fragmented ground reality" (97).

> Built of recycled waste, plastic sheets, scrap metal, canvas, waste wood—
> all juxtaposed with dish antennas, webs of electric wire, cable, et al.—it
> is a kaleidoscope of the past, present and future compressed into an
> organic fabric of alleys, dead ends and a labyrinth-like, mysterious
> streetscape that, like any organism, constantly modifies and reinvents
> itself. (Mehrotra, 97)

The kinetic city cannot be detected or understood through its architectural design. In the kinetic city, space is marked by its relationship to people. Large processions, festivals, hawkers, street vendors, and dwellers are all part of this streetscape that is in constant motion. The kinetic city is energetic and dense; space and the urban crowd converge here, creating a unique site of tension that is both productive and unproductive.[31] It is the kinetic city that struggles for visibility in *Satya*. For instance, the use of the Ganesh Festival[32] procession at the end of the film to stage Bhau Thakarey's death evocatively highlights the place of the kinetic city. Varma's choreography combines the urban crowd with religious fervor and emotional intensity to stage the murder. Thakarey is performing religious rites at the Ganesh Festival procession. Holding a knife, Satya moves through the dense crowd of the festival. Aerial shots of the festival and religious chanting add to the tension. He finally reaches the site where Thakarey is praying, and he kills him with the knife. Within the din of the dense crowd, Satya not only manages to kill but also to escape. The killing sequence suggests that in the kinetic city, motion and density both produce and hide the spectacle of violence. The entire narrative presents an urbanscape of alleys, religious processions, and makeshift dwellings to play out the everyday world of urban living and survival.

The modus operandi of the gang is driven by a logic of survival. In the disenchanted city of *Satya,* it is survival and not a great desire for wealth that constitutes the heart of the gang's operation. This is conveyed throughout the film, from its spaces, to its people, to the desires of the gang members. Even technology is deployed for survival. Cell phones aid in the chain of communication that connects all the gang members and they inevitably play a crucial role in either planning an assassination or planning some form of intervention. The role of technological debris is also crafted through a conscious effort to dot the film with second-grade technology. Instead of new cars, which flooded the market after globalization, we see aging Fiats, Ambassadors (India's eternal version of the Oxford Morris), auto-rickshaws, and a Maruti (Suzuki) van. The car as an emblematic symbol of freedom and fantasy is deliberately undercut.[33] Cars do not glint, their texture is not fetishized—rather, they perform the role of mundane technology and its use value. A music director threatened by the gang is shown with a harmonium, as opposed to the giant music mixer we usually associate with contemporary music production. Satya's hesitancy about his ability to shoot and kill is countered by the gang leader, who says, "You don't need to win a competition; all you need to do is place the gun close to the head." The vehicles used by the assassins are a two-wheeler and an auto-rickshaw. This effort to downsize the paraphernalia within which the narrative of crime unfolds in the film becomes part of the larger context of the residual city. None of the gang members are experts at anything in particular. What binds

Bhiku Mahatre (*left*, Manoj Bajpayee) and Satya (*right*, Chakravarthy) in *Satya* (1998). Courtesy Ram Gopal Varma's Factory.

them together is their will to survive. Their identity and friendship is based on an association within the city. Where and how did these people get together? What is their past? How did they come to the city? The film steers clear of this kind of sociological analysis, moving instead in the direction of a psychological narrative of violence.

When a rival gangster creates problems for Satya's gang, Varma stages an elaborate shootout sequence in an apartment block. The presence of children in the enclosed playground of the apartment block provides a routine, everyday space of playfulness as the backdrop. The shootout here between two gangs is a speedy combination of dynamic steady-cam movements and stillness, with corridors, stairways, and railings becoming the stage for the action. Like a theatrical performance, the play of bodies in this space presents a violent narrative inside an innocuous building. Instead of car chases, which inform many action films, *Satya*'s action sequences are deliberately played out as "realistic," "routine," and "everyday."

The action is not spectacularized through technological extravaganza; rather, the brutality of the violence becomes excruciating because of its existence within the banality of everyday routine. The theatricality that marks the ritual act of killing in action films is deliberately undercut. With a decrepit city as the backdrop, purged of all spectacular com-

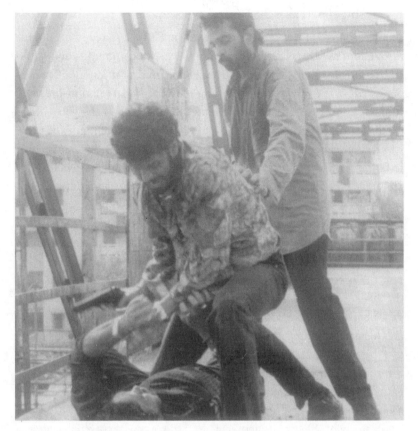

Gang rivalry in *Satya*. Courtesy Ram Gopal Varma's Factory.

modities and the conscious use of an aesthetics of decay, we are in many ways provided with a metaphor of the city as garbage dump, a metaphor that treats the bodies as unwashed, unruly, and irrational, walking through a space of abundant waste. Instead of mounting the idea of a "speed city," *Satya* plays out a spatial topography of slums, *chawls*, and dark alleys, invoking the plebeian world of violence and vernacular modernity that Blom Hansen so skillfully recounts. In *Satya*, Bombay is a disenchanted city where the gang becomes part of an everyday violence that can help them escape the boredom of their existence, the banality of their situation, and the degradation befalling each one of them. By philosophically approaching death as the climactic theatrical performance of urban violence, *Satya* constantly thwarts the desire for a healing touch that can help provide closure. All the protagonists, except one, die at the end of the film.

Friendship, Love, and the Desire for Escape

The alternative ethical world mounted in *Satya* is a recurring theme throughout the film elaborated through a sense of community and familial bonding. Kallu Mama's presence as the head of a family of men is deployed inventively to craft the gang's interpersonal relationships and camaraderie. As the wise and humane father figure in the gang, Kallu Mama (played by Saurabh Shukla), evokes the bonds of family life. In a spectacular rendering of this community, the song "Kallu Mama" projects the idea of a different kind of family through an overwhelmingly male space. In the song, Varma deploys the perfomative mode of street theater to conduct a conversation between gang members. Shot inventively through what can be described as a swaying camera, the song, with its mood lighting, drunken disposition, sense of irreverence, and conversational lyrics, projects a world of male friendship and bonding.

If the presence of Kallu Mama helps evoke a family-like space, then the friendship between Bhiku Mahatre and Satya encapsulates the experience of brotherhood in the gang. Satya's friendship with Mahatre and his romantic involvement with Vidya function in the best tradition of the genre to express a restless inner world. The friendship track and the romance track alternate in the narrative, providing us access to Satya's insecurities, anxieties, and inner life. Satya's friendship with Mahatre operates in a sense as a microcosm of the bond that keeps the community of the gang together. The friendship narrative operates as a journey that begins with Satya and Mahatre's encounter in prison, followed by their developing closeness and Satya's induction into the gang.

Some of the most interesting conversations between the two men are staged against a mise-en-scène that depicts a longing for a romantic myth of the city on the sea. There are two moments staged against the landscape of the sea and Bombay's faded skyline. In the first of these scenes, the skyline is not clearly visible and we just see some dilapidated buildings against the water. Mahatre expresses his anger at having been prevented by Bhau Thakarey from killing a rival. Satya listens, and persuades Mahatre to take revenge. This is played out against the seascape, with Mahatre's raw and insecure masculinity on display through his performance. It is immediately followed by a shootout sequence in which a rival gang member is killed on a railway bridge.

The landscape of the sea is enhanced in a later sequence, with more expansive shots of the skyline and sea. In the earlier sequence, Satya

Satya (Chakravarthy), Kallu Mama (Saurabh Shukla), and Bhiku Mahatre (Manoj Bajpayee) in *Satya*. Courtesy Ram Gopal Varma's Factory.

expresses his solidarity with Mahatre and persuades him to take revenge; in the second sequence, the roles are reversed. Satya wants to confess to Vidya about his profession. He is worried about Vidya's safety and wants to exit the gang. Mahatre takes the active role here, persuading Satya to not say anything. Mahatre wants him to go away to Dubai with Vidya. Like an older brother, Mahatre seems to oversee Satya's interests throughout the film. There is homoerotic energy friendship. Both men are not only drawn to each other but also trust each other. Mahatre's constant concern for Satya's safety and Satya's desire to support Mahatre's anxieties function within the structure of a romantic relationship. The friendship narrative in *Satya* is given a spatial language wherein the poetics of the sea provide the space for the development of the bond, while at the same time introducing the cityscape as the site of violence. The inexplicable bond between the two men symbolizes both the desire for community and the community's insecure formation in the gang. The friendship signals both the high point and the crisis point for the gang, ultimately leading to mayhem in the city.

The romance between Satya and Vidya runs almost parallel to the rest of the narrative. Satya's relationship with Vidya is fragile, since Vidya has no access or knowledge of Satya's gang life. Within the context of the narrative, the deception works like in many other gangster films, with the yearning to start a family presented as an impossible dream.

The impossibility of intimacy is also spatially suggested. Vidya's home is a small room, but the camera almost never provides us access to the whole space. When Vidya comes into Satya's apartment, the two look out of the window, and Vidya talks of the lost view of the sea because of the tall building now standing opposite their apartment. This passing remark mounts the idea of a city constantly changing through building construction, disrupting both the perception of expanse and also the lives of the inhabitants. The most private moments between the couple take place on the terrace of their building. Even the street is not a place that provides any freedom from claustrophobic space. During the two love songs, the couple romance against a tranquil backdrop that is almost deliberately separated from the density of the city. The Bombay Poona Highway and tunnel, the beach and the rocks, the terrace and the gardens—these are the spaces within which romance is possible. Since the city cannot offer leisure spaces to its residents, romance is virtually a problem of space. An alternative topography of space needs to be produced for the performance of romance, since *Satya*'s overall screen space is decrepit and dirty.

When the couple decides to negotiate the city for their romantic pursuit, we are taken into a vortex of violence. This is precisely what happens when Satya takes Vidya to the theater to watch a film called *Border* (ironically, a patriotic film). As *Border*'s nationalist and patriotic zeal unfolds on-screen, a crisis lurks within the crowd watching the film. During the film's interval, a rival gang member who spots Satya, calls the police. Soon the cops are swarming the theater. All the exits to the theater are blocked, barring one. The inspector makes an announcement for the crowd inside, asking people to be calm and to leave in an orderly fashion. At the exit, the rival gang member is waiting to identify Satya for the police. Knowing that he will be caught unless he acts, Satya fires a shot in the ground. In the panic and turmoil that follows, Satya manages to escape with Vidya, but a stampede leaves thirteen people dead and several injured. The violence inside the movie theater becomes the turning point for Satya. Tired of deception, Satya wants to confess to Vidya and then leave the gang. At this point, however, Mahatre stops him, suggesting that Satya instead leave for Dubai, where he will be ensured a legal job. But such endings are never really possible within the genre of the gangster film.

Satya (Chakravarthy) and Vidya (Urmila Matondkar) against the Bombay skyline in *Satya*. Courtesy Ram Gopal Varma's Factory.

In many ways, *Satya* plays out a romantic track within a classical format. Romance brings out the good person, the tender and nurturing personality. It also makes Satya dislike his own identity as a gang member, leading to deception. The proximity to violence makes him fear not so much for himself, but for his beloved. The desperation to end this life of deception and ensure a safe life for Vidya makes Satya yearn for escape from the brutal existence he has become part of. Romance becomes a process through which Satya wants to redeem himself. Satya's journey in the film, then, becomes the story of a migrant, his involvement with a gang, and his subsequent desire for escape and redemption. Within the framework of the film, this is an impossible dream. You can never return to the space of legality after having crossed it to the extent Satya does. In the film, Satya's demise takes place in tandem with the collapse of the gang.

The Postmodern Landscape of *Company*

Ram Gopal Varma's *Company* closely followed the release of *Satya*. *Company* is an epic saga of the rise and fall of a criminal cartel and the men and women who ran it. The film is based loosely on Dawood's highly publicized friendship and conflicts with Hindu gangster Chota

Rajan. Unlike *Satya, Company* takes a macro view of the international crime scene, constructing a modern epic about crime as a capitalist enterprise. For Varma, *Satya*'s narrative strategy was to play out a film in which the creators moved with the gangsters at the street level. In *Company,* Varma wanted a perspective that emerged from the top of or outside the frame. *Satya* developed a low-angle approach that tried to stay in the middle of the action. *Company* has a clear design, a philosophy, and an aerial perspective.[34] "*Satya* grips you by the throat and sucks you into the narrative. It deals with characters who are uneducated. It's like the difference between *Goodfellas* and *Godfather. Satya* gives you an adrenaline rush that *Company* doesn't. In *Company* the viewer is detached."[35]

Company mounts an elaborate landscape that moves seamlessly from Bombay to Hong Kong, from Switzerland to Kenya. In *Company,* space is fluid and almost virtual, producing the postmodern city of the contemporary gangster world. While the street is a site of action, the major part of the film traverses flashy hotels, expensive cars, airports, and monumental streets. It is a lavish, larger-than-life crime story inspired by real-life gangsters and the stories about them. *Company* creates a geography of transience by forging a travel-narrative structure in which mobility and the exploration of urban spaces, both exterior and interior, presents us with a sense of energy and speed. Borders and boundaries either do not exist or appear as porous lines that do not stand in the way of this new global mobility.

Essentially *Company* is the story of two gangster friends, their relationship with each other, their conflict, and their final split. Chandu (played by Vivek Oberoi), the younger of the two men, lives in a *chawl* area with his mother. He is invited to join the gang by Mallick (played by Ajay Devgan). Mallick is in love with Saroja (played by Manisha Koirala), while Chandu falls in love with his friend's sister, Kannu (played by Antara Mali). The two women have an interesting friendship in the film.

Mallick and Chandu together create havoc and terror in Bombay, as gang activities move across the world, with different members looking after their respective territorial responsibilities. What makes *Company* different from the other two films discussed in this chapter is its syndicate gangster world, which is structured as a well-oiled totalitarian machine with immense international power. As some have pointed out,

Saroja (Manisha Koirala), Mallick (Ajay Devgan), and Chandu (Vivek Oberoi) in *Company* (2002). Courtesy Ram Gopal Varma's Factory.

syndicate films do not recognize individuality (Mason). The gangster is part of an object world, a thing, and any notion of defiance or aberrant behavior is seen to merit punishment. In the syndicate world, the individual gangster is a foot soldier who inhabits a system from which no exit is possible. Displaying an anxiety wherein the rescue of the individual from a totalizing corporatization becomes the primary narrative conviction, syndicate films embody the individual's peculiar relationship to a mechanized system in order to reflect on modern man's existence within a world overwhelmed by homogenizing processes. Chandu's life in *Company* is essentially portrayed as the journey of an individual with a mind of his own, into the world of gang life.

Chandu's rise in the gang, his differences with Mallick, and their final conflict ultimately take Chandu on a path of renunciation that will make him redeem himself of his criminal past. In this journey, the individual is rescued from the larger space of the gang and removed to another space where legal order can be restored. This process is structured in such a way as to elaborate on the contemporary world of network and surveillance, postmodern desires and anxieties.

Technological Network and Surveillance

The logic of the gang in *Company* is that of a corporation. Nothing can stand in the way of business. The scriptwriter, Jaideep Sahani, says he merged two different kinds of worlds in the film: the world of gangs in student politics and the world of competitive commercial advertising. These worlds were brought together to create a unique site of male aggression and conflict. The turf battles between advertising magnates were transplanted onto the gang. To a large extent, the philosophical vision of *Company* came from Sahani's own experiences as a student involved in politics, and from his later life as a consultant for major advertising corporations.[36] For Sahani, the story of a crime syndicate was literally like the story of a corporation. Using a hierarchical formation, the gang in *Company* has seamless global mobility and connectivity, with ancillary groups becoming part of the circuit in different parts of the world.

The international character of the gang is mounted throughout the film. This is what makes *Company* an international syndicate film, as opposed to films like *Satya* and *Parinda,* where the localized action within the city of Bombay provides the gang with a different set of codes. In *Company,* the first move made by the gang outside of Bombay is sequentially structured around the song "Ganda Hai, Sab Dhandha Hai Ye." The shot of an airplane and postmodern architecture transitioned through car interiors create a seamless landscape of geographical transitions. The close-up of a car wheel, moving at speed as buildings pass by, creates the hyperbole of speed and travel linked to a globalized landscape, which at the same time provides a sense of connectivity to the "good life."

Gloss and spectacle emerge as a destination away from the alleys and dark spaces of Bombay. The airport at which the gang arrives embodies the gestural and spatial economy of the gangster's world. Walking in style, inhabiting the lavish spaces of international airports that function as zones of transit, and being received by other members at different ports gives the gang a cosmopolitan and powerful structure. Speed and movement through a range of spaces shows how the logic of the gang is structured to achieve this higher status and access to the "good life." Again, this is a different logic from that of *Satya,* in which the gang inhabits a social space only to exist and survive, not to empower themselves with the object world of the "good life." Barring cell phones and old used cars, *Satya* essentially underplays the gangster's paraphernalia.

Company, on the other hand, revels in the gang's ability to inhabit and access the iconography of the "good life." Cars, hotels, airports, architectural grandeur, and aerial photography become the iconic markers through which the "good life" is cinematically mobilized. This mise-en-scène differs from the panoramic interior of the family films. In *Company*, the "good life" is dependent on connections with the streets, and it exists in the realm of illegality, something that is foregrounded in most syndicate films.

As the gang becomes more and more global, its connectivity to Bombay and the city's streets operates through remote control. This is powerfully placed several times in the film. When the gang's activity expands, a documentary-like sequence in the film encapsulates the tentacles and power of the gang. The "objective" voice of a narrator informs the audience of the gang's expansion and the role of the phone in this enterprise. In a sense, the documentary sequence performs the role of a bird's-eye "objective" view that Varma wanted to present in the film. The sequence climaxes with a montage of phone shots edited to the sound of phones ringing. Here the phone instrument itself takes on a larger-than-life quality as it is framed in imaginative ways against dazzling skylines and interiors, shabby cars, and decrepit spaces. The phone becomes the technological highway that will help the gang to be international and also maintain links with and control over the streets of Bombay. Sahani was intrigued by the work of Sam Petroda, known for revolutionizing the telecommunications network in India in the 1990s. Petroda set up phones in various parts of the country, and became identified as the man who transformed the region into a modern networked society. Petroda's vision of connectivity was playing at the back of Sahani's mind when he developed the phone sequence in *Company*.[37]

Syndicate films tend to move across nations, through an expansive territorialization of international space. Because these films mimic the functioning of the corporate world, the process of planning takes on a predominant function in the genre (Mason; Shaodian). This is creatively rendered in one of the major assassination sequences in *Company*, in which both the plan and the nature of the contract that binds the syndicate are put to the test. In Switzerland, Chandu meets with a politician, Raute, who wants the current home minister of Maharashtra out of the picture, without his death looking like murder. The gang in Hong Kong is shown on the terrace trying to plan this death without staging it as murder. This discussion is placed within an expansive mise-en-scène of architectural grandeur that forms the backdrop as a skyline. Chandu is asked to monitor the killing of the minister. The plan is to make it look like an accident. The plan is prepared on paper with precision, as the route and the movement of the car are worked out. On the fateful day, Chandu gets a call from his compatriots, who are waiting outside the minister's house on Peddar Road in Bombay. Chandu is informed that the minister's children are also in the car with him. Mallick at this moment is in a meeting with a group of foreign gangsters on a ship somewhere in South Africa. Chandu is confused and feels the money was paid to kill one man, not to kill two innocent children. He calls Mallick, who insists the killing should go according to the plan and that they may not get another chance. Chandu, however, decides to take things in his own hands, and asks his friends to call off the action. Meanwhile, Yadav, another member of the gang, informs Mallick of the crisis. Mallick then calls Bombay directly and tells the gang members to go ahead with the plan. This entire sequence is filled with mounting tension. Phones play an important role, and the movement from Bombay to Chandu at the gang's headquarters to Mallick on the ship presents the audience with three different kinds of spaces.

Kannu (Antara Mali) and Chandu (Vivek Oberoi) in *Company*. Courtesy Ram Gopal Varma's Factory.

Chandu inhabits a space where the sky outside and the high-contrast lighting inside evoke a psychological expressionism. Mallick inhabits a cold, clinical space where monetary transactions are being discussed on a ship. The Bombay streets and highways are clearly controlled by forces outside, and, in this connectivity, technology plays a crucial role. The simultaneous editing between these different spaces, where time is crucially organized through a technological network, shows that disruption in the chain of connection can obviously cause problems. The disruption takes place when Chandu decides to change the plan. However, Mallick's entry restores the plan, with the gang's hierarchy put back in place. This hierarchy, however, comes at a cost, leading to the growing estrangement between two friends. Corporate logic and efficiency is threatened when the well-oiled machine is disrupted, and this is precisely when brotherhood and friendship get tested.

Another logic of the disciplinary mechanism of the corporation works through a culture of surveillance. Technological surveillance, however primitive, is at work within the gang. When the balance of power linked to territorial control of Bombay is seen to heavily tilt in favor of Chandu, Pandit (Mallick's advisor) suggests that Krishnan, who is Chandu's friend, be brought over to help with the control of Bombay. Much to Chandu's surprise, Krishnan arrives in Hong Kong to become his partner. The rivalry between Krishnan and Varsi, another gangster friend in Bombay, becomes a point of conflict that Chandu tries to manage. In a drunken stupor, Varsi, sitting in his *chawl* in Bombay, lets out his frustration to his group of friends, claiming he's going to follow no one's orders, since he is the man really connected to the streets of Bombay. Unknown to him, his voice is recorded on a tape, which is later played in Mallick's and Chandu's presence. Chandu is distraught, realizing that this means death for his friend for having defied the logic of the company's hierarchical management.

The staging of Varsi's drunken outburst is akin to the performance of betrayal in many other gangster films. But betrayal works through a complex network of surveillance that combines the "old" with the "new." Surveillance here is acoustic, traveling as sound to another part of the world, keeping the techniques of power in control. Unlike the general ways in which technological surveillance works within everyday life, here the eavesdropper is a gang member unknown to his friend. The partner in crime becomes a stranger as soon as efficiency and discipline are threatened. With the hierarchical management of the gang through surveillance, a balance of power is maintained and restored.

Surveillance technology functions in *Company* like an allegorical rendering of the postmodern condition, worked out through an intricate journey into gangland psychology and management. The streets of Bombay are not free of surveillance. The presence of technological debris circulates in these spaces, making the possibility of uninhibited space impossible. In Blom Hansen's description of the Muslim *Mohalla,* the presence of phones and low-grade technology is overwhelming, making the street function through complex and unpredictable networks. Varsi's voice is recorded on a cassette tape and physically transported to another part of the world. The tactility of sound travel here is evocative of technological debris and its role in the cityscape. The metaphoric use of the phrase "walls have ears" comes to life in a stunning moment in *Company,* leading to death, mayhem, and a subsequent split within the gang. The narrative of betrayal works precisely because of surveillance. It is only through surveillance that the act of defiance can be given the title of betrayal, creating an alternative ethical world where everything is justified in the interest of a higher order, that of gang efficiency.

Playing with the Genre

If postmodernism or postmodern culture is defined as the pursuit of pure form, where style and performance mimic other representations, where the sense of the original is not easily retrievable, where representation is self-conscious and the desire is to highlight the form of duplicity (Hutcheon), then *Company* displays the characteristic codes of a postmodern text while at the same time traversing the sense of Bombay's alleys and darker side. This engagement with the city is not attempted directly, but through a play with genre and style and through the deployment of a technological network that makes the specificity of the street operate by remote control. *Company* thus functions both as a postmodern representation and as a film that renders for its audience the experiential realm of the postmodern condition. It is this double movement that makes *Company* an interesting archive of the city, playing as it does with gangland psychology through a formal play with the genre, while at the same time addressing the culture of technology and surveillance that marks the global movement of space and time today.

Company is in many ways a gangster film that pays tribute to the iconography of well-known gangster films from around the world. *Company* seems to combine Francis Ford Coppola's panoramic sweep with Martin Scorsese's emotional intensity. The first admission of a play with style is made right at the beginning of the film when Urmila Matondkar, dressed like a *femme fatale,* performs an MTV-like dance number with a group of men dressed in black trench coats and hats. Urmila has no other role in the film. She appears in a dance sequence in which the codes and signs of the gangster film and film noir are mobilized to create a spectacular performance. The play and performance of style follow a brief introduction to the culture of profit and success that drives the gang, rendered to the audience in a stylized, impressionistic montage with Malick's voice on the audio track. This cuts immediately to Urmila and the male dancers who directly address the spectators as the screen is bathed in expressionist lighting against a red backdrop. The dancers sensuously invite the audience into the narrative universe of the film. The existence of the song, standing in as a prologue or citation that refers to the role of cine/film history itself, is something that Varma deployed in *Rangeela.* Unlike the attempt at "strategic realism" in *Satya, Company* departs to create a unique journey into Bombay though a rich engagement with the gangster genre.

The use of the wide-angle lens throughout *Company* is consistent with the choreographic style mounted in the film. Space is explored via a camera perspective that defies the acceptable framing of the ordinary lens. Expanding the frame on the sides, distorting perspective, and creating imaginary horizons, the camera adopts the role of a protagonist whose vision is playful and angular. Through this angular vision, we enter a range of urban spaces where distortion is spectacularized to evoke dread, decay, and the pleasurable engagement with commodity aesthetics. The seamless movement from Bombay to Hong Kong to Kenya creates the necessary speed and spatial transitions that help bring together a range of spaces. Car interiors, hotel rooms and lobbies, airports, and bridges exist in relation to a Bombay of *chawls,* dark alleys, police interrogation rooms, brothels, shabby train compartments, and abandoned factory sites.

The actors in the film deploy the characteristic gestures of well-known cinematic gangsters. Mimicking the walk, the swagger, the posturing, and the stylized rendering of dialogue, the characters take on a

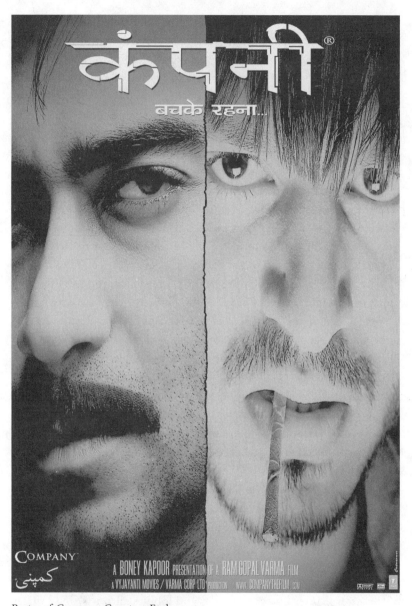

Poster of *Company.* Courtesy Endeavour.

hyperperformative mode to express themselves. As the film quite self-consciously seeks to engage with the representation of the gang world within cinematic history, we learn to see the specific role of the gangster genre in providing access to forms of masculinity and urban space. The framing of all the conversations is done through tilted frames, which evokes a sense of layeredness. The self-conscious lighting strategies, use of foregrounding techniques, and fluid movement through claustrophobic space are all part of this negotiation with the genre.

The attempted assassination on Chandu, staged in Kenya, is one such sequence where the codes of the genre are explored with stylish verve. Combining architectural mise-en-scène with creative use of the steady cam, the sequence presents us with a choreography of violence that is markedly different from *Satya*. Here, all the codes of the gangster genre are mobilized. The camera swings and glides through corridors, spiral staircases, and narrow alleys, moving from interior to exterior views, climbing buildings, and using aerial perspectives, as a badly injured Chandu makes an attempt to escape the bullets of Mallick's gang members. Barefoot and unarmed, Chandu evokes the world of Bruce Willis in *Die Hard*, where interior architecture is navigated through the protagonist's careful movements. Such staged and choreographed sequences that combine stylized camera movements with a cinematic exploration of architectural space are possible only in the cinematic medium. The mimicry of iconic images from well-known action films is scattered throughout this sequence. Style drives the mise-en-scène of action, making *Company*'s narrative universe a self-conscious exploration of generic codes of the gangster genre. Moving away from the simple unfolding of a story, the assassination sequence, like many other sequences in the film, stands out for its visual virtuosity and style, taking the viewer through a dazzling array of familiar images. Technology, architecture, and chase sequences—all central to the gangster genre—are mobilized here for a momentous performance of stylized violence. Space here is both dynamic and violent. The building does not appear as a still object, but becomes an architectural experience that combines the dynamics of space, movement, and narrative, thus embodying the primary effect of cinema (Bruno 2002, 57). The cinematic exploration of architectural space challenges the "notion of buildings as a still, tectonic construct," allowing the possibility of imagining space as practice (57).

Crime and the City

The representation of crime in literature, theater, and film has historically provided, and continues to offer, a fairly complex look at the relationship between legality and illegality, individual empowerment versus the establishment, and the futility of the justice system. In the context of the modern city, crime narratives help us navigate not only the topography of the city, but also the mental cartography of an urban consciousness ravaged by social conflict. From questioning the fragility of the social contract to expressing psychological despair and challenging the establishment, crime films have a metaphorical power that appeals to audiences because of the different ways in which these films seek to redraw the established rules that govern our everyday existence. Representations of crime, in their own particular ways, try to concern themselves with issues like police brutality, prison rules, the judiciary, corruption, and the individual victim's crusade against an unfair world. At the same time, these representations also provide us with some resolution through a performative triumph over corruption. This ambivalence of identification and distance lies at the heart of crime narratives, because they work through a dialectic of pleasure and revulsion.

The gangster film as a subgenre of the crime film becomes significant in the context of the urban. If the city is a space of intoxication, magic, and spectacle, it is also the home of the gangster. Fran Mason, in an interesting analogy, draws attention to the difference between the classical flâneur and the gangster (14–15). Unlike the flâneur, who merely looks and gazes, the gangster seeks control with his gaze. He traverses every part of the city and physically attempts to territorialize its spaces. Through the gangster's movement and location within the city, we are taken to both physical and imagined urban spaces that evade our gaze of urban distraction. As legitimate and illegitimate societies intermingle within the gangster's world, an excessive logic empowers these figures to move with great fluidity. The significance of the gangster genre lies in its ability to evoke a world of strife where normative codes of morality, legality, rationality, and identity are challenged. In this journey of urban exploration, chaos, disorder, violence, death, and despair, the city as the site of rationality and reason is challenged. Despite its checkered and complicated history, the gangster genre has played an important role in addressing the volatile conflicts of city life, particularly the spaces of illegality, decadence, commodification, corporate corruption, and economic depression. Like most gangster films, the crime narrative does not express exhilaration for life, but rather a fundamental state of desperation that is constantly the backdrop within which the crime world enfolds.

Writing about the drive for commercial architecture in Bombay, John Lang, Madhavi Desai, and Miki Desai suggest that in the post-independence period, the aesthetic concern of builders in Bombay was to present a "modern face to the world" (236–37). Thus, glass façades and other symbols of wealth were used both in five-star hotels and in domestic architecture to enhance the projection of Bombay as "modern" and "international." Display was central to this aesthetic drive, and architects in India have been inspired by photographic material exhibited in international architectural and popular magazines, without taking into account its appropriateness for a country like India. Nariman Point, located on Marine Drive in Bombay, is an example of a place where prestigious commercial and state government buildings have made this site in some ways the symbolic heart of Bombay (Lang, Desai, and Desai 236–37). To the naked eye, Nariman Point is like a series of high-rise buildings magically placed against the sky and the expanse of the sea. This image is quite frequently captured in cinema, in tourism photography, and in travelogue films. However, the symbolic appeal of this dreamscape of urban modernity and desire is challenged by the urbanscape of gangster cinema. Through an evocation of Bombay as a city of claustrophobic and violent spaces, films like *Company, Parinda,* and *Satya* operate as fragments that chart out an elaborate archaeology of urban fear. In these films, friendship and betrayal provide the landscape for a new ethical world. Through a radical rewriting of earlier narratives of crime and the figure of the outlaw, the gangland experience situates Bombay as the site of *ruin,* to powerfully remind us that the glitter of consumption comes at a price.

In *The Arcades Project,* Benjamin posed *ruin* as the opposite of the phantasmagoria of the city. *Ruin* enables one to see history not as a chain of events, marked both by linear time and the glory of civilization, but as a narrative on death and catastrophe. The modern city, which presents itself as the glorious culmination of industrial culture, hides behind the spectacular and seductive world of the commodity. Yet the city as ruin can be excavated through the allegorical gaze that allows one to deal with estrangement, alienation, and spatial displacement within the city. Like Benjamin's evocation of ruin, the gangster genre becomes one of the ways to cast shadows on the routine movements of the city.

In many ways, the performance of violence operates in all three films to draw attention to a crisis of the everyday in which random, unpredictable events challenge the mundane world of repetition. In this space, the "death drive" of a community of men comes to signify both the nature of Bombay's everyday and the crisis generated within its routine. If the everyday is the realm of the routine, the mundane, the habitual, then where do we locate the terrain of unpredictability, violence, and spectacular disruption? These are questions whose answers can be only tentatively advanced through forms that can help us journey through the subjectivity and the psychological terrain that forms the core of city life. The landscape of Bombay's gangster cinema provides us insight into a world of despair, degradation, and violence. This is a world that cannot be quantified. It is a world that is fluid, dangerous, and shrouded in mystery. But it is a world that resides in the city both as fact and as fiction.

CONCLUSION

After Life

In his classic work *The Fall of Public Man*, Richard Sennett writes, "A dialectical enquiry means that the argument is complete only when the book has come to an end. You cannot state 'the theory' all at once and then lay it like a map over the historical terrain" (1974, 6). Sennett's position is deeply modernist in that it gestures to the notion of a "complete" argument at the end of the narrative. My own agenda in this book has been less emphatic about the idea of an "end." However, I would go along with Sennett's prescription that theoretical understanding cannot precede the narrative; it must be embedded in the narrative itself.

I have argued in this book that cinema is perhaps the major reservoir of the urban experience in India. If cinema archives the city contemporaneously, it does so in an unusual manner, drawing on historical contexts as they mediate the generic patterns of popular cinema. However, at this current juncture, is it possible to imagine the city in entirely new ways that challenge the very framework of the dominant cultures of popular cinema? Is it possible for Bombay cinema to move in directions not yet taken, to look at experiences and lives hitherto untouched? In some ways, both the family and the gangster genres have reached a kind of imaginative impasse in engaging with the urban. As globalization makes its presence felt in more powerful ways than ever, the need to record the transformations of this period in inventive ways has become imperative. The rapid diversification of audiences, the rise of multiplexes, and the strengthening of institutional networks influencing formal and informal censorship in recent years have pushed the cinematic archive to innovate and adopt new modes of engagement with the city. A cluster of films made in recent years has started exploring the city in ways that stand out from many of the films discussed in this book. This small and emerging body of "fringe cinema" has engaged the city without resorting to the classic masculine form of the gangster genre. *Paanch* (Five, 2000), *Chameli* (2003), and *Ek Haseena Thi* (The one who was beautiful, 2004) can be placed within a small body of films that have hesitatingly emerged to offer an entirely different perceptual entry into the city experience. Unlike gangster cinema, women play a critical role in these films, drawing audiences into an unusual spatial experience of the city.

Urban Nihilism in *Paanch*

The controversy linked to Anurag Kashyap's debut film *Paanch* reveals the complexities and difficulties involved in contemporary engagements with the city. The Indian Film Censor Board initially thought the film was excessively violent and lacked a "social" message. They added that the film did not have a single positive character. Finally, when *Paanch* was cleared for release, with many cuts, financiers blocked its release because the producer owed them money. *Paanch* has, however, been shown at a couple of film festivals, and has also managed to circulate unofficially on DVD among select audiences. *Paanch* creates an urban landscape where nihilism and the uncanny are narrated through a novel architectural journey. A critic said of the film, "In *Paanch* the city is a merciless adversary that pulverizes every good quality in the man on the street" (Jha 2001).

The film narrates the story of a rock band called "The Parasites," who live in a Bombay *chawl*. One day, a man who claims to represent a music company tempts the band with the possibility of cutting their first CD. But the band needs money to do it. The group decides to stage a fake kidnapping of Nikhil, the wealthiest in the group, with his permission, to extract money from his father. This simple plan turns into a nightmare, soon striking the heart of the band. The father informs the police and trouble follows. Luke, the domineering head of the band, murders Nikhil in a fit of temper. As one thing leads to another, the band members lose control, leading to four other murders. Violence, betrayal, death, and destruction unravel in this film that enters heterotopic architectural and psychological spaces of Bombay. The band is made up of Joy (played by

The Parasites in *Paanch* (2000). Courtesy Tutu Sharma.

Joy Fernandes), Pondy (played by Vijay L. Maurya), Murgi (played by Aditya Srivastava), Shiuli (played by Tejaswini Kolhapure), and Luke (played by Kay Kay).

The film opens with images of Bombay stylized through strobe-like shots. Edited to the rhythm of music, the sequence conveys energy, diversity of space, a sense of the crowd, and an air of decrepit gloom. In this initial urbanscape, the story is unraveled through flashbacks that move temporally between the past and the present. The police are interrogating Pondy and Murgi. Murgi's narrative becomes the journey into the past through which we access the history of the band. The film plays with the classic features of detective noir; acts of confession, replay flashbacks, and the figure of the femme fatale are all integrated into the narrative, although for different purposes. The use of Murgi's personal narration to the police of the band's history is the device used to structure a selectively revealed, complicated plot. In many ways, *Paanch* is a fresh effort to question and stretch the parameters of conventional cinematic practice as it engages with the lives of five desperadoes of Bombay. The characters are part of a generation of post-globalized urban youth who are living in *chawls* and "doing the rounds" of media producers, struggling to make it on the margins of Bombay's media industry. *Paanch*'s characters enter the world of violence not because they are part of a world that has been bypassed by the global city. The protagonists in *Paanch* are invested in the dreams of the new city, of succeeding in a cutthroat media industry. Educated and nontraditional, *Paanch*'s characters generate an internal, almost primordial violence, in which mutual slaughter becomes functional for success. Unlike gangster films, which offer a street-side view of violence, *Paanch* shows the slow, inevitable, inner destruction of the dreams of post-global success. The flashy, glamorous world of music production that boomed via television after globalization has little place in *Paanch*. Instead we see greed, petty dreams, and uninhibited ambition that seems to have no limits.

The process that goes into the disposal of the murdered bodies in *Paanch* draws attention to the claustrophobic architectural layout of cities. A dead body in the village can easily be buried, says Anurag Kashyap,[1] but in *Paanch,* the bodies are chopped as in a butcher shop, and then distributed throughout the city. Invoking the gothic sensibility of haunting and horrifying spatial landscapes, the visual expressionism of detective noir, and the experience of the architectural uncanny in a new ensemble genre, *Paanch* defies easy analysis. The film neither draws on the Bombay underworld of crime nor on other notions of criminality popularized by Hindi cinema. Rather, a complex network of psychological forces emerging out of the urban experience produces a world of instability, nihilism, and death. The city in *Paanch* seems to spare no one—even westernized middle-class youth enter a world of discursive violence on their path to success. The difference between this film and gangster films, in which violence is perpetrated by social groups or criminal organizations, is significant.

Most of the narrative in *Paanch* is located in the home where the members of the band live. This is a space that is shot inventively in order to highlight the architectural layout of the building. Kashyap uses architecture to emphasize the psychological world of the band. Walls play a significant role in the film. The walls seem to stand for feelings that cannot be articulated or as "metaphors for a distanced soul" (Schwarzer, 205). The graffiti and colors that adorn the walls express a disturbed emotional world; the walls in *Paanch* are ornamentalized through desecration. This is particularly true in Luke's room, which is hidden from all the other band members, as well as from the spectators, and is not revealed until much later in the film. The spatial complexity and textured density of the *chawl* home is bold and evocative of the film's nihilistic surge. The spectator's eye travels across walls, ceilings, staircases, carved railings, balconies, and an assortment of decrepit furniture and mattresses on the floor. This is a space that will witness the dramatic performance of sex, graphic violence, and death. The architectural design seems to uncannily suggest what lies ahead in the narrative.

The most striking element in the film is the representation of Shiuly. As the femme fatale, she does not get punished at the end of the narrative (as in most classic Hollywood film noir), but instead journeys through the film with a sexualized performance, ultimately emerging as the victorious figure. This is a rare feat for Hindi cinema, to have a woman enter the space of masculinity with confidence and then participate in an intriguing plot to get all the money. As a singer in the band, she is independent, making her own decisions. Her final collaboration with the

Shiuly (*center,* Tejaswini Kolhapur) as the femme fatale in *Paanch.* Courtesy Tutu Sharma.

policeman implicates the forces of legality as an extension of the crime world. Within the classic structure of Hindi cinema, *Paanch* establishes many feats as it breaks the narrative codes of what is socially acceptable.

Paanch journeys into areas of urban life unaddressed by given generic structures. It flouts certain conventions of Hindi cinema in order to create an expressionistic tapestry on urban life. This is neither a perfect portrait nor a falsification of urban life. *Paanch* is a film that is struggling to articulate something that has not yet been captured within the Bombay film industry. It does not offer us a causal narrative, nor does it suggest a way out of the depraved form of urban living that affects the lives of the film's protagonists. What makes *Paanch* interesting is its desire to flout norms and taboos. The victory of the femme fatale within a cinematic practice that has always morally coded women is the most striking feature of the film. *Paanch* does not exist as an alternative form but makes a conscious attempt to break out of the generic dominance within popular culture.

The Encounters of the Street in *Chameli*

Sudhir Mishra's *Chameli* offers the experience of the Bombay street through an intense portrayal of one night. Chameli (played by Kareena Kapoor) is a prostitute who walks the streets. On a fateful rainy night, she encounters an investment banker who is stranded because his car has broken down. Contact between the two leads to an unusual connection, drawing them into a vortex of subterranean violence that tells a story of desperation, sex work, underworld encounter killings, transsexuality, and police brutality. Instead of mounting the density of the city, Mishra creates a simulated architectural design of the street that combines pillars, arches, streetlights, and an open corridor. In this architectural mise-en-scène, memories and the fleeting encounters of the night, innocence and the bewildering forces of the street, and dim lighting and the dazzling expressiveness of Chameli all combine to produce an unusual mood.

Aman (played by Rahul Bose) is introduced as a slightly melancholic, impatient, and naive man whose comfortable existence as a corporate executive does not prepare him for what he will go through when he meets Chameli. Chameli is a seasoned prostitute who walks with confidence and has an irreverent impishness about her. The film spatially contrasts the lives of the two protagonists. Aman's first-person narrative, as he navigates through his office, a bathroom, and a nightclub party, is laced with a desire to transcend his melancholic disposition, the cause for which is revealed later in the film. A woman sings at the nightclub as Aman laments the life he lives, surrounded by mediocre, boring, and incompetent people. We see Aman standing next to a window that reveals the force of the downpour outside. The rain provides the transition to Chameli's quarters and becomes the metaphor to signal the stormy nature of the night ahead. Chameli and her friends live in a claustrophobic space that has peeling walls and a run-down, shabby look. As the prostitutes talk about their nighttime experiences, someone from the street calls out for Chameli, but she refuses to go down. A man named Nayak wants Chameli, but she refuses to go to him because he is ill and could infect her. The reference to AIDS is deliberately understated.

Aman's car stops dead in the middle of a street as he is returning from a party. He gets out of the car and runs to a covered arcade area for shelter from the rain. Chameli, who is waiting here for customers, assumes Aman is a prospective client and walks up to offer her services. Aman shirks away, leaving Chameli in a listless state, as she has not yet earned any money this night. However, the two soon start chatting and sharing their life experiences, some true, some false. Their conversation

Aman (Rahul Bose) and Chameli (Kareena Kapoor) in *Chameli* (2003). Courtesy Pritish Nandy Communications.

is constantly interrupted by various elements of the night—a cop who wants to collect extortion money from the pimp under whom Chameli works, a boy on a cycle selling cigarettes and tea, a transvestite and his lover, and pimps and hoodlums who are looking for Chameli.

Throughout the night, Aman and Chameli reminisce about their lives and get to know each other. The conversation has an existential quality driven by each person's perceptions and personal revelations. Each character perceives the other through circulating stereotypes. As the conversation continues, Mishra subverts the moral discourse of tragedy associated with the stereotypical prostitute narrative of Hindi cinema. Underscoring the melodramatic power of tragic circumstances as a way to explain women's entry into sex work, Chameli narrates three different stories, to explain her own entry into sex work, and then trivializes these same three stories, admitting that tragic stories help her get more money from her clients. Mishra, however, does not leave us with this subversion of a popular image of the cinematic prostitute. The film develops an ambivalence about Chameli's past in an interesting way that is revealed briefly during a memory sequence while she is hiding with Aman in a shack. It is this typically urban experience of a constant play of complex pasts and memories triggered by the intensity of the night that makes *Chameli* unusual within the generic form of Hindi cinema. The past is not a site for a causal explanation for the present, but is something that keeps intruding into the present in sudden flashes. Aman's memories are also impressionistically encapsulated in flashes, as he tells Chameli about his pregnant wife, their romance, her fear of cockroaches and dislike of the city, and her final death in a car accident on a rainy night.

The street is a typically urban space where strangers brush past each other, where violence can suddenly snowball into something spectacular, and where memories exist to refract everyday life. If the dominant iconography of the street in urban literature is that of the street as a space of consumption and distraction, to be patrolled through surveillance (Crouch, 161), then *Chameli* moves away from this iconography to create a new iconography of street. The two protagonists embody the street through traces of intimacy, memories, and a fleeting sensuality of the body. Mishra stages the street in a stylized manner in order to trigger memories for both protagonists. Inventively intruding into the nar-

Chameli (Kareena Kapoor) in *Chameli*. Courtesy Pritish Nandy Communications.

rative as fragmented flashes from the past, memories live alongside the present in the midst of a strange encounter between two people. The street becomes the zone for a process of engaging with two members of the urban crowd, each inhabiting and embodying different kinds of spatial practices. Sudhir Mishra's set design helps create the inner lanes of the fountain area, the space behind the Gothic façade. Chameli's relationship to the streets is born out of her profession, making her embody the language of the street differently than Aman. When the two protagonists are taken to the police station, the power dynamics of the city emerge through conversations, police negligence, deals, and the sound of encounter-killing gunshots. The night moves on, and the two protagonists part company in the morning. A prostitute and a corporate executive have spent a whole night together, carving for themselves a new kind of interaction and conversation in the street.

Chameli is neither a romantic film nor a film that wants to present the city as dark and ruinous. The interesting thing about the film is that it actively shies away from a resolution, allowing spectators the chance to experience something new in the city. The film does not follow a generic pattern. Neither is it an ensemble genre like *Paanch*. Rather, it offers a surprisingly quasi-existential experience of the city street as a space where individuals can carve out values and questions about life as they inhabit different urban worlds. The larger experience and context of the city unfolds in the form of cameo figures, the police station where the protagonists are taken, the nightclubs, and the encounter killings. Chameli's mark is its evocative exploration of the night street experience to stage the context of a changing city in all its diversity.

Revenge and the Everyday in *Ek Haseena Thi*

Sri Ram Raghavan's *Ek Haseena Thi* is in many ways a straightforward plot that uses many of the classic features of the revenge narrative. But unlike many other female revenge narratives, in which questions of moral subjugation and sexual humiliation are settled through the revenge plot in order to restore stability to the idea of romance and the family (for example, *Anjaam, Zakhmi Aurat, Khoon Bhari Mang*), *Ek Haseena Thi* journeys into the spatial and psychological meeting ground of the everyday.

Sarika (played by Urmila Matondkar) lives in Bombay as a single woman in an apartment block. The film begins with vignettes of her daily routine as she is shown watching TV, painting her nails, lounging around after her bath, talking on the phone, and moving around aimlessly in the house. Overtures by a male neighbor are a source of constant irritation for Sarika. This mini portrait of Sarika's life reveals the ordinariness of a middle-class single woman's existence in the big city. The film plays out the anxieties associated with neighbors and the insecurities of everyday life. Sarika's daily life is suddenly given a twist when she meets Karan (played by Saif Ali Khan), who has come to her office to buy an airline ticket. He asks her to go out on a date with him, but she refuses because of her own insecurities and lack of confidence. Then one day Karan nabs a few thieves after they snatch Sarika's purse. This draws Sarika to Karan and they soon start meeting regularly. Karan is allowed entry into her house, and the film spends considerable time developing their relationship.

Conversations, Sarika's display of her fear of rats, and the movement toward a passionate physical relationship are all deployed to carve a different kind of romance. This relationship emerges outside of marriage and, unlike other films where romantic intimacy is displaced in the narrative through songs and spectacular landscapes, *Ek HasSena Thi* firmly locates the romance in the very intimate spaces that Hindi cinema is

Publicity stills of *Ek Haseena Thi* (2004).

unable to handle. Thus, Sarika's home, her bedroom, her kitchen, and her daily experience of intimacy are presented with a calm confidence. This world of romance also holds the specter of the uncanny, quite vividly stoking the spectator's curiosity. This is particularly evident as the film begins with a Gothic noir image of Sarika in prison, and then moves into the flashback of the main story. We are made to wonder about the image, and the flashback is supposed to provide us with the plot. Karan's entry into Sarika's life is a chance encounter, presented like a random, routine story of many couples in the city. Sarika's experience as a single woman will prove to be dangerous, drawing her into the depths of a nightmare situation from which she will finally emerge victorious through revenge. The film shows how Karan uses Sarika in an underworld operation that leads to her false implication in a murder. In prison, Sarika is advised by Karan's lawyer to confess in court, an act that leads to a seven-year sentence for her. Raghavan subsequently narrates Sarika's experience in prison and her escape to seek revenge.

Ek Haseena Thi's uniqueness lies in the way the revenge plot is grafted onto a vivid urban landscape of iconic city spaces, department stores, crowds in Delhi's Jama Masjid area, alleys, claustrophobic jail spaces, hotel lobbies, and Sarika's home. The desire to mount the narrative as a journey that moves from Bombay to Delhi gives the film an unusual look, as Sarika's escape from prison is followed by walks, rickshaw rides, car travel, and leisure activities like shopping. Throughout this journey, Sarika is intelligently and methodically planning her revenge. Her movement in the film from a meek, subdued, and ordinary woman to an adventurous, revenge-seeking, and defiant woman is structured like a journey of empowerment that is both physical and psychological.

The early part of the film concentrates on Sarika's mundane life of limited movement within the city, as she moves from her apartment to her workplace and back. After her escape from prison, the film shows Sarika moving through a vast urban landscape with the confidence of a woman who can occupy and devour any space. This strategy is effective because the spatial expansion of her physical movements go hand in hand with her psychological journey toward a carefully worked out confidence. This strategy is also developed through editing techniques. The first part of the film has a slow pace as Sarika's daily life is excavated for the spectator. Nothing spectacular happens in this early section. The everyday is routine and uneventful. This world is suddenly disrupted by a turn of events that catapults Sarika onto a journey of destruction and self-discovery. It is the nature of this journey and its vivid mise-en-scène that make the film interesting.

Sarika's life in prison is developed in classic prison-film style, with the protagonist having to face a hard life not of her own making. The prison becomes the site where innocence is destroyed as Sarika is forced to confront a world of complicated social spaces. Her encounter with a bully, her relationship with the prison guards and other inmates, and her unusual bond with a female don create a choreography of urban encounters located within the prison. In prison, Sarika loses her fear of rats, and develops a physical and psychological strength. The prison performs the role of a microcosmic space of strangers that shapes the spatial journey Sarika will embark on. Raghavan's inventive play with the prison is developed through a subtle combination of character looks, small conflicts, Sarika's lonely reflections, flashbacks, and Sarika's conversations with Karan and the lawyer. As Karan's callous plot is unveiled, the strangers in the prison, a group of female outcasts, provide Sarika with a strange kind of comfort and strength.

The first person Sarika meets after she escapes from prison is a friend of the female don; this friend gives her a gun and ammunition. In order to find this friend, Sarika has to walk through alleys into the heart of Bombay, a space never before encountered by her when she was a workingwoman. Subsequently, Sarika leaves for Delhi, where she explores and navigates various parts of the city. During this time, her mind is working out the nature of her revenge. She stays in a hotel where Karan is also staying. He occupies the room next to her, but is unaware of her presence. Shots of the lobby area reveal this hotel space as a transit zone for strangers. As members of a crowd, each person moving through the lobby has an interesting story and life, and we are provided detailed access to the lives of some.

Raghavan also uses stylized shots of flyovers, both at ground level and through aerial perspectives, to mark recent transformations in Delhi. The use of farmhouses, the airport, the old city near Jama Masjid, and Connaught Place gives the second half of the film a spatial identity distinctly different from Bombay. Crime and the journey of crime bring all these spaces together. The police function as detectives in the film, but even here Raghavan creates a complex web of characters who convey their suspicions and feelings through subtle but expressive looks. An unwritten respect and bond develop between a female cop and Sarika, something that is settled only at the end of the film, when Sarika surrenders to the police. .

Sarika leaves Karan chained in a cave full of rats in Tuglakabad just before she surrenders. This graphic mounting of death by someone who began her journey in the film as an insecure and timid woman becomes significantly empowering in narrative terms. For Sarika, nothing matters after this event, and she makes her way back to prison, her future uncertain. The exhilaration in the film lies in the way Sarika draws us into a journey of revenge where the navigation of urban space becomes critical to the unfolding of the revenge plan. In narrative terms, the destruction of her innocence and her forced venture into unfamiliar terrain gives the film a mise-en-scène that is new for Sarika and for the spectator. As urban space expands in the film, Sarika is endowed with a new kind of knowledge as the city emerges both as character and as a space for her psychological empowerment.

Looking Ahead, Looking Back

All the three films discussed in this chapter subvert some kind of prevailing trope of popular cinema. In this act of subversion, what unites the three films is their use of women as major protagonists. *Paanch* moves against the grain of male friendship and its melodramatic pronouncements, as is generally depicted in popular cinema. The language of friendship and its emotional reservoir of heroic sacrifice, estrangement and reunion, and pleasurable camaraderie are twisted beyond recognition. The female protagonist has the upper hand who achieves her victory through a carefully planned-out plot that depends on the destruction of male friendship. In so doing, the image of the female vamp and her punishment in popular narratives is also reinvented. Similarly, in *Chameli*, as I have shown, the dominant representation of the prostitute/courtesan is subverted by a woman who questions the very premise of tragedy associated with sex work. In *Ek Haseena Thi*, female revenge unfolds as a journey that does not end in fulfillment or the reestablishment of the family and romance. Revenge ends in an ambivalent future but makes a single woman feel empowered through her ability to navigate a diversity of urban spaces.

All three films use urban space inventively to craft a cinematic archive that is refreshingly different. As a form of fringe cinema, these low-budget films exist on the periphery of popular cinema. Unique in their form, style, and purpose, fringe films depict an unstable urban world where resolutions are not easily found or even desirable. Perhaps this will be the beginning of a different kind of journey into the cinematic city, a journey that must never fail to surprise us.

Looking back at the architecture of my narrative in this book, I would reiterate that the power and insights of the cinematic city as a mode addressing the issues of the day is one of the more interesting features of Bombay cinema. In the exploration of the cinematic city, *Bombay Cinema* charts a series of journeys into both the practice of cinema and the urban experience in India. I have argued that for the "angry man" in *Deewar,* the appeal is to a sense of loss of the early visions of nationalism, the dreams of equality and redistribution, and the end of familial solidarity that freedom promised. As the city became the typical space in which this critique was mounted, the narrative of the "national" lost its sense of stability. It must be stressed that films like *Deewar* were hugely popular and addressed widespread social transformations of the period. In later editions of anger in the city, as in *Baazigar,* the "national" recedes as a necessary point of dialogue; instead, we witness the logic of violence taking on a tactile form in a city unhindered by moral claims. In the figure of the tapori, the relationship to the larger context of "nationalism" and "secularism" is negligible. The tapori's street-rebel persona moves through the city using gesture, symbol, and comic performance. Some of these gestures are clearly taken from African American styles in the United States and then combined with the *Bambayya* street language. Issues of morality and justice are negotiated through a marginal youth subculture outside the periphery of the new consumption space that emerged in the 1990s.

Earlier distinctions between the heroine and the vamp served to mark the domains of purity/excess, national/foreign, sexual order and disorder. By the 1990s, the new heroine adopted an aggressive sexualized display that rendered the old distinctions problematic. This new sexual excess was, of course, within a new commodity economy of globalization where display and spectacle held out possibilities of global consumption and mobility. Sexual independence goes hand in hand with an emphasis on elite lifestyles.

The other side of this consumption experience has been the emergence of the panoramic interior in the family films, which show virtual urban spaces with affluent global families as reference points. In these films, marriage becomes the space for new tensions (as in the case of forced arrangements), and also the site for new displays of wealth and attention to detailed ritual. In the context of new insecurities and anxieties stemming from globalization, the family is seen as the marker of stability and ritual, but it is modernized and redeployed in the narrative.

The most striking development in the cinematic city after globalization has been the rise of films on the Bombay underworld. Here the city loses its abstract character, investing in mobile forms of violence that result in the destruction of subjectivity. The gangster films are significant in their deep engagement with the underworld. The new gangster films show a greater investment in forms of violence, shorn of the sociology of criminal behavior that was typical of movies like *Deewar* in the 1970s. Few people have direct access to the space of the underworld, but folklore circulating within the city of Bombay, the events, the killings, and the extortion rackets are all part of an everyday knowledge system that seems to have been captured *only* in cinema. We see a psychological exposition of the underworld in Ram Gopal Varma's *Satya*, in which Bhiku Mahatre is a charged soul, while Satya is a man with no past or family. The emergence of these characters on the margins of the city, imbricated within a vortex of violence, has been a significant narrative development in recent years. The gangster films retain an existential relationship to the characters; their location within the city is neither causally nor sociologically explained.

Women have finally started playing an important role in the cinematic city of fringe cinema. Perhaps this tiny but growing body of fringe cinema can lead to a different landscape of the cinematic city whose imaginary possibilities can never be fully exhausted.

The film industry in Bombay is large, churning out a range of seven hundred films a year, of which the films I deal with in this book are just a small part. It would be excessive to suggest that most films today deal with the urban, or that nationalist themes are now disappearing. Instead, *Bombay Cinema* follows Benjamin in generating "profane illuminations," in which aspects of the urban experience burst through fragments of the cinematic cities' recent past. As India moves unsurely into the next few decades of globalization, often touted as pathbreaking, the cinematic city of ruin may offer a window into its bleaker future.

Notes

Introduction

1. Unlike Hollywood cinema, popular Indian cinema did not emerge as a linear narrative based on cause and effect. Instead, creative work in the film industry was done within a framework of attractions based on musical, performative, and narrative elements. There is a clear indication of a sense-making mechanism operating here that has been referred to as "a circuit of communication, of narrative and performative intelligibility in the relationship between films and their audiences" (Vasudevan 2000, 7). This distinction between the Hollywood and the Indian film experience points to the need for a deeper understanding of "local" cinematic cultures, in which performative, musical, and linguistic idioms complicate the narrative form (8). The "circuit of communication" is nothing but a repetitive narrative that encompasses a polyglot multigenre ensemble that cannot be easily classified into distinct generic forms.

2. In the case of predominantly agrarian societies like India and China, the negotiation with the non-urban is particularly interesting. For instance, in India large slums in cities like Bombay and Calcutta create "mimic villages" that are rarely like the original, "but the re-construction can be an impressive cultural enterprise" (Nandy 1998).

3. Ashis Nandy describes Indian popular cinema as the articulated expression of the "slum's point of view." The slum is a metaphor for popular cinema because both negotiate everyday survival in the city and both are "low" forms of the modern. "Studying popular film is studying Indian modernity at its rawest, its crudities laid bare by the fate of traditions in contemporary life and arts" (Nandy 1998, 7). Nandy sees the slum as a mix of ethnicities, the "unintended city," that was not part of the "master plan," but a space that emerges as the other of the official plan (1998, 7). The point here is not to resort to a Western–non-Western grid of distinctions, but to map out the differences that form the imaginative landscape of the urban in Bombay cinema.

4. South Asia has been increasingly linked to the capitalist world economy since the eighteenth century. The colonial encounter introduced a wide range of temporal

and spatial transformations, as well as commodity cultures and advertising. What is distinctive about the contemporary constellation many have called *globalization* is a new regime of visuality and consumption, informed by constant acceleration. In the history of independent India, the 1990s will be seen as the decade of restructuring, as liberalization in trade and the opening of the market ushered in a new era. Structural adjustment eased regulatory mechanisms on international trade and the movement of commodities. The economy witnessed rapid privatization of government-owned companies. With India entering the World Trade Organization regime, multinational companies entered the Indian market. After globalization, the economy obviously experienced major changes.

5. The Nehruvian model argued that a state-centered accumulation strategy based on import substitution would lead to rapid national growth. Thirty years of import substitution had cut off India from global commodity and consumption culture. Public culture in independent India tended to be hostile to spectacular consumption, which was partly the legacy of anticolonial struggle and partly the regime's own rhetoric (Sundaram 1997).

6. For more information on globalization in India, see Sundaram (2004).

7. The notable exception is B. R. Ambedkar, who was one of India's preeminent lower-caste *(Dalit)* leaders. He saw the village as the repository of "localism," which prevented lower castes from transcending their place in the caste hierarchy. Ambedkar called the village "a den of ignorance, narrow mindedness and communalism" (13: 62). It was the lack of anonymity in the village that made Ambedkar such a critic of its routines, wherein the "untouchable" was clearly marked and identified by the people of the village (5: 22).

8. While nineteenth-century narratives addressed a small print-public, the Gandhian period changed the addressee of Indian nationalism to include the majority of the population.

9. Partha Chatterjee has called the Nehru-Gandhi strategy against colonial rule the "passive revolution," which, he argues, is the generalized form of the transition from colonial to postcolonial rule in the twentieth century. Chatterjee also argues that anticolonial elites preferred to wage a protracted "war of maneuver" that included compromises and alliances with traditional elites rather than an instantaneous "war of position" (1993).

10. For orthodox Indian Marxists, "the party" emerged as the substitute subject-object of history, within which the negotiation with daily life operated through a narrow ideological prism. The main debates revolved around the mode of production and the nature of the state (Patnaik 1972; Desai 1975; Dutt 1955; Singh 1990). The work of historian D. D. Kosambi stands out as an exception within the Marxist tradition. Less concerned with fitting Indian society into a preconceived schema, Kosambi showed a remarkable concern for the dynamic histories of South Asia, often breaking from the predictions of classical Marxism (1965).

11. India never saw the independent intellectual space that emerged after 1956 in Europe and that pushed varied ex-party thinkers like E. P. Thompson (1966) and Henri Lefebvre (1991) to look at issues of daily life outside old-style structural narratives. The political in India was very narrowly conceived around issues of the state, despite the fact that the "state was of a curious marginality to the fundamental processes of everyday life of society" (Kaviraj 2000, 62). Commenting on the

durability, intensity, and complexity of daily-life forms on the subcontinent, despite changes in political structure, Sudipta Kaviraj suggests that the political, as defined in our modern language, "is distributed across levels and layers of the social formation in a very unfamiliar manner" and cannot be directly attributed to state structures or political regimes (2000, 42). Yet this was never the focus of Marxism in India.

12. The Indian National Congress was once the preeminent nationalist party. It led the country's struggle for independence and came to power immediately after independence under the prime ministership of Jawaharlal Nehru. In 1969, the Congress split, with a faction led by Nehru's daughter, Indira Gandhi, emerging as the dominant faction. It was this faction that ruled the country from 1970 to 1977, at which time it was defeated.

13. The Emergency saw the emergence of a coterie around the son of Indira Gandhi, then the Congress prime minister. This coterie effectively functioned as an inner cabinet, running the daily affairs of the regime.

14. After its defeat in 1977, the Congress returned to power in 1980 and retained power intermittently thereafter.

15. Through juxtapositions that combine the new with the old, fashion with death, antiquity with modernity, modernity with myth, and fashion with the commodity, Benjamin's methodology focuses on tracing the past within the contemporary (Frisby, 212).

16. It is important to point out that Nandy's insights often stem from a position that evokes "critical tradition" as a counter to modernity. What emerges in the process are fleeting encounters with modernity that are unique among the various voices in postcolonial India. See chapter 1 for a critical discussion of Nandy.

17. A major part of my primary research comes from detailed interactions with professionals in the film industry over the course of the last decade. Some of this research went into a twelve-part television series on Bombay cinema that I codirected with Shikha Jhingan. The series, titled *The Power of the Image*, was subsequently broadcast on Indian television.

18. Serious academic writing on Indian cinema is a recent development, barely two decades old. While work on auteur filmmakers such as Satyajit Ray and Ritwik Ghatak had been done earlier, popular cinema originally received scant attention from critics and academics alike. Always dismissed as the falsifying mechanism of an underdeveloped aesthetic form, elitist criticism became the norm to judge the popular (Vasudev and Lenglet 1983; Dasgupta 1991). Chidananda Dasgupta's *The Painted Face* was one such important study that sought to establish and reveal the "premodern," irrational, and unrealistic form of popular Hindi cinema. For Dasgupta, popular cinema needed to be countered by a realistic cinema that would generate a rational form of perception. For an interesting study of Dasgupta and Ashis Nandy as opposing voices in the debate on issues of popular culture, see Vasudevan 2000, 4–6. What Dasgupta sees as premodern and irrational is precisely what makes popular cinema interesting for Nandy.

19. In using the term "iconic," Vasudevan is drawing from a category that emerged from Indian art historical writing. Iconicity relates to a form of condensation of symbolic and mythic material in the construction of the frame (Vasudevan, "You Cannot Live in Society—and Ignore It" 1995).

20. Here Vasudevan's use and definition of the tableau is drawn from the work of both Peter Brooks and Roland Barthes.

21. In the field of film studies, Hollywood cinema tends to get classified according to genres. Then there are the canonical film movements of the world: Russian avant-garde, French new wave, Italian neorealism, German expressionism, etc. However, Third World cinema is usually studied or classified along the lines of a "national" cinema. It was to try and escape the boundaries of such a classification that I chose the city as the vantage point for my investigation of Bombay cinema. This is precisely why my book is not titled "Indian cinema."

1. Rage on Screen

1. Salim Khan, in discussion with the author, April 1995.

2. I am using a broad definition of *psychosis* to refer to the figure on-screen. Psychosis is usually defined as a major mental disorder identified by seriously disturbed behavior and lack of contact with reality.

3. As Raymond Williams states, "Our thinking about tragedy is important because it is a point of intersection between tradition and experience, and it would certainly be surprising if the intersection turned out to be a coincidence" (Williams 1966, 15).

4. I will elaborate on this in a later section.

5. I am referring to the films of Raj Kapoor and Guru Dutt. Both these directors celebrated the state of homelessness to present their critique of the inequality and crisis of cities in newly independent India.

6. For an interesting and fairly detailed account of the different ways in which urban development in Bombay has adversely affected the lives of the poor, see Guha Bannerjee, 100–120. Guha Bannerjee argues that the history of urban development in Bombay shows that, while in the past "it echoed the voices of the rulers—in the early years, the British and their Indian collaborators," in recent years, local finance and industrial capital have played the major role. However, in the post-independence period, workers and a growing middle class have been demanding more space in the city. While politicians and urban managers have pretended to respond to this growing demand, in reality they have continued to ally themselves with business and commercial interests. Guha Bannerjee reveals, through a detailed analysis of three different projects, the process that goes into the making of the "unintended city."

7. For a fresh new look at the memories of the Emergency, see Emma Tarlo's *Unsettling Memories* (2003). Focusing on the forced sterilization and slum clearances conducted during the Emergency, Tarlo weaves in a web of information gathered from anthropological and archival material. Tarlo explores the experiences of men and women who became the primary targets of sterilization and demolition drives.

8. To be sure, the crisis of the regime did not begin in the 1970s. In the late 1960s, the Congress suffered an erosion of power in regional centers. There was also a distinct radicalization of Leftist politics, with the emergence of Left governments in Bengal and Kerala. In 1967, a new splinter from one of India's communist parties (CPI-M) emerged, starting an armed uprising in Naxalbari in northern Bengal. The movement spread to different parts of India and faced strong repression. Sympathetic

to the Chinese Cultural Revolution, this stream was part of the global upsurge from 1968 to 1973 (Bannerjee 1980; Dasgupta 1974).

9. Salim Khan and Javed Akhtar together wrote scripts, dialogues, and screenplays using the screen name "Salim Javed." They wrote some of the most enduring films of the 1970s. Their popularity and stature allowed them to command a fee that was sometimes higher than those of the stars acting in the films they wrote. Some of their best-known films are *Deewar* (1974), *Sholay* (1975), *Trishul* (1978), *Zanjeer* (1973), *Kala Patthar* (1979), and *Yadon Ki Baraat* (1973). Bachchan's rise to stardom has often been attributed to the power of the scripts penned by Salim and Javed.

10. Shyam Benegal, in discussion with the author, May 1997.

11. An ancient pilgrimage center, Allahabad acquired modern-city status as an important railway junction, a center of higher education, and the political home of the Nehru family.

12. What was unique about Bachchan in comparison with his predecessors was his novel use of space, an economy of words in his dialogue, a restraint in his anger, and an immense and total control over his body. It is this resistant posturing through an evocation of a new set of performative codes that seemed to mark the "beginning" of the "angry man" image and a rupture with the romantic persona of the former superstar, Rajesh Khanna.

13. *Suta* is the caste name for the community of charioteers in the time of the *Mahabharata*. *Sutas* were low-caste people.

14. *Kshatriya* is the name for the warrior caste. It is a powerful group in the caste hierarchy, second only to the *Brahmins*. The *Kshatriya* caste is primarily a northern Indian phenomenon.

15. Both Ashis Nandy and Sudhir Kakkar agree that Karna is the underlying myth of the Bachchan phenomenon.

16. In Nandy's words, "*Deewar*'s hero is the prototypical urban man, more at home in slums than in palaces, fighting for, losing, but posthumously winning his mother's acceptance. It is a significant endorsement for an identity inextricably linked to South Asia's discovery of the modern metropolis. The hero finds for the viewers mitigating circumstances that absolve the metropolis of its moral culpability" (1997, 26).

17. Yash Chopra was born in 1932 in Lahore. He began his film career as an assistant director. He collaborated with his brother B. R. Chopra on several productions, including *Waqt* (1965), until their split in 1973, when Yash Raj Films was launched. Two of Chopra's best-known Bachchan films of the 1970s, *Deewar* (1975) and *Trishul* (1978), were written by the scriptwriter duo, Salim Javed. In the 1990s, Chopra metamorphosed into a new kind of director and his films started doing extremely well with the Indian diaspora around the world. Today, Yash Raj Films literally dominates the landscape of the film industry as a powerful production house, because of their success at the box office and their access to the major stars. Many films are now commissioned to outsiders under the Yash Raj banner. Yash Raj Films is also one of the most successful distributors of Indian DVDs today.

18. Madhava Prasad treats this flashback as an unofficial story lodged within the official narrative. The flashback begins when Ravi calls his mother onstage to receive the award being given to him. Once onstage, his mother is "distracted by a memory." Since the subsequent unfolding of the narrative is linked to the mother's memory, it acquires the quality of an unofficial story (Prasad, 148).

19. Nandy sees in the recent invocations of Karna, "a remarkable testimony to the way a living myth in an epic culture—as against myths in cultures that have epics—can act as an alternative record of, and commentary upon, the shifting psychological contours of a culture" (1997, 21). Nandy presents the South Asian experience as derivative of *epics*, rather than as a historical vision. History, says Nandy, "tames time in a manner that myths, legends and epics do not. In a massified society, it gives certitudes about the past and thus, a secular sense of continuity previously ensured only by faith" (1997, 3). Nandy sees in history the projection of absolute truths, which are invoked to perpetrate violence and killings in the modern world (1997, 3). While Nandy may have a point here, the clear opposition between myth and history seems sweeping and even problematic. Nandy, however, tends to reduce history to *ideology*, rather than to a set of complex practices that sometimes resist the violent architecture of metanarratives. The problem in modernity has been the attempt by the discourse of the *historical* to offer a series of simple, rational renderings of social and cultural practices. This is the moment of ideology that Nandy conflates with history itself. His movement to place myth outside history would make sense if history were purely an ideological movement. Myth as a belief that is embedded in social and cultural practices can be read as speaking to the historical, albeit shorn of its ideological moment.

20. I will elaborate on this later.

21. Vijay is offered money just before he makes his transition to criminality by the same man (Iftekhar, the head of one of the underworld gangs). Iftekhar throws the money on the table. Vijay reminds him about his childhood and how he still refuses to accept money that is thrown at him. Childhood images keep coming back to Vijay in his adult life.

22. When Ravi is looking for a job, he meets a young unemployed youth. Ravi feels sorry for the youth and gives up his own job for him.

23. In one of the childhood sequences, Ravi is drawn to children singing the same song at a school assembly meeting. Ravi becomes a good student at school only because his brother sacrifices his own childhood to ensure an education for Ravi.

24. Barthes draws on Kevin Leach's work to elaborate on the city as a place of marked and unmarked elements.

25. In *Deewar*, there is significant discussion concerning the badge when Vijay talks with Rahim Chacha, who informs Vijay about the sacred power of the number 786 in Islam. The sacred meaning of 786, combined with its everyday functionality as an identification number for Vijay, enhances the role that the badge plays throughout the film. Interestingly, the same number was used in Manmohan Desai's film, *Coolie* (1983), in which Bachchan plays the role of a Muslim worker.

26. Today, Shahrukh Khan is Hindi cinema's biggest star. *Baazigar* was Khan's debut film. After the success of *Baazigar*, Khan played the psychotic in *Darr* and in *Anjaam*. With his rising popularity and star status, Khan later reinvented his persona as a successful upmarket icon of the post-globalization period. His stardom today is legendary. Bachchan and Khan have often been compared for their ability to sway the box office.

27. The director duo Abbas Mastan has been in the industry for a while. Known for their fascination with thrillers (*Aitraaz* 2004; *Badshah* 1999; *Humraaz* 2002) and with characters with a dark side, the duo has made a number of successful films at the box office.

28. In 1993, following the demolition of a mosque in Ayodhya, the city of Bombay was torn apart by pogroms against the large Muslim minority instigated by the Hindu nationalist Shiv Sena party.

29. This is where the "circuit of communication" between the film industry and the audience (defined by Vasudevan 2000) faces a disruption.

30. This production of repetitive elements in Bombay cinema derives its principal force from the codes of melodrama. The narratives are usually structured around a set of social and cultural codes or signs, loosely put together to form what is colloquially referred to as the "formula." These codes repeat themselves within specific historical configurations. In other words, the "formula" is in a dynamic relationship with historical codes of representation at any given time. The use of the word "formula" here is deliberate as the phrase is part of the film public's perception of film texts.

31. *Zanjeer* is the first of Bachchan's vendetta films. In this film, however, Bachchan, a police inspector, is part of the establishment. With *Deewar*, Bachchan crosses over to the other side and becomes an outlaw.

32. This is again drawing on Nandy and Das's argument.

33. The psychotic image coexists with other images in Bombay cinema today. In the Bachchan era, the "angry man" narrative was overwhelming in its power. Today, this older iconic image has imploded into various fragments, the psychotic being one of them. It is therefore the critic's task to provide an allegorical reading of this new constellation.

34. Williams makes the same point in a different context.

2. The Rebellious Tapori

1. In both *Ghulam* and *Rangeela,* the actor Aamir Khan plays the role of the tapori. Khan's screen persona, right from the beginning of his career, was that of a soft, romantic, youthful hero popular with teenage audiences. In the two tapori films discussed here, Khan displays a disavowal of his other persona through a body discourse of masculinity.

2. Hindustani is a vernacular blend of the official languages of Hindi and Urdu, combined with several local dialects. Urdu developed under the Mughal Empire in South Asia (1200–1800), with Arabic, Hindi, Turkish, and Sanskrit influences. Today, it is the national language of Pakistan and one of the twenty-three national languages in India. The role of the British government in fueling the language divide during the nineteenth century is now an established fact documented by several historians. Vasudha Dalmia shows the role of the colonial administration in using local intra-elite conflict to ensure a split in Hindustani, which led to the creation of Urdu and Hindi as the separate languages of Muslims and Hindus (146–221). While encouraging and patronizing both Hindi and Urdu, the government often played one against the other. By perceiving Indian society as irreconcilably divided on the basis of religious differences, colonial discourses shaped the emerging sectional and communal identities of Hindus and Muslims. Historical commonalities and shared domains between Hindus and Muslims weakened as a result (King 1994, 17). Emerging Hindu nationalism and colonial policy were working within the context of a rapidly growing print culture, which generated several voluntary language associations. These

associations played a key role in promoting Hindi and the Devnagari script. Many of the members of these associations worked closely with the colonial administration to ensure Hindi's role in the educational policies of the government. In Northern U.P., which was the center of the Hindi movement, political victory was attained when the government declared Hindi equal to Urdu at the end of the nineteenth century.

3. By the 1930s, the divisions between the Hindi- and Urdu-language elites became firmly entrenched as a political battle (Rai, 262). The Bombay talkies begin in 1931, right in the middle of this polarized conflict.

4. Javed Akhtar claims that most of the writers still write in Urdu, and his own scripts are converted to the Devnagari script later, for the actors and actresses (Kabir, 49).

5. *Amar Akbar Anthony* is the story of three brothers who are separated as children and subsequently adopted by families of different religions. Anthony, the tapori in the film, is adopted by a priest and raised Christian. In this chapter, I do not focus on *AAA* only because the film has many other themes woven into it. To focus only on the tapori's character would not do justice to the film.

6. In the case of other urban figures like the "angry man," the speech and diction, the prose and quality of the hero is markedly urbane. Elsewhere, I have argued specifically about Bachchan's trans-class aura in the "angry man" films, generated through his body language and speech (Mazumdar 2000). In the "angry man" films, dialogues have a poetic quality, which is missing from the tapori's lines.

7. Dilapidated buildings with small rooms connected to a shared balcony. A *chawl* of five to seven stories can have almost a thousand people living in it.

8. While Singh's description of the street appears like a utopian metaphor for the cinema, Ravi Vasudevan has shown how the same street was also conjured up as a dystopian space in the 1950s. The street was the site of uprootedness, instability, and criminality, particularly in crime melodramas like *Aar Paar* (1954) and *CID* (1956). Even in *Awara*, the street is where the hero, Raj, meets the criminal, Jagga (Vasudevan 2000).

9. Trained as a civil engineer and the former owner of a video store, Ram Gopal Varma made his entry into the film industry by choice. Known as a maverick filmmaker whose films are often compared with Hollywood films, Varma made his mark in the industry not only through his creative work, but also through his business strategy of running a corporation of young filmmakers making slightly offbeat and low-budget films like *Satya* (1998), often without big stars. Varma's current outfit is known as the Factory, under whose aegis several films are made every year in Hindi and Telegu. The Factory also commissioned Sri Ram Raghavan's *Ek Haseena Thi* (2004), discussed in the concluding chapter of this book. *Rangeela* was Varma's first Hindi film. For a discussion of two gangster films directed by Varma, see chapter 5.

10. For an extended discussion of the flâneur, see chapter 3.

11. Performing artists and actors who formed the backdrop of the film narrative, playing minor cameo roles as part of a crowd or other such situations, were called "extras." In the last two decades, the unionization of these professionals has led to the creation of a new title: junior artists.

12. Taporis tend to celebrate the present through style and gesture. For instance, in *Ghulam* the tapori's memory is deliberately repressed.

13. In the early 1990s, when the stock exchange was booming in India, a number of brokers and bankers siphoned off public money from government securities trans-

actions to speculate in the market. Harshad Mehta was one of the key figures in the biggest financial scandal in India's history, which resulted in the resignations of several senior officials and ministers. Thousands of investors, attracted to rocketing stock prices driven higher by the scam, lost fortunes when the fraud was discovered and the market collapsed. Following public outcry, the government set up the Janakiraman Committee to probe the scam, which broke out between April 1991 and June 1992. At least ten commercial banks, including Standard Chartered Bank, the SBI, and National Housing Bank, an RBI subsidiary, were hit by the scam.

14. Anjum Rajabali, in discussion with the author, April 2003, Bombay.

15. In *Deewar*, Vijay is the uneducated but older brother. While the conversation does not favor one brother over the other, Ravi counters Vijay's pompous declaration of his wealthy lifestyle with the statement that he (Ravi) has the mother, thereby declaring his moral superiority. In *Parinda*, Karan and Kishen have a similar conversation on a motorboat. Here Karan (the educated brother, like Ravi) retains the upper hand. *Ghulam*, however, tilts the balance clearly in Sidhu's favor.

16. The Shiv Sena (Shiva's army) began in the early 1970s as a chauvinist movement against non-Maharashtrians in the city of Bombay. Initially used by the elite to attack the Left labor movement, the Shiv Sena metamorphosized into an aggressive Hindu nationalist party in the 1980s, playing a key role in the pogroms against Muslims during the 1992–93 Bombay riots. For a longer discussion on the Shiv Sena, see chapter 5.

17. Anjum Rajabali, in discussion with the author, April 2003, Bombay.

18. Partly because actor Aamir Khan plays both roles. However, even the body gestures of the two screen characters are similar.

3. Desiring Women

1. The vamp is usually pitted against the heroine. The film industry makes a distinction between vamps and heroines even for the actresses. Actresses playing vamp roles can never be the lead "heroine" of a film.

2. Wilson argues that both the Left and the Right have participated in creating a long history of anti-urbanism, which has adversely affected the way we view women's relationship to cities. Many feminists have also been hostile to the city, focusing on issues of safety, crime, and other dangers women might face in the city. This has led to patronizing discourses and policies regarding women's place in the city.

3. Ravi Vasudevan has suggested that the cinema of the 1950s deployed techniques through which film narratives tried to contain the issue of female desire, particularly in films where the woman is most directly situated in relation to desire. In his analysis of *Andaaz* (1949), Vasudevan argues that the "film uses its woman character to set limits to the image of modernity." However, the complexity of the narrative enables transgressive elements to filter through as an alternative to the dominant ideology embedded in the film narrative (Vasudevan 1993, "You Cannot Live in Society—and Ignore It").

4. Translation taken from Cooper and from Griffith.

5. Needless to say, this imagination has no base in Indian history. As in all ancient cultures, the courtesans—who were independent professionals and prostitutes driven by poverty—have roots traceable to South Asia's distant past. For some, it was a

caste occupation, often sanctioned by religion and social acceptance. Classical literature also acknowledged female sexuality, though a fear of this female power began to manifest itself from about the fifth century BC, apparently to reinforce the hierarchical structure of caste society and the increased social control over upper-caste women (Srinivasan; Mukta; Altekar).

6. There have been other images of sexualized, scheming women in India's cultural past. But the westernized vamp in cinema seems to be linked to the emergence of modern Indian nationalism.

7. A direct address is a common technique of Brechtian alienation and is also common in many devotional films.

8. I am drawing on Peter Brooks's definition of the tableau. For Brooks, the tableau compositionally organizes the character's/actor's attitudes and gestures, which, when "frozen for a moment, give, like an illustrative painting, a visual summary of the emotional situation" (48). The concept of the tableau has also been used in the context of popular Indian films of the 1950s (Vasudevan, "You Cannot Live in Society—and Ignore It").

9. The white sari also indicates simplicity, austerity, and purity. The white sari, however, is not the widow's symbol in southern India or in Maharashtra.

10. There are exceptions and conscious disruptions in the binary narrative of sexuality. In the film Caravan, for instance, the gypsy image of Aruna Irani as an aggressively sexual being does not fit into the binary logic being discussed here, since she is not presented as westernized. Some representations of stars like Sharmila Tagore, Babita, and Mumtaz also defy the binary logic. However, there still remains the issue of repetition and recurrence, which makes it possible to draw on the overall pattern for analysis rather than focus only on the disruptions.

11. As the work of Virilio (1977, 1994), Harvey (1990), and others point out, contemporary capitalism has a tendency toward the annihilation of space by time. Harvey calls this "temporal acceleration" and Virilio calls it the "logic of speed." For the Indian subcontinent, speed/temporal acceleration has emerged from the transformations unleashed by contemporary globalization.

12. A well-known fact about Indian cinema is that almost all the popular productions are musicals. While in the past, the song sequences were remotely linked to the story line, many of the songs today are shot and released before the film. They can be seen as part of countdown shows on television.

13. The narrative no longer displays an urge to link its overall movement to the songs. Song sequences are now played as independent entities within the film.

14. In recent years, there has been considerable work on speed. Some of the most interesting writing has come from French theorist Paul Virilio, who argues that a new vision machine emanates from the new temporal configurations. Virilio writes that in the new electronic space, time has been industrialized and is effectively simultaneous. A notion of "arrival without departure" informs his thesis. There are various problems with Virilio's somewhat flamboyant positions, but there is no doubt that the proliferation of new electronic technologies has transformed the nature of the image. Virilio can be critiqued for assuming a homogeneity of industrialized time on a world scale with something that he hints will be broken only by an apocalyptic crash of the network. This scenario is a violent abstraction when dealing with the diverse realities of Third World societies (1994, 1995).

15. There are some exceptions. Calcutta, which was the capital of British India

until 1911, had two well-known department stores, Whiteway Laidlaw and Hall & Anderson. Whiteway Laidlaw also sold goods via mail-order. In Bombay, there was Evans Fraser, an upmarket department store that was later called Handloom House. The aesthetic projection of these stores resembled that of Western stores, because the English set up these stores. After independence, the stores were shut down, as foreign-made goods became one of the primary targets of Indian nationalism. For a picture of the front window of Evans Fraser, see Mehrotra and Dwivedi, 226.

16. Throughout this period of the 1990s, censorship issues were being passionately debated in the media. The debate was polarized around issues of "obscenity and vulgarity" and the loss of "Indian culture."

17. The Miss World contest in India was mired in controversy throughout the decade of the 1990s. Opposition to the contest came from a range of political and social forces. While the commodification of the female body was the concern of some, others saw the contest as an affront to "Indian culture." Protests against the contest were sometimes violent.

18. Choreographers like Saroj Khan, Farah Khan, and Ganesh are now powerful players within the film industry. They also work very closely with fashion designers to work out the costumes for the dance sequences.

19. This argument is borrowed from Angela McRobbie's analysis of dance culture. While McRobbie looks at dance in a different context, her argument seems to hold for the ways in which contemporary dance sequences in Bombay films have carved out an entirely new space and disposition for the Indian heroine (McRobbie, 45).

20. Made in the style of the new family films of the 1990s, *Dilwale* was the biggest hit of 1995.

21. Karan Johar and Manish Malhotra, in discussion with the author, Bombay, November 2002.

22. Art director Sharmishtha Roy and dance choreographer Farha Khan, in discussion with the author, Bombay, November 2002.

23. It is perhaps counterproductive to trace an originary point in any analysis of fluid transitions, but such moments need to be tentatively discussed to substantiate one's claims. The point of rupture within the larger narrative seems to be *Tezaab* (1988), a film that introduced a new notion of space for the heroine's dances. In *Tezaab*, the heroine (played by Madhuri Dixit) is forced to dance on the stage by her father. The song "Ek Do Teen," which became a big hit, catapulted Madhuri Dixit to stardom. The dance number made a significant and novel use of space, creating a direct relationship between the dancer and the camera and evoking overt and clear reference to the dances of Helen (through the use of top-angle shots to capture a writhing body on the floor). Madhuri, however, was no vamp; she was instead the heroine, projected in a direct relationship to the audience, a crowd of spectators cheering the dance. Interestingly, the last part of the song shows Madhuri catwalking as she displays a range of clothes.

4. The Panoramic Interior

1. The genre of family films that I discuss in this chapter emerged in the 1990s as a form that addressed both a large audience in India and the diaspora across the world.

2. I use the word *panoramic* here with deliberation. The panorama was an early visual technology, prior to the birth of cinema. The panorama enabled fluid mobility across space and time, bringing the country to the town dweller and the past to the present. For the panoramic spectator, distance and space did not matter because the panorama offered "illusionist immersion" through sheer scale and immensity. This history of the panorama has become the metaphor for a kind of vision that is expansive and mobile. The cinema as the prime site for this mobility became the ideal vision machine for the expansive unfurling of the panoramic vision. Film also became the prime medium through which interior architecture could be given a larger-than-life image (Friedberg, 20–25).

3. Some of this was discussed in chapter 2.

4. The presence of television in public space has been traced back to as early as the postwar period in the United States (McCarthy).

5. The term *ambient television* is taken from Anna McCarthy's work on the role of television in public life.

6. The anxiety is expressed through the demand for removal of slums and hawkers by the middle class and the elite (Rajagopal, 91–113).

7. This was my experience when I went to interview a scriptwriter living in Andheri, Bombay.

8. For a vivid account of the French middle-class withdrawal into a comforting domestic world of consumption in the period of decolonization, see Kristen Ross.

9. These magazines include *Sunset Homes for Western Living* and *American House Today.*

10. "Indianness" is being defined here as a conservative and regressive ideology that seeks to construct a national identity through religious and cultural iconography that is largely Hindu. For an interesting account of how the film industry adapts Hollywood films through "Indianization," see Ganti, 281–300. For an account of the anxiety about loss of "Indian" values, particularly around the changing representation of women in the media after globalization, see Ghosh 1999, 233–59.

11. The recurring need to assert "Indianness" as a cultural value was first recognized by the advertising world. When foreign brands entered the Indian market in the 1990s, many Indian brands altered their advertising strategies to address the new situation (Mazzarella, 152). "Indianness" and globalization both became important to the image of the commodity. For instance, the Ericsson Mobility World (EMW) group, a powerful consumer electronics company in India, briefed its advertising agency to address both the sharp corporate value of its products and the issue of "Indianness" (157). "Indianness" was needed, but it had to be "world class." The focus here is to search for an identity, a consumer identity (159).

12. I am not suggesting a pre-given reality of urban life that cinema feeds into. On the contrary, I see the cinema as an essential component of the delirium of consumer display.

13. Publicity in the era of globalization is determined by an understanding of the importance of the visual in a world where images saturate our everyday lives. The entry of television, the transformation of urban space, the expansion of the Internet, the wide circulation of interior-design magazines, and the arrival of new technologies have made their mark on the film industry, shaping both its aesthetic impulse and its marketing strategy. The role of film publicity, which was important even in the past, has today reached an entirely different level. Rajesh Grover, the

head of *Endeavor*, a marketing company set up in 1998, suggests that publicity and marketing have traditionally represented only 5 percent to 10 percent of a film's success or failure at the box office. But today it determines 40 to 50 percent of a films success. Grover suggests that in the contemporary landscape, the media becomes a place for competitive promotion and marketing. The coming together of fashion designers, art directors, and choreographers is now part of this strategy to promote films. Rajesh Grover, in discussion with the author, April 2003.

14. Sharmishtha Roy, in discussion with the author, Bombay, November 2002.

15. For a short history of Bombay's set-design strategies, see Dwyer and Patel, 42–100.

16. Almost 30 percent of total production money is allocated for the sets of the family films. Sharmishtha Roy, in discussion with the author, Bombay, November 2002.

17. Ibid.

18. India has five major film-distribution territories; Bombay is the largest of these territories. Given the scale of diversity and the vast interiors of the country, audiences are often segmented and fragmented according to what the distribution network sees as culturally and socially specific. Therefore the A, B, and C centers have come to represent three different streams of audience composition for the distributors. The A centers constitute big metros such as Delhi, Bombay, Calcutta, Bangalore, Chennai, and other big cities. The B centers are the smaller towns, also known as the interiors, and the C centers are the places where a special group of films circulate (usually low-budget, semi-porn films). Among the A centers, Bombay has always been the biggest territory. In the 1990s, the overseas market became the biggest territory. This territory includes the United States, the United Kingdom, South Africa, and the Middle East. The Indian diaspora living abroad form the largest chunk of the overseas audience, thus pushing the film industry to respond to their tastes and desires.

19. The film *Taal* (Rhythm, Subhash Ghai, 2000) made 2 million rupees (about $44,000) in the overseas market, which is 50 percent more than what the film made in the domestic market.

20. Sooraj Barjatya is the son of Tarachand Barjatya, who set up the very successful production house called Rajshree Productions. Known for its conservatism and its promotion of the myth of the Hindu joint family, Sooraj Barjatya made three very successful films in the same tradition. His first was *Maine Pyar Kiya* (1989), followed by the big hit *Hum Apke Hain Kaun,* and then *Hum Sath Sath Hain* (1999). His most recent film, *Main Prem Ki Diwani Hoon* (2003), did not do so well.

21. Amit Khanna, interviewed in Mazumdar and Jhingan, "The Return of the Family" 1998.

22. Sharmishtha Roy, in discussion with the author, Bombay, November 2002. Also see Dwyer and Patel, 80–81.

23. Sharmishtha Roy, in discussion with the author, Bombay, November 2002.

24. Karan Johar is one of Bombay cinema's most successful directors today. Formerly an assistant director, then an actor, Johar has made several films under his company banner, Dharma Productions. Johar's first film, *Kuch Kuch Hota Hai,* started a new trend of films that combined stories about the family and romance with lavish sets. His second film, *Kabhie Khushi Kabhie Ghum,* was almost as successful as his first film and used the same aesthetic strategy of dazzling the spectator with the

grandeur of lavish set design. He also ran a successful TV show called *Koffee with Karan* that showcased all the major stars of the industry. All Johar's films have been made with actor Shahrukh Khan in the lead role.

25. Sharmishtha Roy, in discussion with the author, February 2005. South Bombay is the older part of the city, known for its architecture, history, and elite apartments.

26. Karan Johar, in discussion with the author, November 2002.

27. Sharmishtha Roy, in discussion with the author, February 2005.

28. Chandni Chowk (Silver Square) was built in 1650 AD. The area grew into a fabulous and prosperous trading center, which spread along a wide road and branched into a number of byroads in all directions. More than 900,000 people now populate a space that once housed an estimated 2,000,000. Old routes and roads, used for hundreds of years, have disappeared, and old buildings have given way to modern structures. Today, Chandni Chowk is a crowded, chaotic, and dirty bazaar space.

29. Karan Johar decided on the family portrait as the best way to market the film. Johar's brief to Soham Shah, the designer of the film's poster, was crucial: "the poster should have a combination of glamour, familial love, star power and elegance" (Soham Shah, in discussion with the author, April 2003). The use of stars like Amitabh Bachchan and Jaya Bhaduri (husband and wife in real life) as the parents added to this public desire for cohesion. Given the fact that gossip about their marriage in crisis has circulated through tabloids for almost three decades, conflict and harmony, both off-screen and on-screen, was mobilized in the film to create a sense of unity against all odds. This is precisely what the *K3G* poster came to signify—a desire for cohesion, located in narratives of conflict and anxiety. As a symbolic articulation, addressing the anxieties and the pleasurable desires unleashed in the post-globalization period, *K3G* functions like a cultural document, providing us access to a range of cultural tensions. The poster's desire to overlook the conflict that is central to the story, through the deployment of the family album, draws attention to the tensions and the cultural turmoil within which the contemporary family genre has emerged.

30. Diwali is a Hindu festival of lights that symbolizes the victory of good over evil. Lamps are used to celebrate the victory over darkness. There are many different legends associated with the Diwali, but the festival broadly marks the celebration of life. On this day, many wear new clothes, distribute sweets, and play with firecrackers.

31. The Rajputs were a group of warrior clans who lived in what is now Rajasthan and Madhya Pradesh. As *Kshatriyas* (members of the warrior caste), they saw themselves as people whose divine duty was to fight. There are legendary stories of their courage on the battlefield. Under British rule, they were constituted as one of the principal "martial races." But despite their preoccupation with war, the Rajputs were known as patrons of art and architecture. Some of the finest examples of their crafts are forts and palaces. Seen as a fusion architectural form that drew on many traditions, Rajput palaces are compositions built as inner citadels surrounded by the city. The inner walls are usually intricately carved and inlaid with mirrors. The Rajput style is simulated to highlight the exclusivity of many five-star hotels in India.

32. Bankimchandra Chatterjee (popularly known as Bankim) wrote "Bande Mataram" in 1875. The song evokes images of the countryside and worship of the motherland and also makes reference to the Hindu goddess, Durga. Bankim used the song in his controversial novel *Anandmath.* The novel was replete with glorification

of incidents of "cleansing" of Muslims. "Bande Mataram" has since been embroiled in many controversies. Today it is popularly known as a nationalist song.

33. Sharmishtha Roy, who did the sets of *K3G*, has this to say about Johar: "Karan cannot handle dirt, he cannot deal with grime, he went to Chandni Chowk and almost fainted." Roy recalls, and I quote, "Once, Karan Johar came to the living room sets of *K3G* to check out everything before shooting the next day. I had used prints, not original paintings, to decorate the walls. Karan went into a state of shock. He then borrowed the originals on canvas from his friends. Paintings of Hussain, Anjolie Ela Menon, etc., were put up, and we finally had to get special security to look after that one wall" (Sharmishtha Roy, in discussion with the author, Bombay, November 2002). Pankaj Khandpur, the main special-effects consultant for *K3G* working for an organization called Western Outdoors in Bombay, is now working on a number of film projects. Khandpur said Johar asked him to make sure the dirt of even the upmarket Chandni Chowk set in *K3G* was removed through color correction. Khandpur worked on *K3G* after the film was completed. His job was to digitally coordinate and correct the colors, make fat people look slightly thinner, and also work on Amitabh Bachchan's age lines (Pankaj Khandpur, in discussion with the author, Bombay, November 2002). This kind of post-production work is completely new in Hindi cinema and comes primarily from the world of advertising.

34. Farhan Akhtar is the son of scriptwriter and lyricist Javed Akhtar. *Dil Chahata Hai* was his first film, followed by *Lakshaye* (2003). Formerly employed in the advertising world, Akhtar has often claimed that *Dil Chahata Hai* was a salad tossed together with the personality traits of his many friends (Farhan Akhtar, in discussion with the author, August 2002).

35. Nikhat Kazmi, review of *Dil Chahata Hai*, *Times of India*, August 12, 2002.

36. Suzanne Meherwanji, interviewed by Debashree Mukherjee for the author, March 2004.

37. Farhan Akhtar, in discussion with the author, August 2002.

38. Amir Khan, interviewed in *The Making of Dil Chahata Hai*, DVD, 2002.

39. Suzanne Meherwanji, interviewed by Debashree Mukherjee, for the author, March 2004.

40. Farhan Akhtar, in discussion with the author, August 2002.

5. Gangland Bombay

1. The arrest of one of the most powerful film financiers, Bharat Shah, because of his connections with the underworld has clearly established the role of gang money in film production. See Najmi and Jathar and see Crawford.

2. While the gangster genre has its antecedents in the Hollywood silent-film era, the classic cycle takes off with three films made after the arrival of sound. In his comprehensive look at the American gangster film, Jonathan Munby suggests that the arrival of sound technology and the rise of the gangster genre enabled ethnic minorities the ability to play out their rebelliousness on-screen. Clearly, the use of language and accent found adequate articulation through the arrival of new technologies. *Scarface*, *Public Enemy*, and *Little Caesar* have leading men who play bootleggers of the Prohibition era. All the characters were glorified, which led to many censorship controversies. The initiation of the Production Code in 1930s Hollywood

(the code was most actively enforced after 1934) put pressure on studios to explicitly take a moral position on criminals. As many film historians have indicated, the gangster genre was one of the main targets of the Production Code (Munby).

3. In 1993, following the demolition of a mosque in Ayodhya, the city of Bombay was torn apart by pogroms instigated by the Hindu nationalist Shiv Sena party against the large Muslim minority. These pogroms were followed by a bomb blast, supposedly masterminded by Dawood Ibrahim, at Bombay's stock exchange. S. Hassan Zaidi, a reporter for *Midday* (a Bombay-based newspaper), wrote a book based on his investigation of the blast. The book, *Black Friday,* traces the events and the conspiracy that led up to the blast. Filmmaker Anurag Kashyap adapted the book to film.

4. For information on Dawood's criminal activities, see Sharma and see Najmi and Jathar.

5. Restructuring and mechanization led to a crisis in the textile industry from the 1960s onward. Technological backwardness and low-capacity utilization made it difficult to run many of the mills efficiently.

6. The strike started over the issue of bonuses. Subsequently, it became the expression for a number of other grievances. The closure of several mills in the aftermath of the strike left many workers unemployed. Over 100,000 workers lost jobs. Some mills were abandoned, while others functioned in dilapidated condition with few workers still on the job. The mill district acquired the look of a ghost town, and, in a state of desperation, workers made their way into the informal sector.

7. For a critical account of the strike, see Van Wersch, 64–85.

8. Also see Patel, 9–13. For an opinion that links criminality to the crisis of the textile union, see Virani.

9. See Narayan Surve's poem titled "Mumbai" in Patel and Thorner 1995, 147–50. Sayed Mirza's film *Salim Langde Pe Mat Ro* deals with Central Bombay in the post-strike period.

10. For a detailed account of the decline of the textile mills, see Monte.

11. For a vivid account of the Shiv Sena, see Blom Hansen and see Lele.

12. This *dada* culture lies at the heart of performance in the gangster films.

13. The term *Supari* has a long history in the Maratha warrior tradition. *Supari* was a mode of honor that acknowledged someone as a great warrior. It is intriguing that gangland Bombay deploys a term of honor to designate the fee for contract killing.

14. *Bambayya,* as discussed in chapter 2, is a hybrid language of the street that is inflected with the resonance of multiple tongues. The bulk of the people who use this language belong to the working classes.

15. Anurag Kashyap, in discussion with the author, March 2003. Anurag Kashyap is a scriptwriter and filmmaker who first shot to fame with the script for Ram Gopal Varma's film *Satya,* which was coauthored with Saurabh Shukla. Kashyap's directorial debut, *Paanch* (2003), was initially blocked by the censor board, for its violence, and later got caught in a battle between the producer and the film's financiers. To date, the film has not been released. Kashyap's second film, *Black Friday* (2005), is also stuck in litigation. Despite both films being unreleased, Kashyap has become known for his talent both as a director and as a script and dialogue writer. He has written for such films as Mani Ratnam's *Yuva* (2004) and Deepa Mehta's *Water* (2005).

16. Both *Midday* and *Afternoon Dispatch* are known for their crime reporting.

17. Ram Gopal Varma, interviewed in *Rediff on the Net,* Movies, http://www
.rediff.com, October 13, 1999.

18. Ram Gopal Varma, in discussion with the author, February 2005.

19. Vidhu Vinod Chopra graduated as a filmmaker from the Film and Television
Institute at Pune. Many of his films have received critical acclaim, including awards
at film festivals. *Parinda* was his first commercial film with big stars. He has made
several films since then, including *Kareeb* (1998) and *1942: A Love Story* (1993). He
turned producer in 2003 with an immensely successful film, *Munna Bhai, MBBS.*

20. In India, photographs on the wall are garlanded only when the person is dead.

21. Eisenstein believed that montage was produced by the collision of two pieces
of film unrelated to each other. The content of a film should unfold in a series of
shocks linked together in a sequence and directed at the emotions of the audience
(45–63).

22. In a slightly different reading, Lalitha Gopalan suggests that the gangster
genre's obsession with the past is narrativized in a way that makes these films "analogous to biographies of the post-colonial state" (107). For Gopalan, the spatio-temporal
deconstruction of the gangster film can enable rich insights into the ways in which
memory and history work within these popular narratives. Through detailed analysis of Mani Ratnam's *Nayakan* and Chopra's *Parinda,* Gopalan draws on the specific
cinematic conventions that work to articulate themes of nostalgia, memory, and
history. *Parinda* highlights a different approach to memory, one that is characterized not by the coherent linear logic of *Nayakan,* but by temporal discontinuities.
This makes *Parinda* a film whose temporal organization can serve as a "model for
writing the history of the modern nation that is less developmental and progressive" (Gopalan, 141).

23. Collision is central to Eisenstein's theory of art. The intensity and meaning
such collision takes depends on the qualities of the opposing forces in the colliding
shots. Eisenstein developed an interesting relationship between the city and cinema
in his theory of montage. The relationship between Manhattan's unique grid and the
experience of moving through space and time in film was significant in the development of Eisensteinian montage. Eisenstein said that Manhattan's spatial organization
lends itself to a range of perspectives that has enabled the city to emerge throughout the twentieth century as the quintessential cinematic city (Mazumdar 2003).

24. The steady cam is a brace used to fix the camera on the shoulder of the cam-
eraperson to capture speedy movements without the jerks normally associated with
handheld shots. The steady cam is usually used to capture chase sequences. In fact,
Ram Gopal Varma was the director who first introduced the steady cam in India,
with his film *Shiva* (1989).

25. Vinod Chopra, in discussion with the author, October 1997.

26. Gerrard Hooper, in discussion with the author, May 2005.

27. *Midday,* May 10, 1998.

28. Girija Jain, *Hindu,* January 15, 1999.

29. Ram Gopal Varma, interviewed by Jyoti Venkatesh, *Afternoon Dispatch,* taken
from Web reviews and interviews on *Satya.*

30. Gerrard Hooper, in discussion with the author, May 2005.

31. Mehrotra sees the kinetic city as a form that needs to be acknowledged for its
energy and for its ability to offer work and shelter to so many people. At the same

time, Mehrotra does not romanticize this space, instead urging planners to recognize and acknowledge the power of the kinetic city in their visions of the future in South Asia (2002, 95–108).

32. The Ganesh Chaturthi festival is Bombay's most popular festival. It is the birthday of the elephant god Ganesh. During the festival celebration, which lasts for about ten days, a number of deities of Ganesh, made in clay in all possible sizes, are bought and sold. The deities are kept in the house for a few days and then submerged in the ocean. The submersion is spectacular, as crowds of people in thousands of processions converge on the beaches of Bombay carrying the idols of Ganesh to be immersed in the sea. Accompanied by drumbeats, dancing, and devotional songs, the submersion marks the end of the festival. For more information on the festival, see Kaur.

33. For a discussion on the use of cars in another gangster film, *Nayakan,* see Gopalan. Gopalan establishes the relationship between time and the commodity through a discussion of the use of cars in the film. Developing a powerful argument, Gopalan suggests that the presence of different cars in the mise-en-scène not only signals the passage of time, but, through their collage-like presence as cars from different time periods, they also "perform the ambivalence of writing post-colonial history that cannot escape its own investment in nostalgia" (116).

34. Ram Gopal Varma, in discussion with the author, February 2005.

35. Ibid.

36. Jaideep Sahani, in discussion with the author, January 2006.

37. Ibid.

Conclusion

1. Anurag Kashyap, in discussion with the author, March 2005.

Bibliography

Abbas, Khwaja Ahmad. 1987. *Bombay, My Bombay! The Love Story of the City*. Delhi: New Ajanta.

Abel, Richard. 1995. "The Perils of Pathe, or the Americanization of the American Cinema." In *Cinema and the Invention of Modern Life*, ed. Leo Charney and Vanessa Schwartz. Berkeley: University of California Press.

Affron, Charles, and Mirella Jona Affron. 1995. *Sets in Motion: Art Direction and Film Narrative*. New Brunswick, N.J.: Rutgers University Press.

Ahmad, Aijaz. 1987. "Jameson's Rhetoric of Otherness and the 'National Allegory.'" *Social Text*, no. 17 (Autumn): 3.

Aitkin, Stuart, and Leo Zonn, eds. 1994. *Place, Power, Situation, and Spectacle*. Lanham, Md.: Rowman & Littlefield.

Akhtar, Jan Nissar. 2004. *Shaad Aur Akhtar Ki Shayari*, selected by Amar Dehalavi. New Delhi: Diamond Books.

Albrecht, Donald. 1986. *Designing Dreams: Modern Architecture and the Movies*. New York: Harper & Row.

Altekar, A. S. 1959. *The Position of Women in Hindu Civilization from Prehistoric Times to the Present Day*. Delhi: Moti Lal Banarasi.

Ambedkar, B. R. 1994. *Writings and Speeches*. Vols. 5 and 13. Bombay: Government of Maharashtra.

Appadurai, Arjun. 2000. "Spectral Housing & Urban Cleansing: Notes on Millenial Mumbai." *Public Culture* (December 3): 627–51.

———. 1996. *Modernity at Large: The Cultural Dimension of Globalization*. Minneapolis: University of Minnesota Press.

———. 1987. "Street Culture." *India Magazine* 8 (December): 2–23.

Appadurai, Arjun, ed. 1986. *The Social Life of Things: Commodities in Cultural Perspective*. New York: Cambridge University Press.

Bachelard, Gaston. 1994. *The Poetics of Space*. Trans. Maria Jolas, with a new foreward by John R. Stilgoe. Boston: Beacon Press.

Bagchi, Amiya. 1982. *The Political Economy of Underdevelopment*. New York: Cambridge University Press.

Bakhtin, Mikhail. 1986. *Speech Genres and Other Essays.* Austin: University of Texas Press.

Bakshi, Rajni. 1986. *The Long Haul: The Bombay Textile Workers Strike.* Bombay: Build Documentation Centre.

Bamzai, Kaveree. 1993. "Sold on Sex." *Express: Sunday Magazine* (India), March 14.

Bannerjee, Sumanta. 1997. "Marginalization of Women's Popular Culture in Nineteenth Century Bengal." In *Recasting Women: Essays in Colonial History,* ed. Kumkum Sangari and Sudesh Vaid. New Delhi: Kali for Women.

———. 1989. *The Parlour and the Street: Elite and Popular Culture in Nineteenth Century Calcutta.* Calcutta: Seagull Books.

———. 1980. *In the Wake of Naxalbari.* Calcutta: Subarnarekha.

Bardhan, Pranab. 1984. *The Political Economy of Development in India.* New Delhi: Oxford University Press.

Barnouw, Eric, and S. Krishnaswami. 1980. *Indian Film.* 2d ed. New York: Oxford University Press.

Barthes, Roland. 1997. "Semiology and the Urban." In *Rethinking Architecture,* ed. Neil Leach. New York: Routledge.

———. 1993. *Image, Music, Text.* London: Fontana Press.

———. 1983. *Empire of Signs.* New York: Hill and Wang.

———. 1977. *Image Music Text.* New York: Hill and Wang.

———. 1973. *Mythologies.* New York: Hill and Wang.

Baudelaire, Charles. 1986. "The Painter of Modern Life." In *My Heart Laid Bare and Other Prose Writings.* London: Soho Book Company.

Baudrillard, Jean. 2002. "The Ecstasy of Communication." In *The Anti-Aesthetic: Essays on Postmodern Culture,* ed. Hal Foster. New York: New Press.

Bauman, Zygmunt. 1995. "The Stranger Revisited and Revisiting." In *Life in Fragments: Essays in Postmodern Morality.* Cambridge, Mass.: Blackwell.

Bayly, C. A. 1992. *Rulers, Townsmen and Bazaars.* Bombay: Oxford University Press.

Benjamin, Walter. 1999. *The Arcades Project.* Cambridge, Mass.: Harvard University Press.

———. 1992. *One Way Street and Other Writings.* New York: Verso.

———. 1977. *The Origin of German Tragic Drama.* New York: Verso.

———. 1969. "On Some Motifs in Baudelaire." In *Illuminations.* New York: Schocken.

———. 1969. "The Work of Art in the Age of Mechanical Reproduction." In *Illuminations.* New York: Schocken.

Berlant, Lauren. 2000. *Intimacy.* Chicago: University of Chicago Press.

Berman, Marshall. 1988. *All That Is Solid Melts into Air: The Experience of Modernity.* New York: Penguin Books.

Berry, Sarah. 2000. *Screen Style: Fashion and Femininity in 1930s Hollywood.* Minneapolis: University of Minnesota Press.

Blom Hansen, Thomas. 2001. *Wages of Violence: Naming and Identity in Postcolonial Bombay.* Princeton, N.J.: Princeton University Press.

Blumemberg, Hans. 1990. *Work on Myth.* Trans. Robert M. Wallace. Cambridge, Mass.: MIT Press.

Bordwell, David, Janet Staiger, and Kristin Thompson. 1985. *The Classical Hollywood Cinema: Film Style and Mode of Production.* New York: Columbia University Press.

Brass, Paul R. 1990. *The Politics of India since Independence*. New York: Cambridge University Press.

Brecht, Bertolt. 1977. "Uber gestische Musik." In *Schriften zum Theater,* 283–84. Berlin: Henschelverlag Kunst und Gesellschaft.

Brooks, Peter. 1976. *The Melodramatic Imagination: Balzac, Henry James, Melodrama, and the Mode of Excess*. New Haven: Yale University Press.

Brosius, Christiane, and Melissa Butcher, eds. 1999. *Image Journeys: Audio Visual Media and Cultural Change in India*. Thousand Oaks, Calif.: Sage Publications.

Bruno, Giuliana. 2002. *Atlas of Emotion: Journeys in Art, Architecture, and Film*. New York: Verso.

———. 1993. *Streetwalking on a Ruined Map: The City Films of Elvira Nottari*. Princeton, N.J.: Princeton University Press.

Buck-Morss, Susan. 1990. *The Dialectics of Seeing: Walter Benjamin and the Arcades Project*. Cambridge, Mass.: MIT Press.

———. 1986. "The Flaneur, the Sandwichman, and the Whore: The Politics of Loitering." *New German Critique* 39: 99–140.

Bukatman, Scott. 1997. *Blade Runner*. London: BFI Publishing.

Chakrabarty, Dipesh. 1991. "Open Space/Public Place: Garbage, Modernity, and India." *South Asia* 14, no. 1.

Chakravarty, Sumita. 1996. *National Identity in Indian Popular Cinema, 1947–1987*. Bombay: Oxford University Press.

Chandra, Anupama. 1994. "It's a Mad, Bad World." *India Today*, July 31, 88–89.

Charney, Leo, and Vanessa Schwartz, eds. 1995. *Cinema and the Invention of Modern Life*. Berkeley: University of California Press.

Chatterjee, Gayatri. 1993. *Awara*. New Delhi: Wiley Eastern.

Chatterjee, Partha. 1997. "The Nationalist Resolution of the Women's Question." In *Recasting Women: Essays in Colonial History,* ed. Kumkum Sangari and Sudesh Vaid. New Delhi: Kali for Women.

———. 1997. *A Possible India: Essays in Political Criticism*. Mumbai: Oxford University Press.

———. 1995. "A Bit of Song and Dance." In *Frames of Mind: Reflections on Indian Cinema,* ed. Aruna Vasudev. Bombay: UBS Publishers.

———. 1993. *The Nation and Its Fragments: Colonial and Postcolonial Histories*. Princeton, N.J.: Princeton University Press.

———. 1986. *Nationalist Thought and the Colonial World: A Derivative Discourse*. Delhi: Oxford University Press.

Chatterjee, Partha, ed. 1998. *Wages of Freedom: Fifty Years of the Indian Nation-State*. Mumbai: Oxford University Press.

Chatterjee, Saibal. 1994. "A Bawdy Blow." *Times of India*, April 24.

Chowdhary, Anuradha. 1997. "Nostalgia: The Untold Story behind the Making of the Angry Young Man." *Filmfare*, February.

Clarke, David B., ed. *The Cinematic City*. New York: Routledge, 1997.

Conlon, Frank E. 1995. "Dining Out in Bombay." In *Consuming Modernity: Public Culture in a South Asian World,* ed. Carol Breckenridge. Minneapolis: University of Minnesota Press.

Cooper, Darius. 1988. "The Hindi Film Song and Guru Dutt." *East-West Film Journal* 2, no. 2 (June).

Craik, Jennifer. 1994. *The Face of Fashion: Cultural Studies in Fashion*. New York: Routledge.

Crawford, Reavis. 2002. "Bullets over Bombay: Exposing the Underworld of Hindi Cinema (Both Onscreen and Offscreen)." *Film Comment*, May–June, 53–55.

Crouch, David. 1998. "The Street in the Making of Popular Geographical Knowledge." In *Images of the Street: Planning, Identity, and Control in Public Space*, ed. Nicholas R. Fyfe. New York: Routledge.

Dalmia, Vasudha. 1997. *The Nationalization of Hindu Traditions: Bharatendu Harishchandra and Nineteenth-Century Banaras*. Mumbai: Oxford University Press.

Das, Veena, and Ashis Nandy. 1985. "Violence, Victimhood, and the Language of Silence." In *Contributions to Indian Sociology*, 177–95. Thousand Oaks, Calif.: Sage.

Dasgupta, Biplab. 1974. *The Naxalite Movement*. Bombay: Allied Publishers.

Dasgupta, Chidananda. 1991. *The Painted Face: Studies in India's Popular Cinema*. New Delhi: Roli Books.

———. 1981. *Talking about Films*. New Delhi: Orient Longman.

de Certeau, Michel. 1998. *The Practice of Everyday Life*. Vol. 2. Trans. Timothy J. Tomasik. Minneapolis: University of Minnesota Press.

———. 1984. *The Practice of Everyday Life*. Vol. 1. Trans. Steven Rendall. Berkeley: University of California Press.

Debord, Guy. 1994. *The Society of the Spectacle*. Brooklyn, N.Y.: Zone Books.

Desai, A. R. 1975. *State and Society in India: Essays in Dissent*. Bombay: Popular Prakashan.

———. 1966. *Social Background of Indian Nationalism*. Bombay: Popular Prakashan.

Dhumil. 1972. "Shahar, Shyam Aur Ek Burha: Mai." In *Sansad Se Sadak Tak*. New Delhi: Rajkamal.

Diamond, Elin, ed. 1996. *Performance and Cultural Politics*. New York: Routledge.

Dimendberg, Edward. 1997. "From Bunker Hill: Urban Space, Late Modernity, and Film Noir in Fritz Lang's and Joseph Losey's *M*." *Wide Angle* 19, no. 4 (October).

Dissanayake, Wimal, ed. 1993. *Melodrama and Asian Cinema*. New York: Cambridge University Press.

D'Monte, Darryl. 2005. *Ripping the Fabric: The Decline of Mumbai and Its Mills*. New York: Oxford University Press.

Donald, James. 1999. *Imagining the Modern City*. Minneapolis: University of Minnesota Press.

Doraiswamy, Rashmi. 1995. "Hindi Commercial Cinema: Changing Narrative Strategies." In *Frames of Mind: Reflections on Indian Cinema*, ed. Aruna Vasudev. Delhi: UBSPD.

Dutt, Rajni Palme. 1955. *India Today and Tomorrow*. London: Lawrence and Wishart.

Dwyer, Rachel, and Divia Patel. 2002. *The Visual Culture of Hindi Film*. Reaktion Books.

Eckert, Charles. 1990. "The Carole Lombard in Macy's Window." In *Fabrications: Costume and the Female Body*, ed. Jane Gaines and Charlotte Herzog. New York: Routledge.

Eisenstein, Sergei. 1977. *Film Form: Essays in Film Theory*. New York: Harcourt Brace Jovanovich.

Ellin, Nan. 1997. *Architecture of Fear*. New York: Princeton Architectural Press.

———. 1996. *Postmodern Urbanism*. Cambridge, Mass.: Blackwell.

Elsaesser, Thomas. 1991. "Tales of Sound and Fury." In *Imitations of Life: A Reader on Film and Television Melodrama*, ed. Marcia Landy. Detroit: Wayne State University Press.

Evenson, Norma. 1996. "An Architectural Hybrid." In *Bombay: Mosaic of Modern Culture*, ed. Sujata Patel and Alice Thorner, 165–81. Delhi: Oxford University Press.

Ezekiel, Nissim. 1989. *Collected Poems, 1952–1988*. Bombay: Oxford University Press.

Felski, Rita. 1995. *The Gender of Modernity*. Cambridge, Mass.: Harvard University Press.

Fernandes, Naresh. 2000. "Urban Fabric." In *Elsewhere: Unusual Takes on India*, ed. Kai Friese. New York: Penguin Books.

Foster, Hal. 2002. *Design and Crime and Other Diatribes*. New York: Verso.

Foucault, Michel. 1984. *The Foucault Reader*, ed. P. Rabinow. Harmondsworth.

Frankel, Francine R. 1978. *India's Political Economy, 1947–77: The Gradual Revolution*. Princeton, N.J.: Princeton University Press.

Friedberg, Ann. 1993. *Window Shopping: Cinema and the Postmodern*. Berkeley: University of California Press.

Frisby, David. 1986. *Fragments of Modernity*. Cambridge, Mass.: MIT Press.

Fuller, C. J., and Veronique Benei. 2000. *The Everyday State and Society in Modern India*. New Delhi: Social Science Press.

Gaines, Jane. 1989. "The Queen Christina Tie Ups: Convergence of Show Window and Screen." *Quarterly Review of Film and Video* 2, no. 1 (Winter).

Gandhi, M. K. 1938. *The Hind Swaraj*. Ahmedabad: Navjivan Trust.

Gandhy, Behroze, and Rosie Thomas. 1991. "Three Indian Film Stars." In *Stardom Industry of Desire*, ed. Christine Gledhill. London: Routledge.

Ganghar, Amrit. 1996. "Films from the City of Dreams." In *Bombay: Mosaic of Modern Culture*, ed. Sujata Patel and Alice Thorner. New York: Oxford University Press.

Ganti, Tejaswini. 2002. "And Yet My Heart Is Still Indian: The Bombay Film Industry and the (H)Indianization of Hollywood." In *Media Worlds: Anthropology on New Terrain*, ed. Faye Ginzburg, Lila Abu-Lughod, and Brian Larkin, 281–300. Berkeley: University of California Press.

Gehlot, Deepa. 1995. "The Stars Call the Shots." In *Frames of Mind: Reflections on Indian Cinema*, ed. Aruna Vasudev. UBS Publishers.

Gelder, Ken. 1997. Introduction to part 7. *The Subcultures Reader*. New York: Routledge.

Gelder, Ken, and Sarah Thornton, eds. 1997. *The Subcultures Reader*. New York: Routledge.

Ghosh, Avijit. 1996. "India's Journey with Amitabh Bachchan." *Pioneer*, November 24.

Ghosh, Shohini. 2000. "*Hum Apke Hain Kaun*: Pluralizing Pleasures of Viewership." *Social Scientist* 28, no. 3–4 (March–April).

———. 1999. "The Troubled Existence of Sex and Sexuality: Feminists Engage with Censorship." In *Image Journeys*, ed. Christiane Brosius and Melissa Butcher, 233–59. Thousand Oaks, Calif.: Sage Publications.

Gilloch, Graeme. 1996. *Myth and Metropolis: Walter Benjamin and the City*. Polity Press.

Gleber, Ancke. 1998. *The Art of Taking a Walk: Flanerie, Literature, and Film in Weimar Culture*. Princeton, N.J.: Princeton University Press.

Gledhill, Christine, ed. 1987. *Home Is Where the Heart Is: Studies in Melodrama and the Woman's Film*. London: British Film Institute.

Gopalan, Lalitha. 2002. *Cinema of Interruptions: Action Genres in Contemporary Indian Cinema.* BFI Publishing.

Goswami, Shama. 1981. *Nagarikran aur Hindi Upanyas.* Delhi: Jaishree Prakashan.

Grant, Barry Keith. 1986. *Film Genre Reader.* Austin: University of Texas Press.

Griffith, Alison. 1996. "A Moving Picture in Two Senses: Allegories of the Nation in 1950s Indian Melodrama." *Continuum* 9: 2.

Grumbach, Antoine. 1978. "The Theatre of Memory." *Architectural Design Profile* 48: 8–9.

Guha, Ranajit, and Gayatri Spivak, eds. 1988. *Selected Subaltern Studies.* New York: Oxford University Press.

Guha Bannerjee, Swapna. 1996. "Urban Development Process in Bombay: Planning for Whom?" In *Bombay: A Metaphor for Modern India,* ed. Sujata Patel and Alice Thorner. Bombay: Oxford University Press.

Gunning, Tom. 2000. *The Films of Fritz Lang: Allegories of Vision and Modernity.* London: BFI Publishing.

———. 1997. "From the Kaleidoscope to the X-Ray: Urban Spectatorship, Poe, Benjamin and the Traffic in Souls." *Wide Angle* 19, no. 4 (October).

———. 1986. "The Cinema of Attraction(s): Early Film, Its Spectator, and the Avant Garde." *Wide Angle* 8, no. 3–4.

Harvey, David. 1990. *The Condition of Postmodernity.* Cambridge, Mass.: Blackwell.

Hasan, Zoya, ed. 2000. *Politics and the State in India: Readings in Indian Government and Politics.* Thousand Oaks, Calif.: Sage Publications.

Hebdige, Dick. 1997. "Posing . . . Threats, Striking . . . Poses." In *The Subcultures Reader,* ed. Ken Gelder and Sarah Thornton, 393–406. New York: Routledge.

———. 1997. "Subculture: The Meaning of Style." In *The Subcultures Reader,* ed. Ken Gelder and Sarah Thornton, 130–44. New York: Routledge.

———. 1979. *Subculture: The Meaning of Style.* New York: Methuen.

Heuze, Gerard. 1995. "Cultural Populism: The Appeal of the Shiv Sena." In *Bombay: Metaphor for Modern India,* ed. Sujata Patel and Alice Thorner. New York: Oxford University Press.

Higson, Andrew. 1989. "The Concept of National Cinema." *Screen* 30, no. 40: 36–46.

Hirsch, Marianne. 1997. *Family Frames: Photography, Narrative, and Postmemory.* Cambridge, Mass.: Harvard University Press.

Horkheimer, Max, and Theodor W. Adorno. 1988. *Dialectic of Enlightenment.* New York: Continuum.

Hutcheon, Linda. 1989. *The Politics of Postmodernism.* New York: Routledge.

Huyssen, Andreas. 1986. *After the Great Divide.* Bloomington: Indiana University Press.

Jameson, Fredric. 1986. "Third World Literature in the Era of Multinational Capitalism." *Social Text,* no. 15 (Autumn): 65–88.

———. 1981. *The Political Unconscious: Narrative as a Socially Symbolic Act.* Ithaca, N.Y.: Cornell University Press.

———. 1971. *Marxism and Form.* Princeton, N.J.: Princeton University Press.

Jha, Subhash. 2001. "Living on the Edge." Rediff India Abroad. http://www.rediff.com (August 24, 2001).

John, Mary E. 1998. "Globalization, Sexuality, and the Visual Field: Issues and Non-Issues for Cultural Critique." In *A Question of Silence: The Sexual Economies of Modern India,* ed. Mary E. John and Nair Janaki. New Delhi: Kali for Women.

John, Mary, and Nair Janaki, eds. 1998. *A Question of Silence: The Sexual Economies of Modern India.* New Delhi: Kali for Women.

Julier, Guy. 2000. *The Culture of Design.* Thousand Oaks, Calif.: Sage Publications.

Kabir, Munni. 1999. *Talking Films: Conversations on Hindi Cinema with Javed Akhtar.* New York: Oxford University Press.

Kakkar, Sudhir. 1992. *The Inner World: A Psycho-Analytic Study of Childhood and Society in India.* New York: Oxford University Press.

———. 1989. *Intimate Relations: Exploring Indian Sexuality.* New Delhi: Penguin.

Kapur, Geeta. 1987. "Mythic Material in Indian Cinema." *Journal of Arts and Ideas,* nos. 14–15: 79–107.

Karve, Iravati. 1991. *Yuganta: The End of an Epoch.* Disha Books.

Kaur, Raminder. 2003. *Performative Politics and the Cultures of Hinduism: Public Uses of Religion in Western India.* Permanent Black.

Kaviraj, Sudipta. 2000. "The Modern State in India." In *Politics and the State in India,* ed. Zoya Hasan. Thousand Oaks, Calif.: Sage Publications.

———. 1997. "Filth and Practices about Space in Calcutta." *Public Culture* 10, no. 1: 83–113.

———. 1996. "Dilemmas of Democratic Development in India." In *Democracy and Development: Theory and Practice,* ed. Adrian Leftwich. Polity Press.

———. 1988. "A Critique of the Passive Revolution." *Economic and Political Weekly,* 2429–43.

———. 1986. "Indira Gandhi and Indian Politics." *Economic and Political Weekly* 21, no. 38–39: 1697–708.

Kazmi, Nikhat. 1998. *The Dream Merchants of Bollywood.* Delhi: UBS Publishers.

Kearns, Gerry, and Chris Philo, eds. 1993. *Selling Places: The City as Cultural Capital, Past and Present.* Oxford: Pergamon Press.

Keller, Alexandra. 1995. "Disseminations of Modernity: Representation and Consumer Desire in Early Mail Order Catalogs." In *Cinema and the Invention of Modern Life,* ed. Leo Charney and Vanessa Schwarz. Berkeley: University of California Press.

Kesavan, Mukul. 1994. "Urdu, Awadh, and the Tawaif: The Islamicate Roots of Hindi Cinema." In *Forging Identities: Gender, Communities, and the State,* ed. Zoya Hassan. Kali for Women.

King, Barry. 1991. "Articulating Stardom." In *Stardom: Industry of Desire,* ed. Christine Gledhill. New York: Routledge.

King, Christopher. 1994. *One Language, Two Scripts.* New York: Oxford University Press.

King, Ross. 1996. *Emancipating Space: Geography, Architecture, and Urban Design.* New York: Guilford Press.

Kosambi, D. D. 1965. *The Culture and Civilization of Ancient India in Historical Outline.* London: Routledge and Kegan Paul.

Kothari, Rajni. 1989. *Politics and the People: In Search of a Humane India.* 2 vols. Delhi: Ajanta Publications.

Kracauer, Siegfried. 1995. *The Mass Ornament: Weimar Essays.* Ed. and with an introduction by Thomas Y. Levin. Cambridge, Mass.: Harvard University Press.

Kudchedkar, Shirin. 1996. "Poetry and the City." In *Bombay: Mosaic of Modern Culture,* ed. Sujata Patel and Alice Thorner, 126–64. Delhi: Oxford University Press.

Kumkum, Sangari, and Sudesh Vaid, eds. 1997. *Recasting Women: Essays in Colonial History.* New Delhi: Kali for Women.

Lal, Vinay, ed. 2000. *Dissenting Knowledges, Open Futures: The Multiple Selves and Strange Destinations of Ashis Nandy.* Oxford University Press.

Lang, John, Madhavi Desai, and Miki Desai. 1997. *Architecture and Independence: The Search for Identity: India, 1880–1980.* New Delhi: Oxford University Press.

Lefebvre, Henri. 1997. "The Production of Space." Extracts. In *Rethinking Architecture: A Reader in Cultural Theory,* ed. Neil Leach. New York: Routledge.

———. 1996. *Writings on Cities.* Cambridge, Mass.: Blackwell.

———. 1992. *The Production of Space.* Cambridge, Mass.: Blackwell.

———. 1991. *Critique of Everyday Life.* New York: Verso.

Lehan, Richard. 1998. *The City in Literature: An Intellectual and Cultural History.* Berkeley: University of California Press.

Lele, Jayant. 1995. "Saffronization of the Shiv Sena: The Political Economy of the City, State, and Nation." In *Bombay: Metaphor for Modern India,* ed. Sujata Patel and Alice Thorner. New York: Oxford University Press.

Lungstrum, Janet. 1999. "Window Designs and Desires of Weimar Consumerism." *New German Critique* 76 (Winter).

Mani, Lata. 1998. *Contentious Traditions: The Debate on Sati in Colonial India.* Berkeley: University of California Press.

Martin, Randy. 1998. *Critical Moves: Dance Studies in Theory and Politics.* Durham, N.C.: Duke University Press.

Marx, Karl. 1977. *The German Ideology.* New York: International.

Mason, Fran. 2002. *American Gangster Cinema: From Little Caesar to Pulp Fiction.* New York: Palgrave Macmillan.

Masselos, Jim, ed. 2003. *Bombay and Mumbai: The City in Transition,* 9–13. New York: Oxford University Press.

Mazumdar, Ranjani. 2000. "From Subjectification to Schizophrenia: The 'Angry Man' and the 'Psychotic' Hero of Bombay Cinema." In *Making Meaning in Indian Cinema,* ed. Ravi Vasudevan. Oxford University Press.

Mazumdar, Ranjani, and Shikha Jhingan. 1998. "The Journey from the Village to the City." In *The Power of the Image.* Twelve-part television series on Bombay Cinema. BITV.

———. 1998. "The Legacy of the Angry Man." In *The Power of the Image.* Twelve-part television series on Bombay Cinema. BITV.

———. 1998. "The Return of the Family." In *The Power of the Image.* Twelve-part television series on Bombay Cinema. BITV.

———. 1998. "The *Tapori* as Street Rebel." In *The Power of the Image.* Twelve-part television series on Bombay Cinema. BITV.

———. 1998. "Whatever Happened to the Vamp?" In *The Power of the Image.* Twelve-part television series on Bombay Cinema. BITV.

Mazumdar, Vina. 1990. "The Social Reform Movement in India from Ranade to Nehru." In *Indian Women from Purdah to Modernity,* ed. B. R. Nanda, 41–66. Radiant Publishers.

Mazzarella, William. 2003. *Shoveling Smoke: Advertising and Globalization in Contemporary India.* Durham, N.C.: Duke University Press.

McCann, Graham. 1994. *Rebel Males: Clift, Brando, and Dean.* New Brunswick, N.J.: Rutgers University Press.

McCarry, John. 1995. "Bombay: India's Capital of Hope." In *National Geographic* 187, no. 3 (March).

McCarthy, Anna. 2001. *Ambient Television: Visual Culture and Public Space.* Durham, N.C.: Duke University Press.

McRobbie, Angela. 1990. "Fame, Flashdance, and Fantasies of Achievement." In *Fabrications: Costume and the Female Body,* ed. Jane Gaines and Charlotte Herzog. New York: Routledge.

Mehrotra, Rahul. 2002. "Bazaar City: A Metaphor for South Asian Urbanism." In *Kapital and Karma: Recent Positions in Indian Art,* 95–110. Vienna: Kunsthalle Wien.

Mehrotra, Rahul, and Sharda Dwivedi. 1995. *Bombay: The Cities Within.* Book House.

Mehta, Gita. 1997. *Snakes and Ladders: Glimpses of Modern India.* New York: Doubleday.

Mehta, Suketu. 2004. *Maximum City: Bombay Lost and Found.* New York: Alfred A. Knopf.

Miller, Daniel. 1987. *Material Culture and Mass Consumption.* Oxford: Basil Blackwell.

Miller, Toby. 1998. *Technologies of Truth: Cultural Citizenship and the Popular Media.* Minneapolis: University of Minnesota Press.

Misra, Vijay. 1985. "Towards a Theoretical Critique of Bombay Cinema." *Screen* 26, no. 3–4: 133–46.

Mitra, Ashok. 1979. *The Hoodlum Years.* New Delhi: Orient Longman.

Mukta, Parita. 1994. *Upholding the Common Life: The Community of Mirabai.* New Delhi: Oxford University Press.

Mulvey, Laura. 2000. "Visual Pleasure and Narrative Cinema." In *Film and Theory: An Anthhology,* ed. Robert Stam and Toby Miller. Cambridge, Mass.: Blackwell.

Munby, Jonathan. 1999. *Public Enemies, Public Heroes: Screening the Gangster from Little Caesar to Touch of Evil.* Chicago: University of Chicago Press.

Najmi, Quaied, and Dnyanesh Jathar. 2001. "Don in Twilight Zone." *New Statesman,* March 12.

Nandy, Ashis. 2001. *The Ambiguous Journey to the City: The Village and Other Odd Ruins of the Self in Indian Imagination.* New Delhi: Oxford University Press.

———. 1998. "Indian Popular Cinema as a Slum's Eye View of Politics." In *The Secret Politics of Our Desires: Innocence, Culpability, and Indian Popular Cinema,* ed. Ashis Nandy. Oxford University Press.

———. 1995. "An Intelligent Critic's Guide to Indian Cinema." In *The Savage Freud and Other Essays on Possible and Retrievable Selves.* Bombay: Oxford University Press.

———. 1983. *The Intimate Enemy: Loss and Recovery of Self under Colonialism.* Bombay: Oxford University Press.

———. 1980. *At the Edge of Psychology: Essays in Politics and Culture.* Mumbai: Oxford University Press.

Naremore, James. 1998. *More Than Night: Film Noir in Its Contexts.* Berkeley: University of California Press.

———. 1990. *Acting in the Cinema.* Berkeley: University of California Press.

Neale, Steve. 1980. *Genre.* London: British Film Institute.

Nehru, Jawaharlal. 1972. *The Discovery of India.* Mumbai: Vikas Publishing House.

Nichols, Bill, ed. 1976. *Movies and Methods.* 2 vols. Berkeley: University of California Press.

Olalquiaga, Celeste. 1992. *Megalopolis: Contemporary Cultural Sensibilities.* Minneapolis: University of Minnesota Press.

Pandian, M. S. S. 1992. *The Image Trap.* Delhi: Sage.

Parekh, Bhikhu. 1992. "The Poverty of Indian Political Theory." *History of Political Thought* 13, no. 3 (Autumn).

Patel, Sujata. 1995. "Bombay's Urban Predicament." In *Bombay: Metaphor for Modern India,* ed. Sujata Patel and Alice Thorner. Delhi: Oxford University Press.

Patel, Sujata, and Alice Thorner, eds. 1996. *Bombay: Mosaic of Modern Culture.* Delhi: Oxford University Press.

———. 1995. *Bombay: Metaphor for Modern India.* Delhi: Oxford University Press.

Patnaik, Prabhat. 1972. "Imperialism and the Growth of Indian Capitalism." In *Studies in the Theory of Imperialism,* ed. Roger Owen and Bob Sutcliffe, 210–29. Pantheon Books.

Patnaik, Utsa. 1986. *The Agrarian Question and the Development of Capitalism in India.* New Delhi: Oxford University Press.

Pendse, Sandeep. 2003. "Satya's Mumbai, Mumbai's Satya." In *Bombay and Mumbai: The City in Transition,* ed. Sujata Patel and Jim Masselos, 301–36. Oxford University Press.

———. 1996. "Toil, Sweat and the City." In *Bombay: Metaphor for Modern India,* ed. Sujata Patel and Alice Thorner. Delhi: Oxford University Press.

Pensky, Max. 1993. *Melancholy Dialectics: Benjamin and the Play of Mourning.* Amherst: University of Massachusetts Press.

Polan, Dana. 1986. *Power and Paranoia: History, Narrative, and the American Film, 1940–50.* New York: Columbia University Press.

Prakash, Gyan. 2006. "The Idea of Bombay." *American Scholar* (Spring).

———. 2002. "The Urban Turn." In *Sarai Reader 2: The Cities of Everyday Life.* New Delhi: Centre for the Study of Developing Societies and Society for Old and New Media.

———. 1999. *Another Reason: Science and the Imagination of Modern India.* Princeton, N.J.: Princeton University Press.

Prasad, M. Madhava. 1998. *Ideology of the Hindi Film: A Historical Construction.* New Delhi: Oxford University Press.

Raban, Jonathan. 1998. *Soft City.* London: Harvill Press.

Rabinovitz, Lauren. 1998. *For the Love of Pleasure: Women, Movies, and Culture in Turn-of-the-Century Chicago.* New Brunswick, N.J.: Rutgers University Press.

Rai, Alok. 1999. "Making a Difference: Hindi, 1880–1930." In *Multiculturalism, Liberalism, and Democracy,* ed. Rajeev Bhargava et al. New Delhi: Oxford University Press.

Rajadhyaksha, Ashis. 1993. "The Epic Melodrama: Themes of Nationality in Indian Cinema." *Journal of Arts and Ideas* 25–26: 55–70.

———. 1987. "Neo-Traditionalism: Film as Popular Art in India." *Framework* 32–33: 20–67.

Rajadhyaksha, Ashish, and Willeman Paul. 1999. *Encyclopedia of Indian Cinema.* New rev. ed. London: BFI/Oxford University Press.

Rajagopal, Arvind. 2001. "The Violence of Commodity Aesthetics: Hawkers, Demolition Raids, and a New Regime of Consumption." *Social Text* 19, no. 3: 91–113.

Rajendran, Girija. 1999. *Hindu,* January 15.

Rao, M. S. A., ed. 1974. *Urban Sociology in India.* Hyderabad, India: Orient Longman.

Raqs Media Collective. 2005. "X Notes on Practice: Stubborn Structures and Insistent Seepage in a Networked World." In *Data Browser 02: Engineering Culture,* ed. Geoff Cox and Joasia Krysa. New York: Autonomedia.

Renov, Michael. 1993. "The Truth about Non-Fiction Film." In *Theorizing Documentary,* ed. Michael Renov. New York: Routledge.

Rosen, Philip, ed. 1986. *Narrative, Apparatus, Ideology.* New York: Columbia University Press.

Ross, Kristen. 1996. *Fast Cars, Clean Bodies: Decolonization and the Reordering of French Culture.* Cambridge, Mass.: MIT Press.

Sahai, Malti. 1987. "Raj Kapoor and the Indianization of Charlie Chaplin." *East-West Film Journal* 2, no. 1.

Sahani, Roshan. 1996. "Polyphonous Voices in the City: Bombay's Indian-English Fiction." In *Bombay: Mosaic of Modern Culture,* ed. Sujata Patel and Alice Thorner. Delhi: Oxford University Press.

Sangari, Kum Kum, and Sudesh Vaid, eds. *Recasting Women: Essays in Colonial History.* New Delhi: Kali for Women.

Scarry, Elaine. 1985. *The Body in Pain: The Making and Unmaking of the World.* New York: Oxford University Press.

Schivelbusch, Wolfgang. 1988. *Disenchanted Night: The Industrialization of Light in the Nineteenth Century.* Berkeley: University of California Press.

Schneider, Sara K. 1995. *Vital Mummies: Performance Design for the Show Window Mannequin.* New Haven, Conn.: Yale University Press.

Schrader, Paul. 1996. "Notes on Film Noir." In *Film Noir Reader,* ed. Alain Silver and James Ursuni. New York: Limelight Editions.

Schwarzer, Mitchell. 2000. "The Consuming Landscape: Architecture in the Films of Michelangelo Antonioni." In *Architecture and Film,* ed. Mark Lamster, 197–216. New York: Princeton Architectural Press.

Seigworth, Gregory J. 2000. "Banality for Cultural Studies." *Cultural Studies* 14, no. 2: 234.

Sen, Jai. 1976. "The Unintended City." *Seminar,* no. 200 (April).

Sengupta, Saswati, and Shampa Roy. 1995. "Behind the Bold and Beautiful." *Pioneer,* February 22.

Sennett, Richard. 1990. *The Conscience of the Eye: The Design and Social Life of Cities.* New York: W. W. Norton.

———. 1974. *The Fall of Public Man.* New York: W. W. Norton.

Shah, Ghanshyam. 1977. *Protest Movements in Two Indian States: A Study of the Gujarat and Bihar Movements.* New Delhi: Ajanta Publications.

Shaodian, Jack. 2003. *Dreams and Dead Ends: The American Gangster Film.* New York: Oxford University Press.

Sharma, Rajiv. 2002. "D-Company Empire." *Tribune,* December 23.

Sheth, D. L. 2000. "Changing Terms of Elite Discourse: The Case of Reservation for 'Other Backward Classes.'" In *Politics and the State in India,* ed. Zoya Hasan. Thousand Oaks, Calif.: Sage Publications.

Shiel, Mark, and Tony Fitzmaurice, eds. 2001. *Cinema and the City: Film and Urban Societies in a Global Context.* Cambridge, Mass.: Blackwell.

Silver, Alain, and James Ursini. 1996. "Notes on Film Noir." In *Film Noir Reader,* ed. Alain Silver and James Ursini. New York: Limelight Editions.

Simmel, Georg. 1990. *The Philosophy of Money.* New York: Routledge.

———. 1971. *On Individuality and Social Forms.* Ed. and with an introduction by Donald N. Levine. Chicago: University of Chicago Press.

Singer, Ben. 2001. *Melodrama and Modernity.* New York: Columbia University Press.

———. 1995. "Modernity, Hyperstimulus, and the Rise of Popular Sensationalism." In *Cinema and the Invention of Modern Life,* ed. Leo Charney and Vanessa Schwartz. Berkeley: University of California Press.

Singh, Randhir. 1990. *Of Marxism and Indian Politics.* New Delhi: Ajanta Publications.

Sinha, Sachidanand. 1977. *Emergency in Perspective: Reprieve and Challenge.* New Delhi: Heritage Publishers.

Sklar, Robert. 1994. *City Boys.* Princeton, N.J.: Princeton University Press.

Spiegel, Lynn. 1992. "The Suburban Home Companion: Television and the Neighbourhood Ideal in Post War America." In *Sexuality and Space,* ed. Beatriz Colomina. Princeton Papers on Architecture. New York: Princeton Architectural Press.

Srinivasan, Amrit. 1985. "Reform and Revival: The Devdasi and Her Dance." *Economic and Political Weekly* 44: 1869–76.

Stam, Robert. 1989. *Subversive Pleasures: Bakhtin, Cultural Criticism, and Film.* Baltimore: Johns Hopkins University Press.

Subramaniam, Radhika. 1998. "The Crowd in Bombay." Ph.D. diss.

Sundaram, Ravi. 2004. "Uncanny Networks: Pirate, Urban, and the New Globalization." Special issue on globalization, *Economic & Political Weekly (EPW),* January 3.

———. 1997. "Asian Futures and the Paradoxes of Urban Life in India." In *Secession: Cities on the Move,* ed. Hou Hanru and Hans Ulrich Obrist. Hatje.

Swanson, Gillian. 1996. "Drunk with the Glitter: Consuming Space and Sexual Geographies." In *Postmodern Cities and Spaces,* ed. Sophie Watson and Katherine Gibson. Cambridge, Mass.: Blackwell.

Tarlo, Emma. 2003. *Unsettling Memories: Narratives of the Emergency in Delhi.* Berkeley: University of California Press.

Tejpal, Tarun. 1998. "The Mirror Has Two Faces." *Outlook,* July 20, 61–66.

Terdiman, Richard. 1993. *Present Past: Modernity and the Memory Crisis.* Ithaca, N.Y.: Cornell University Press.

Tharu, Suzie. 1997. "Tracing Savitri's Pedigree: Victorian Racism and the Image of Women in Indo-Anglian Literature." In *Recasting Women: Essays in Colonial History,* ed. Kumkum Sangari and Sudesh Vaid. New Delhi: Kali for Women.

Thomas, Helen. 1997. *Dance in the City.* New York: Saint Martin's Press.

Thomas, Rosie. 1985. "Indian Cinema: Pleasures and Popularity." *Screen* 26, no. 3–4.

Thompson, E. P. 1966. *The Making of the English Working Class.* New York: Vintage Books.

Thorner, Alice. 1996. "Bombay: Diversity and Exchange." In *Bombay: Mosaic of Modern Culture,* ed. Sujata Patel and Alice Thorner. Delhi: Oxford University Press.

Thorner, D. 1980. *The Shaping of Modern India.* Bombay: Allied Publishers.

Tripathi, Salil. 2001. "Gangsters Grab the Bluelight." *New Statesman* (March 12).

Turim, Maureen. 1989. *Flashbacks in Film: Memory and History.* New York: Routledge.

Van Wersch, Hub. 1995. "Flying a Kite and Losing the String: Communication during the Bombay Textile Strike." In *Bombay: Metaphor for Modern India,* ed. Sujata Patel and Alice Thorner, 64–85. Bombay: Oxford University Press.

Varma, Rashmi. 2004. "Provincializing the Global City: From Bombay to Mumbai." *Social Text* 81 (Winter): 65–87.

Vasudev, Aruna. 1986. *The New Indian Cinema.* New Delhi: Macmillan.

Vasudev, Aruna, and Philippe Lenglet, eds. 1983. *Indian Cinema Super Bazaar.* Delhi: Vikas.

Vasudevan, Ravi. 1995. "Addressing the Spectator of a 'Third World' National Cinema: Bombay 'Social' Film of the 1940s and 1950s." *Screen* 36, no. 4 (Winter): 312–13.
———. 1995. "You Cannot Live in Society—and Ignore It: Nationhood and Female Modernity in *Andaz*." *Contributions to Indian Sociology* 29, no. 1–2: 83–108.
———. 1994. "Dislocations: The Cinematic Imagining of a New Society in 1950s India." *Oxford Literary Review* 16: 93–124.
———. 1993. "Shifting Codes, Dissolving Identities: The Hindi Social Film of the 1950s as Popular Culture." *Journal of Arts and Ideas* 23–24: 51–84.
———. 1989. "The Melodramatic Mode and the Commercial Hindi Cinema: Notes on Film History, Narrative, and Performance in the 1950s." *Screen* 30, no. 3: 29–50.
Vasudevan, Ravi, ed. 2000. *Making Meaning in Indian Cinema*. New Delhi: Oxford University Press.
Vidler, Anthony. 2002. *Warped Space: Art, Architecture, and Anxiety in Modern Culture*. Cambridge, Mass.: MIT Press.
———. 1992. *The Architectural Uncanny: Essays in the Modern Unhomely*. Cambridge, Mass.: MIT Press.
Vinaik, Achin. 1990. *The Painful Transition: Bourgeois Democracy in India*. London: Verso.
Virani, Pinki. 1999. *Once Was Bombay*. Viking Penguin India.
Virilio, Paul. 1995. *Art of the Motor*. Minneapolis: University of Minnesota Press.
———. 1994. *The Vision Machine*. Bloomington: Indiana University Press.
———. 1986. *The Overexposed City*. Zone 1/2: 20.
———. 1977. *Speed and Politics: An Essay on Dromology*. Foreign Accents Series. New York: Semiotext(e).
Ward, Janet. 2001. *Weimar Surfaces: Urban Visual Culture in 1920s Germany*. Berkeley: University of California Press.
Ward, Stephen. 1998. *Selling Places: The Marketing and Promotion of Towns and Cities, 1850–2000*. London: Routledge.
Walkowitz, Judith. 1992. *City of Dreadful Delight: Narratives of Sexual Danger in Late Victorian London*. Chicago: University of Chicago Press.
Weber, Max. 1930. *The Protestant Ethic and the Spirit of Capitalism*. London: Allen & Unwin.
Wernick, Andrew. 1991. *Promotional Culture: Advertising, Ideology, and Symbolic Expression*. London: Sage.
Williams, Raymond. 1973. *The Country and the City*. New York: Oxford University Press.
Williams, Raymond. 1966. *Modern Tragedy*. Stanford, Calif.: Stanford University Press.
Wilson, Elizabeth. 1995. "The Invisible Flaneur." In *Postmodern Cities and Spaces*, ed. S. Watson and K. Gibson. Cambridge, Mass.: Blackwell.
———. 1991. *The Sphinx in the City: Urban Life, the Control of Disorder, and Women*. Berkeley: University of California Press.
———. 1990. "All That Rage." In *Fabrications: Costume and the Female Body*, ed. Jane Gaines and Charlotte Herzog. New York: Routledge.
Wilson, Kalpana. 1994. "Post Independence Indian State in Marxist Writing." In *State and Nation in the Context of Social Change*, ed. T. V. Sathyamurthy. New Delhi: Oxford University Press.

Wolf, Janet. 1990. "The Invisible Flaneuse: Women and the Literature of Modernity." In *Feminine Sentences: Essays on Women and Culture,* 34–50. Berkeley: University of California Press.

Zukin, Sharon. 1991. *Landscapes of Power: From Detroit to Disney World.* Berkeley: University of California Press.

Index

Abbas, Khwaja Ahmed, 48
adventure: notion of, 31, 33
advertising, xxi, 52, 93; films and, 120;
  language of seduction and, 97
aestheticization: of urban space, 95,
  111–12
Afternoon Dispatch, 159
agit-prop theater, 57
Akhtar, Farhan, 142, 148, 227n34. *See
  also Dil Chahta Hai*
Akhtar, Jan Nissar, xxiv
Akhtar, Javed, 9, 22, 35, 36, 43, 217n9,
  220n4; on Amitabh Bachchan, 10; on
  Bombay film hero, 42
Albrecht, Donald, 119
Allahabad, 10, 217n11
allegory, xxix, xxx, 39
Aman, Zeenat, 90
Amar Akbar Anthony, 44, 220n5
Ambedkar, B. R., 214n7
ambient television, 112
Anamika, 85
Andaaz, 221n3
anger, 1; cinematic articulation of,
  xxxvi; and revenge, 1
angry man, xxxvi, 1, 8, 9, 41, 211
Anjam (The result), 2
antihero, 3, 7. *See also* angry man;
  Baazigar; homelessness
Appadurai, Arjun, 81
architecture, 111; commercial, in
  Bombay, 194–95; concept of window

wall, 116; in family films, 117–18;
  interior-exterior relationship, 116. *See
  also* interior spaces
Arjuna, 13, 25
art directors, 120, 121
Avadhi, 45
Awara, xxiii, 3

Baazigar (The player), 2, 3, 27, 32–35, 37,
  39–40, 211, 218n26; childhood memories in 34, 35; death of protagonist,
  40; expression of interiority, 34–35,
  38; flashback in, 34, 35; homelessness as trope in, 2, 3; protagonist as
  stranger in the city, 2, 40. *See also*
  stranger in the city
Babi, Parveen, 25
Babri mosque, 152
Bachchan, Amitabh, 9–10, 14, 23, 27,
  29, 34, 36, 136, 139; Akhtar on, 10; as
  angry man, 1, 8, 9, 11, 36, 217n12;
  death of, 40; and Karna, 12–13, 14;
  language of, 220n6; as mirror of
  youth disillusionment, 9; as product
  of modernization, 9; psychotic as
  extension of, 36–37, 219n33; and
  psychotic figure, comparison between, 28; as tapori in *Amar Akbar
  Anthony,* 44, 220n5; trans-class aura,
  9–10, 220n6; Vijay as on-screen
  persona, 10–11, 34. *See also Deewar*
Bachchan, Jaya, 139

Ranjani Mazumdar is an independent filmmaker and associate professor of cinema studies at the School of Arts and Aesthetics at Jawaharlal Nehru University, New Delhi, India.